Microsoft FORTRAN

Microsoft FORTRAN

Paul M. Chirlian

Professor
Department of Electrical Engineering and Computer Science
Stevens Institute of Technology

dilithium Press
Beaverton, Oregon

To Barbara, Lisa and Peter

ISBN: 0-918398-46-0
Library of Congress catalog card number: 80-70797

Printed in the United States of America.

dilithium Press
P.O. Box 606
Beaverton, Oregon 97075

Preface

This is an introductory text on FORTRAN. It is intended for readers who have essentially no experience with FORTRAN, or with other programming languages. It is written for users of small computers which use MICROSOFT FORTRAN. This version of FORTRAN was developed by MICROSOFT of Bellevue, Washington. It is exceptionally well suited to these small computers. This is the version of FORTRAN which is usually run on the Radio Shack TRS-80 computer. It can be run on other computers as well. For instance, there is a version which will run with the CPIM operating system. Procedures for running MICROSOFT FORTRAN with various operating systems are discussed.

The various topics of FORTRAN are presented in a very simple manner so as not to confuse the beginner. They will provide him with an understanding of computer programming using FORTRAN.

This book discusses techniques of structured FORTRAN programming. Topics such as top down programming are covered. Motivation for writing structured programs is given.

Material in included in Sections 1.3 and 1.4 which will allow you to begin writing FORTRAN programs immediately. The basic ideas needed to run programs using the MICROSOFT FORTRAN system are discussed in Sec. 1.3. Examples are given for the TRS-80 computer as well as for other computers.

Introductory material on debugging is given in Section 1.4. A more detailed discussion of debugging is given in Chapter 14. The commonly occurring bugs have been illustrated and a discussion of reduction of computation error has been included. This chapter is included not only to indicate debugging techniques to the beginner, but also to show him that bugs often occur in programs and that this should not discourage him personally. A thorough discussion of the MICROSOFT editor is also given in Chapter 14.

Most of the illustrative examples are written to present the ideas of FORTRAN as clearly as possible. However, simple procedures do not always result in optimum programs. Some material on optimizing programs has been included to give the beginner an idea of the problems involved and at least some of the procedures used to optimize programs.

The subject of writing algorithms has been discussed in some detail. Flowcharts are also used with standard notation. The use of comments in computer programs is illustrated in many ways. Examples are given which relate the comments to the algorithm and its associated flowchart.

A complete section is devoted to the important topic of documentation.

The storage and retrieval of data from floppy disks is given considerable attention. Formatted and unformatted input/output is discussed as are sequential and direct access files.

The subject of MICROSOFT FORTRAN is covered rather completely. Thus, when you have gone through the text, you will be familiar with almost all aspects of MICROSOFT FORTRAN. In addition, the complete MICROSOFT FORTRAN system (compiler, linker, library and editor) is discussed in detail.

It is also hoped that the book will serve as a reference so that even advanced programmers can refer to it to refresh themselves on some details. To aid in this, a glossary of MICROSOFT FORTRAN terms and expressions and a list of built-in MICROSOFT FORTRAN subprograms are included in Appendix A and Appendix B, respectively.

The book is organized so that a reader can start running programs almost instantly. Many varied exercises are included at the end of each chapter.

ACKNOWLEDGMENTS

The author would like to express his gratitude to his colleagues Professor Alfred C. Gilmore, Jr., Professor Stanley H. Smith, and Otto C. Boelens for the many helpful discussions held with them during the writing of the book.

Much loving gratitude and heartfelt thanks are again due my wife, Barbara, who not only provided me with continuous encouragement, but who also typed the rough and final drafts of the manuscript and corrected the punctuation and grammar of the copy.

Contents

1 Introduction to Computer Programming

The modern digital computer can perform a remarkable number of tasks. It can, in a matter of second or minutes perform calculations which could take hours, or even years of work if they were performed without using computers. Computers are also used to control widely diverse processes such as the operation of chemical plants and the landing of space ships on the moon. They can play both simple and complex games. However, as powerful as computers may seem, they cannot think. Indeed, they must be instructed to perform each step of their calculations. They can perform these steps very rapidly and accurately but they cannot determine what steps to perform. The computer follows a set of instructions called a *program*. In this book we shall discuss the writing of computer programs. There are many programming languages that can be used. We shall discuss a language that is almost universally used, and which is particularly applicable to mathematical and scientific computations. This language is FORTRAN.

Although the FORTRAN language was originally designed to run on large digital computers, it performs well when run on small microcomputers. There is a version called MICROSOFT FORTRAN that has been developed by MICROSOFT of Bellevue, Washington that is particularly suited for these computers. It is this version of FORTRAN that we shall discuss in this book.

In addition to discussing how to program in FORTRAN, we shall also present the details of how MICROSOFT FORTRAN can be run on a small microcomputer. Such features as the compiler, the editor, and the linker will be explained and their use will be discussed.

1.1 SOME COMPUTER FUNDAMENTALS

In this section we shall discuss some of the fundamental components which are common to almost all digital computers. This discussion will be particularly directed to microcomputers. We shall not consider how these parts work, but shall direct our attention to the type of operations that they perform.

All digital computers have a *central processor*. In a microcomputer this is called the *microprocessor*. It performs all the arithmetic and logical operations of the computer. The data and instructions are stored in the *memory* or *main storage unit*. This is also called the *random access memory* or RAM. The RAM in a microcomputer is made up entirely of semiconductor devices which are incorporated in several chips.

Data can be stored in or read from the memory very rapidly, often in much less than one *microsecond* (10^{-6} second). The size (that is, the number of semiconductor circuits used) of the memory determines the amount of data that can be stored there. Larger memories must be utilized when a great deal of data is to be processed and/or if many instructions are present in the program.

The amount of data that can be stored in the RAM is limited and it is usually lost when the computer is turned off. These memories are said to be *volatile*. Often, we want to store programs or data for further use. Such storage should be nonvolatile and should be able to store great quantities of data at relatively low cost. Various *magnetic storage devices* are used for this purpose. For instance, magnetic *tape* storage is widely used. Here the information is stored on a magnetic tape, often using an ordinary tape recorder. *Magnetic disks, floppy disks,* and *magnetic bubble memories* are also used for this type of storage. The floppy disk is widely used with microcomputers because it is much faster than tape storage. Most microcomputers that use FORTRAN rely on floppy disk storage. We shall discuss its use in this book.

If a program is to be of use, data must be supplied to the computer and the answers must be outputted. Various input and output devices are used for this. We shall consider the ones generally used with microcomputers. Small microcomputers use a *video terminal* to input and output data. The information is typed in on a keyboard that resembles an ordinary typewriter keyboard. The information is displayed on a *video monitor* that resembles an ordinary television screen. In fact, the monitor may actually be a television set. Microcomputers may also use *line printers* for the output of data. We shall discuss FORTRAN programs that can output data using either mode of operation.

A large digital computer is so constructed that it will respond to a sequence of commands called a *machine language* program. Some typical commands are: store a number in a particular part of the memory; add a number stored in one part of the memory to one stored in another part of the memory; print a number stored in a third part of the memory, etc. The computer is directed by this machine language and all programs can be written in machine language. However, it is extremely tedious to program in machine language. For instance, suppose we want to write a program which adds three numbers to obtain a fourth. That is,

$$x = a + b + c \qquad (1.1)$$

where a, b, and c represent the three numbers and x is their sum. We would like to write a program that results in the calculation of Eq. (1.1). This program should resemble Eq. (1.1). However, if machine language were used, this would not be the case. In addition, a storage location in the main storage would have to be specified for each variable. Each location would have to be remembered by the programmer. To relieve the programmer of the tedium of working in machine language, special programs called *compilers* are used in the computer. The compiler translates a program written in more easily used language into machine language. For instance, using the MICROSOFT FORTRAN compiler, a program which would evaluate Eq. (1.1) could be written as

X=A+B+C $\qquad$ (1.2)

The compiler then translates this into the appropriate machine language. Hence, the compiler allows the programmer to work in a simpler and less tedious language called a *programming language*. Note, however, that the computer is still directed by the machine language. (In certain instances, it is desirable to write programs in machine language. However, for the vast majority of programs, programming languages should be used.)

In this book we shall thoroughly discuss the MICROSOFT FORTRAN programming language. But in order to run a FORTRAN program on your computer, you must become familiar with procedures other than those directly involved in FORTRAN programming. For instance, a set of instructions must be given to the compiler to cause it to compile the program. When the program is run, its machine language version is stored in the main memory of the computer. The MICROSOFT compiler does not actually write the final machine language program, but writes an intermediate form called a *relocatable program* or *relocatable*

file or *REL file*. The program is called relocatable since it can be
modified for storage in different parts of the memory. Other programs
that we shall discuss must be combined with the REL program before
it can be run. There is another program called a *linker* or *linking loader*
that actually translates the relocatable file into a machine language
program and combines it with other necessary programs so that the
program can be run. The linker is supplied with the MICROSOFT
FORTRAN package so that you do not have to worry about the actual
details of linking. Actually, as far as the programming is concerned, the
operations of compiling, linking, and loading can be performed with a
simple sequence of commands.

Let us consider some of the details of the linker and loader. There
are certain operations that are performed in many FORTRAN programs.
One such operation is the multiplication of two numbers. Another is
the outputting of data on your terminal. There are programs that
direct these kinds of operations. These programs are supplied in the
MICROSOFT FORTRAN package. They are stored in a file called the
FORTRAN *library*. After you write, compile and link a FORTRAN
program, the linker will automatically get the required programs from
the library and link them with your program. When the linker has
completed its operation, a complete machine language program which
can be run on your computer is obtained.

The MICROSOFT FORTRAN package contains the compiler, linker
and library. These programs are written so that you only have to type
in some simple commands and the operations of compiling and linking
will be performed. Actually, the MICROSOFT FORTRAN package is
arranged so that the only real details that you need concern yourself
with are those directly involved with writing the FORTRAN program.

An *editor* is supplied with the MICROSOFT FORTRAN package.
This is a program which simplifies the actual details of writing a FOR-
TRAN program. The editor allows you to easily type in a program on
your terminal and to change the program if there are errors. The editor
has some very powerful features that make editing of programs particularly simple. In this first chapter we shall discuss some simple details of
editing. These will enable you to write FORTRAN programs and make
changes when necessary. In Chapter 14 we shall discuss the more
advanced features of editing. As you gain more familiarity with FOR-
TRAN, you might want to read the editing sections of that chapter out
of sequence in order to gain more familiarity with the editor. A similar
situation exists in the case of the linker. In this chapter we shall discuss
some simple procedures that will allow you to write and run some
simple programs. Additional details of linking will be discussed in
Chapter 7.

1.2 THE FORTRAN PROGRAMMING LANGUAGE

Computer programs are written in a programming language. The FORTRAN programming language has a set of characters, a vocabulary, and rules of grammar. The designers of FORTRAN developed a language which would be suitable for mathematical computations.

FORTRAN Characters

In the early days of computers, almost all programs were punched on cards using a key punch. These punched cards were originally used, not in computers as we know them today, but in devices which sorted or alphabetized the cards. These cards were then adopted for use in the computer. The characters of FORTRAN were those available on the key punch and in general, they are the characters used in computer programming today. Let us now consider them. FORTRAN uses the 26 upper case alphabet characters.

A B C D E F G H I J K L M
N O P Q R S T U V W X Y Z

In addition, the ten digits† are used

$\emptyset$ 1 2 3 4 5 6 7 8 9

Various punctuation marks and arithmetic symbols are also allowed

. , ' * / + - = $ ( )

Thus, these characters and the blank space make up the elements of the FORTRAN language. In the succeeding chapters of this book we shall discuss how these elements are written into programs.

Program Structure

The written English language has a certain structure. For instance, suppose that we want to print a page of text. The following rules can be used. Leave a space between words; end each sentence with a period; leave two spaces between the period at the end of a sentence and the start of the next one; indent the start of each paragraph by five spaces,

---

† In this text the FORTRAN zero will be represented by $\emptyset$ to distinguish it from the FORTRAN capital letter O.

etc. There are similar rules in FORTRAN called the rules of *syntax*. Each line in a FORTRAN program is called a *statement*. For instance, a sequence of statements is

A=B+C+D

E=A+2.3+B   (1.3)

F=A-E

Each statement is written on a separate line. (Subsequently, we shall discuss how long statements may be written using several lines.) Each line is composed of columns. There are a total of 80 columns that can be used and certain rules must be followed exactly. We shall now state them. The FORTRAN statement is typed in columns 7 to 72. Thus, a single line can only contain 66 characters of a statement. At times, a FORTRAN statement requires more than 66 characters, in which case, additional lines are used and there must be some indication when a line is a continuation of a *previous* one. Column 6 is used for this purpose. If *any* character except a blank or a zero is put in column 6, then it indicates that the line continues the FORTRAN statement of the previous line. For this reason, column 6 is called the *continuation column*. Note that the character in column 6 is not part of the FORTRAN statement. Its only functions is to indicate a continuation.

At times, we want to number FORTRAN statements. As an illustration, consider the sequence of statements shown

15   A=B+C+D
9   E=A+2.3+B   (1.4)
11   F=A-E

The computer executes these statements in the order in which they are written. The statement numbers are ignored in the execution. That is, first A would be calculated, then E and finally, F. The statement numbers *do not* affect the order of execution. However, there are several reasons why some statements may be numbered, and we shall discuss them subsequently.

Statement numbers are typed in columns 1–5. A number appearing here is just a statement number and is not acted upon as part of a statement. The statement number is an unsigned integer. For instance, 15 or ∅∅15 are both valid and equivalent statement numbers. However, +15 and 15.∅ are invalid. The first contains a sign while the second is not an integer (it contains a decimal point).

At times, it is convenient for the programmer to write a statement which is ignored when the program is compiled. For instance, if a program computes the average value of a list of numbers, then it would be convenient if the first line read AVERAGE VALUE. It would then serve as a label. If the letter C is placed in column 1, then the line is ignored when the program is compiled. This is called a *comment*. When the FORTRAN program is printed, however, the comments *will* be printed. Thus, another use for comments is to explain parts of the program. This is often useful when one programmer writes a program which must then be understood by others.

Columns 73 to 80 in the FORTRAN statements are ignored when the program is compiled. They can be used by the programmer for identification purposes. (When punched cards are used, these columns are used to number the cards.) Most programmers using microcomputers ignore columns 73 to 80. However, they are available if you want to use them.

Your video terminal may not have room for 80 characters on a single line. In this case, the FORTRAN statement will appear on two lines. However, as far as the compiler is concerned, the entire statement is on a single line.

Data must usually be entered when a program is to be run. For instance, in the program sequence (1.4), the values of B, C, and D must be supplied. In Sec. 1.4 and in Chapter 3 we shall discuss the entering of data.

1.3 HOW TO WRITE SIMPLE MICROSOFT FORTRAN PROGRAMS

In this section we shall provide you with all the information needed to write simple FORTRAN programs. We shall also discuss simple details of editing and linking so that you can run the programs on your microcomputer.

To show how simple a FORTRAN program can be, let us consider a program which results in the addition of 3 + 4 to obtain 7. Of course, this is very simple. However, we shall soon consider more complex programs. The program is

```
C  A  SAMPLE  PROGRAM
        A=3.
        B=4.
        C=A+B
        WRITE(5,50)C                    (1.5)
50      FORMAT(' ',E14.7)
        STOP
        END
```

Each line of the program is called a statement. Note that many of the statements appear familiar. Let us discuss each statement in turn. The first statement here is called a comment, see Sec. 1.2. Such a statement just serves to provide information to the programmer or to anyone else who reads the program. Remember that if a C is put in the first column, then that statement is ignored by the compiler.

In the second statement we define a *variable* which we call A and set its value equal to 3. (Note that this statement starts in column 7, see Sec. 1.2.) In the next statement we do the same for a variable called B and set its value equal to 4. In the fourth statement we define a variable called C and set it equal to the sum of A and B. Thus, after the program is executed, the value of C will be 7. Arithmetic statements are discussed in detail in Chapter 2.

If the result is to be of use, the value must be supplied to the user of the program. The lines

```
        WRITE(5,50)C
50      FORMAT(' ',E14.7)
```

cause the computed value of C to be printed. Let us consider these statements in detail. They should be written in the form shown. For instance, the WRITE statement should contain the numbers 5 and 50 separated by a comma and enclosed in parentheses. The number 5 indicates that the data is to be printed on the screen of your terminal.

The number 50 refers to the FORMAT statement and must be included. The FORMAT statement is one which indicates the form to be used in printing the data. In Chapter 3 we shall discuss FORMAT statements in much more detail and shall modify some of the statements made here. However, for the time being, let us always use 50 as the second number in the WRITE statement and also use 50 as the statement number, see Sec. 1.2, of the FORMAT statement. Thus, for the present, we shall write the FORMAT statement in the following way. First we write 50 using columns 1 and 2. Then, the word FORMAT starts in column 7. Following this we have a parenthesis, single quote mark, blank space, single quote mark, and then E14.7, followed by a close parenthesis. In Chapter 3 we shall explain the meaning of these terms. For the time being, just use the FORMAT statement as given. If we had wanted the values of A and B to also be printed, we could have changed the WRITE statement to

```
        WRITE(6,50)A,B,C
```

Note the three commas. The line

```
        STOP
```

stops the evaluation of the program. The last line

    END

must also be included. These statements are described in greater detail in Sec. 3.5. Actually the statement STOP can be omitted when MICRO-SOFT FORTRAN is used. However, with most other versions of FORTRAN, it must be included. We shall include the word STOP in most programs so that they can be run with other FORTRAN systems. If the statement STOP is included in a MICROSOFT FOR-TRAN program, the word STOP will be printed on the video screen when the execution of the program is completed.

Note that the computer executes each statement of the program in turn. (Subsequently, we shall discuss exceptions to this.)

When the program is executed, the value of C will be printed. It will appear as

$$\emptyset.7\emptyset\emptyset\emptyset\emptyset\emptyset\emptyset E+\emptyset 1$$

(The leading $\emptyset$ will be omitted on some versions of MICROSOFT FOR-TRAN.) This is actually 7. The value E+$\emptyset$1 represents $10^1 = 10$. Thus, the number is

$$0.7 \times 10^1 = 7$$

In general, E is used to represent a power of 10. For instance

$$E+\emptyset 3 - 10^3 - 1,000$$
$$E+\emptyset 6 = 10^6 = 1,000,000$$
$$E-\emptyset 3 = 10^{-3} = 0.001$$
$$E-\emptyset 6 = 10^{-6} = 0.000001$$

Note that very large or very small numbers can be represented in this way. For instance,

$$E+15 = 10^{15}$$
$$E-21 = 10^{-21}$$

We must describe how to actually write the program in the editor and how to compile and link it if you are to actually run the program. Let us start by discussing the editor. MICROSOFT FORTRAN is usually supplied on two diskettes. These should be placed in your disk drives with the first numbered disk in the first drive. (If you only have one disk drive, we shall modify this statement subsequently.) Now boot the system. To call the editor program, type EDIT. The word

    FILE:

will appear on your screen after the editor program is loaded. We are writing a new program. Type in its name, for instance,

SAMPLE/FOR   (1.6)

The name of the program can be any valid file name for your disk operating system (DOS). For instance, if you are using a Radio Shack DOS, statement (1.6) would be a valid file name. You can also specify a disk drive. For instance,

SAMPLE/FOR:1

specifies that the program named SAMPLE/FOR is to be stored on drive 1. Passwords can also be added to a file. In general, the procedure outlined in your DOS manual for naming files should be used here. We have used the extension FOR to indicate a FORTRAN file. In general, this should be done. On some systems, a period rather than a slash is used to designate an extension, for instance

SAMPLE.FOR

If you are writing a new program, then, after entering the program name, depress **ESC** or **BREAK**. Your terminal will have one or the other. A $ will appear after the name of the program and the edit program will print some information. For instance, the material appearing on the screen might appear as

```
DOS READY
EDIT
FILE: SAMPLE/FOR:1$
CREATING
VERSION 1.Ø                                             (1.7)
COPYRIGHT 1977,78 (C) BY MICROSOFT
CREATED:19-FEB-79
3Ø782 BYTES FREE
::
```

The underlined material was typed by you. The asterisk is a prompt that indicates that the editor is ready to receive data. In response, type **I** and **RETURN**. On some computers, the **RETURN** key is labeled **ENTER**. The editor will respond with

ØØ1ØØ

You can now type in a line. After you hit **RETURN**, the editor will respond with

$$\emptyset\emptyset2\emptyset\emptyset$$

and you can enter another line. For instance, if program (1.5) were entered, you would have

```
ØØ1ØØ     C A SAMPLE PROGRAM
ØØ2ØØ          A=3.
ØØ3ØØ          B=4.
ØØ4ØØ          C=A+B
ØØ5ØØ          WRITE(5,5Ø)C
ØØ6ØØ    5Ø    FORMAT(' ',E14.7)              (1.8)
ØØ7ØØ          STOP
ØØ8ØØ          END
ØØ9ØØ $
*
```

After the **END** and **RETURN (ENTER)** are typed, ØØ9ØØ will appear on the screen. Since you do not want to enter a new statement, type **ESC** or **BREAK**. The $ will appear after the ØØ9ØØ and the asterisk prompt will appear on the next line indicating that the editor is ready to receive a new command.

If you now type E, the editor procedure will be terminated and your FORTRAN program will be saved under the name SAMPLE/FOR on the disk in drive 1.

Note the numbers ØØ1ØØ, ØØ2ØØ, etc. in (1.8). They are called *line numbers* and are *not* part of the FORTRAN program. These numbers are used by the editor. In general, when we list FORTRAN programs in this book, line numbers will not be present. However, the MICROSOFT editor will always include them. They make it very convenient to edit your programs. Note that the program is entered in accordance with the procedure discussed earlier. For instance, in line ØØ1ØØ, the C is typed in column 1 of the FORTRAN statement (i.e. the columns to the left, which contain the line numbers and some spaces, do not exist as far as the compiler is concerned). Similarly, in line ØØ2ØØ, A is typed in column 7. You may have a tab key on your computer (e.g. right arrow) which will tab over seven spaces so that you do not have to keep counting six spaces. The MICROSOFT editor is such that the first column in which *you* can type is column 1. The line numbers and spaces are typed by the computer.

Let us consider some of the basic editing procedures here. In Chapter 14 we shall discuss editing in detail. You can read the editing section of that chapter any time that you want to learn the very convenient and powerful editing techniques that are available. Suppose that you make a mistake in your program and want to change a line. In response to the prompt *, type **R** and the line number (**R** stands for Replace). For instance, to replace line 00500, you would enter

    R500   (RETURN)

The computer would respond with

    00500

and you would type in the new statement which would replace the old statement 500. If there are no lines between 500 and 600, the computer would next respond with

    00600

and you could either enter a new line or type **ESC** or **BREAK**. If there already is a line 600, or there are lines between 500 and 600, the editor would respond with an asterisk prompt.

If you want to add lines between existing ones, the **I** command is used. For instance, in program (1.8), suppose that you want to add a line between 600 and 700. Then, in response to the asterisk, you would type

    I650

or **I** followed by any number between 600 and 700. The computer will respond with

    00650

and you can enter a line as before.

If you want to print a line on the screen, type **P** and the line number (followed by **RETURN**). For instance,

    *P600 (RETURN)

will cause the line number 00600 to be printed on the screen. A range of lines can be printed by typing a colon (:) between numbers. For instance,

P2∅∅:6∅∅ **(RETURN)**

will result in the printing of all lines between ∅∅2∅∅ and ∅∅6∅∅ on the screen. If you have a line printer, and if the **P** is replaced with an **L**, then the lines will be printed on the line printer.

We have assumed that you have been working with a new program. Once you exit the editor and store the FORTRAN program on a disk, it becomes an old program. The procedures for entering and exiting the computer with old programs are slightly different. In response to

FILE:

type the name of the file followed by **RETURN**. Note that **RETURN** rather than **ESC** or **BREAK** is used here. The editing procedure is as previously discussed.

Most editors require that you give the file a new name when you exit. In that way, the old file is saved as a backup. The file is named on exiting. To exit, you type **E** followed by the new name, for instance,

⊁E SAMPLE2/FOR:1

Now the new file will be called SAMPLE2/FOR and it will be stored on the disk in drive 1. Note that the MICROSOFT FORTRAN system is supplied on two disks. In this case, the file will be stored on one of the system disks. There is usually room for this if the programs are not very long. The files can always be transferred to a new disk using the copy procedure of your DOS.

Once the FORTRAN program is written, it must be compiled, linked and run. To compile the program, you must be in the DOS command mode. Then type **F8∅**. The compiler will be loaded and an asterisk will appear as a prompt. Suppose that you want to compile the file called SAMPLE/FOR and that the disk is in drive 1. You could type

⊁=SAMPLE:1 **(RETURN)**   (1.9)

Note that the extension (/FOR) need not be typed. If no extension is given, it is assumed that /FOR is used. The compiler will check the program and determine if there are any syntax errors. If there are, error

messages will be printed on your screen. The statement containing the
error will be referred to by line number, which simplifies the editing
procedure.

If your program has no errors then, after the * prompt, type the
name that you want to give to the relocatable file, followed by an
equals sign and the name of the FORTRAN file that you want to
compile, for instance,

$$\ast ABC/REL:1=SAMPLE/FOR:1 \qquad (1.10)$$

Now a relocatable file called ABC/REL will be compiled. Actually,
it is usually less confusing to have the same name for the relocatable
file and the FORTRAN file, which is also called the *source* file. We
could write (1.10) as

$$\ast SAMPLE/REL:1=SAMPLE/FOR:1 \qquad (1.11)$$

If no extension is given, the relocatable file will be given the extension
/REL, and if no extension is given for the source file then /FOR will be
assumed. Hence, (1.11) can be written as

$$\ast SAMPLE:1=SAMPLE:1 \qquad (1.12)$$

In examples (1.10) to (1.12) we have assumed that the source file was
on the disk in drive 1 and that the compiled file was also stored there.
This need not be the case and different drive numbers could have been
used.

Once the program is compiled, it must be linked and loaded. The
linker performs several functions. It gets the relocatable file and stores
it in the RAM, then links it with any necessary library programs and
loads the linked program into memory or stores it on a disk in a form
that can be executed. To do all of this, the loader program must be
executed. From the command mode, type

   L8Ø

This will load and execute the loader. After the asterisk prompt, type
the relocatable file name followed by –G and **RETURN**. The program
will then be executed. For instance, to load the program from example
(1.11) or (1.12), type

$$\ast SAMPLE/REL:1-G \quad \textbf{(RETURN)} \qquad (1.13)$$

If no extension is given, REL will be assumed. Hence, the following is equivalent to (1.13)

$$\text{*SAMPLE:1-G (RETURN)} \qquad\qquad (1.14)$$

Data indicating the memory locations occupied by the program will be printed on the screen. The program will then be executed.

The linking operation can take several moments. It is sometimes desirable to save the machine language program. It can then be executed without having to go through the linking operation. This can be done by writing the name of the file which is to store the machine language program followed by –N, a comma, and the relocatable file name followed by –G, for instance,

$$\text{*ABC/CMD:1-N,SAMPLE:1-G (RETURN)}$$

Now the program will be executed and stored in a file called ABC/CMD, This file will be placed on the disk in drive 1. Note that the editor will not write over an existing file and you must use a new file name in exiting the editor. This is *not* the case when the compiler or linker is run. For instance, in the above example, if there were an old file called ABC/CMD on the disk in drive 1, it would be written over.

We have used the dash followed by a letter in the linker commands. With some operating systems, a slash may replace the dash. (In such cases, the slash in the extension may be replaced by a period.) For instance, (1.13) and (1.14) would be written as

$$\text{*SAMPLE.REL:1/G}$$

or

$$\text{*SAMPLE:1/G}$$

In the remainder of this section we shall use the dashes. Remember that the operation on your computer may be different. Your MICROSOFT manual will specify the proper form.

If the program is to be run again, then ABC/CMD need only be run from the DOS command mode. Your DOS manual should be consulted to see how this is done. With some computers, the extension CMD will be assumed so that it can be omitted from the specification in (1.14). In this example we have assumed that extensions are specified by a /. Remember that some DOSs use a different procedure. Also, the specification of the disk drive numbers (e.g. :1) may differ. Use the procedures of your DOS here.

We have assumed that there are at least two disk drives. This is convenient, but not necessary. The following is an outline of the procedure that can be used if you only have one drive. The manual that comes with your MICROSOFT FORTRAN system will provide specific details.

Put the FORTRAN system disk with the editor in the drive and type **EDIT**. After the editor has loaded and the prompt, FILE:, has appeared on the screen, remove the disk and place your *working disk* in the drive. (Do this before you type in the file name.) The working disk is the one which contains the program to be edited or, if a new program is being written, the disk where the program is to be stored. Now perform the editing operation and exit as discussed previously.

Now insert the FORTRAN system disk that contains the compiler and type **F80**. (It may be necessary to reboot the system before this can be done.) After the compiler has loaded, remove the system disk and insert the working disk. Now perform the compiler operations to create the relocatable files.

Remove the working disk and insert the disk that has the linker, reboot the system and type **L80 (RETURN)** after the * appears. Put the working disk back in the drive and type the name of your program, for example

 ☼SAMPLE:1   (RETURN)

The program will be loaded into memory and a list of the needed library programs will be listed. (You can ignore this list.) The asterisk prompt will appear again. Now remove the working disk and insert the disk with the FORTRAN library (the same one that has the loader) and type

 ☼FORLIB-S

The necessary library routines will then be obtained and stored in the RAM. After the prompt appears on the screen, remove the disk and put your working disk back in the drive. Now type a file name followed by **-N-E**, for instance,

 ☼SAMPLE/CMD:1-N-E

Now a file called SAMPLE/CMD will be stored on the working disk. This working disk should also have a copy of the DOS on it so that you can run the program.

Note that the disks can only be swapped at certain times and that, if this is not done correctly, then *files can be destroyed*. The disks can only be swapped when:

1. You are in the DOS command mode
2. Before booting the system
3. When the * prompt for the loader or compiler has just appeared
4. When the editor prompt FILE: appears

You cannot swap disks at any other time in the editor. To do so may cause damage to your files or to the system files. Always exit the editor (and return to the command mode) before swapping disks.

1.4 SOME ADDITIONAL SIMPLE PROGRAMS —
ELEMENTARY IDEAS OF DEBUGGING

The simple program (1.5) could only add the numbers 3 and 4. Suppose that you want to add other numbers. It would be awkward, especially for more complex programs, to rewrite the program each time that new data had to be entered. We can eliminate this difficulty by instructing the computer to read any required data from the terminal while the program is being executed. Let us illustrate a program which does this.

```
C A SAMPLE PROGRAM
      READ(5,40)A,B
40    FORMAT(E14.7)
      C=A+B
      WRITE(5,50)C
50    FORMAT(' ',E14.7)                    (1.15)
      STOP
      END
```

(Remember that, when we list a FORTRAN program, we omit the line numbers which are added by the editor. Also remember that MICROSOFT FORTRAN does not require the STOP statement in simple programs such as this one.) When the program is executed, the following will happen. The operation will pause until the data that is called for is entered from the terminal. In this case, two numbers, which provide the values for A and B must be entered. Each number should be entered using exponential notation and each number *must* be on a separate line. In Chapter 3 we shall discuss procedures that allow us to modify the procedure for entering (or outputting) data. However, for the time being, follow these procedures exactly. For instance, when program (1.15) is executed, if we enter

> 3.EØ **(RETURN)**
> 4.EØ **(RETURN)**

then the answer

> .7ØØØØØØE+Ø1

will be printed. *Always include the decimal point*. We could also have entered the data as

> 3. **(RETURN)**
> 4. **(RETURN)**

(Do not use more than 14 spaces on each line.)

There can be more than one READ statement in a program. For instance, suppose that we have

```
      READ(5,4Ø)A,B
      READ(5,4Ø)C,D
4Ø    FORMAT(E14.7)
```

Now the data for A, B, C, and D would be entered on four successive lines.

In a similar way we can have multiple WRITE statements in a program. Let us illustrate these ideas with a program. Two numbers *a* and *b* will be read. Their sum will be computed and printed. Next, two numbers *e* and *f* will be read. Their sum will be added to the sum of *a* and *b*. This value will be printed. Thus, we want to compute

$$c = a + b$$
$$g = c + e + f$$

The program is

```
C A PROGRAM ILLUSTRATING MULTIPLE READ AND
C WRITE STATEMENTS
```

```
        READ(5,4Ø)A,B
 4Ø     FORMAT(E14.7)
        C=A+B
        WRITE(5,5Ø)C
 5Ø     FORMAT(' ',E14.7)
        READ(5,4Ø)E,F
        G=C+E+F
        WRITE(6,5Ø)G
        STOP
        END
```
(1.16)

If we enter the data

```
        .3ØØØØØØE+Ø1
        .4ØØØØØØE+Ø1
        .1ØØØØØØE+Ø1
        .3ØØØØØØE+Ø1
```

the computer would then print on the screen

```
        .7ØØØØØØE+Ø1
        .11ØØØØØE+Ø2
```

We have added numbers in the simple programs. Now let us consider the other arithmetic operations. Subtraction is indicated by a minus sign —, division by a slash /, and multiplication by an asterisk *. Now let us write a program which performs the following algebraic operation

$$x = a + \frac{bc}{d} - e$$
(1.17)

The program is

```
        READ(5,4Ø)A,B,C,D,E
 4Ø     FORMAT(E14.7)
        X=A+B*C/D-E
        WRITE(6,5Ø)X
 5Ø     FORMAT(' ',E14.7)
        STOP
        END
```
(1.18)

For this program, the first line instructs the computer to read the values of A, B, C, D, and E. The next statement causes the value of X to be printed. Remember that, using our simplified procedure, six lines of data would have to be supplied.

We can use parentheses in a FORTRAN program in a way similar to that used in algebra. This subject is discussed in detail in Sec. 2.3. Let us illustrate this with an example. Suppose that we want to calculate the following algebraic quantities:

$$x = (a + b)(c + d)/[(e + f)(g + h)] \qquad (1.19a)$$

$$y = (a - b)/(c + de) \qquad (1.19b)$$

The following program would accomplish this:

```
        READ(5,4Ø)A,B,C,D,E,F,G,H
4Ø      FORMAT(E14.7)
        X=(A+B)*(C+D)/((E+F)*(G+H))
        Y=(A-B)/(C+D*E)
        WRITE(6,5Ø)X,Y
5Ø      FORMAT(' ',E14.7)
        STOP
        END
```
(1.20)

Note the parentheses within parentheses in the second line. An asterisk *must* appear between the two parentheses in multiplication. For instance, $(A + B)(C + D)$ is incorrect FORTRAN. It must be written as $(A + B)*(C + D)$. At the start, relatively simple manipulations should be performed in a single statement. After Sec. 2.3 is read, more complex manipulations can be performed. At the present time, extra statements should be used to reduce the complexity of statements. For instance, we could replace the statement

```
        X=(A+B)*(C+D)/((E+F)*(G+H))
```

by the two statements

```
        Z=(E+F)*(G+H)
        X=(A+B)*(C+D)/Z
```

Parentheses can be used to ensure that operations are performed in the proper order. For instance

```
        A*B-C
```

results in $ab - c$, while

```
        A*(B-C)
```

results in $a(b-c)$. Thus, parentheses are needed in the second case. In Sec. 2.3 we shall discuss this subject in detail. For the time being, if there is any doubt about the order of operations, use parentheses or write several statements rather than just one. For instance, we could write A*B−C as (A*B) − C.

In FORTRAN we signify exponentiation, or raising to a power, by two asterisks ** followed by the power. For instance, the expression x^2 would be written as X**2. Similarly, $\sqrt{x} = x^{1/2}$ would be written as X**0.5. Note that we use the decimal 0.5 and not the fraction ½ as the exponent. In Sec. 2.3 we shall modify this statement.

As a final example, let us write a program which obtains the roots of the quadratic equation

$$ax^2 + bx + c = 0 \qquad (1.21)$$

The roots are

$$x_1 = \frac{-b + \sqrt{b^2 - 4ac}}{2a} \qquad (1.22a)$$

$$x_2 = \frac{-b - \sqrt{b^2 - 4ac}}{2a} \qquad (1.22b)$$

We shall assume here that $b^2 - 4ac$ is a positive number. (Procedures will be introduced in Chapter 4 which will enable us to remove this restriction.) The program is

```
         READ(5,4Ø)A,B,C
4Ø       FORMAT(E14.7)
         D=(B**2-4.*A*C)**Ø.5
         X1=(-B+D)/(2.*A)
         X2=(-B-D)/(2.*A)                    (1.23)
         WRITE(5,5Ø)X1,X2
5Ø       FORMAT(' ',E14.7)
         STOP
         END
```

The value of $\sqrt{b^2 - 4ac}$ is calculated in the second line. We call this variable D. Next X1 is calculated. This is equivalent to $(-b + d)/2a$. Next, X2 is calculated. This is given by $(-b - d)/2a$.

We have used X1 and X2 as variable names. Subscripts are not allowed in FORTRAN. However, variable names can consist of up to six letters or numbers. The first character must be a letter. For the time being, start all variable names with the letters A, B, C, D, E, F, G, H, P, Q, R, S, T, U, V, W, X, Y, and Z. Thus,

```
ABLE
XL
BOOK2
```

are acceptable variable names. Note that the letters I through O are omitted. Actually FORTRAN makes a distinction between integers (i.e., numbers without fractional decimal parts) and real numbers (i.e., those which can have a fractional decimal part). For instance, some integers are 1, 4, and -3 while some real numbers are 1.0, 3.6, and -7.8. Variable names starting with A through H or P through Z are reserved for real numbers while variable names starting with I through O are reserved for integers. At the start, let us consider all variables as real. Subsequently, we shall consider cases where integers are used. A complete discussion of variables' names is given in Sec. 2.5. The reader should not attempt any complicated operations using variable names until that section is read. Integers should not be used for input or output until Chapter 3 is read.

Now you are ready to actually use the computer. At this point, only simple programs can be written. However, the subsequent material in the text will provide you with the information required to write the most complex FORTRAN programs.

Debugging of Programs. When computer programs are written, they often contain errors. Such errors are called *bugs*. The correction of these errors is called *debugging*. In Chapter 14 we shall discuss debugging of programs in detail. For the present, let us consider simple bugs that can occur. The simplest error is a typographical one. For instance, instead of writing

```
WRITE(5,50)A,B,C
```

we might write

```
WRITE(5 50)A,B,C
```

The first comma has been omitted. In this case, the program will not run. Instead, the error will be indicated. An "error message" will be printed on the screen when you attempt to compile the program. The error message will indicate that an error in syntax has occurred. The statement number of the statement with the error will be indicated. Once a statement with an error has been called to your attention, the error can usually be found by carefully proofreading the statement.

When complex programs are written, other types of errors called logical errors sometimes result. In this case, the program is perfectly good FORTRAN but it does not calculate the desired quantity. For instance, suppose that we want to average three numbers. The correct statement would be

$$AVE=(A+B+C)/3$$

Suppose that

$$AVE=(A+B-C)/3$$

were typed instead. This is a perfectly good FORTRAN statement. However, a minus sign was typed instead of a plus sign. In this case, no error message will be given. The computer will simply calculate the wrong value. To "catch" such errors, the results of the program should be *checked using known values*. For instance, the program should be run using $A = 100$, $B = 50$ and $C = 90$. If the answer 80 does not result, then the program should be carefully checked. That is, each statement should be read and its implications carefully considered. Additional helpful debugging procedures are discussed in Chapter 14. The editor is used to modify the program and to remove the bugs. The editing procedures discussed in the last section can be used. In Chapter 14, we shall discuss procedures that make editing easier.

EXERCISES

1.1. Describe the function of the central processor, main storage memory, and magnetic disk memory.

1.2. List the allowable characters used in FORTRAN.

1.3. Describe the function of statement numbers.

1.4. Discuss the layout of a FORTRAN statement card.

1.5 What is a compiler?

1.6 What is a linker?

1.7. Compare a FORTRAN program with a machine language program.

1.8. Write a FORTRAN program which evaluates

$$x = a + 2b + c$$

Run this program on your computer using the values $a = 1$, $b = 3.5$ and $c = 5.1$.

1.9. Repeat Exercise 1.8 for the function

$$x = \frac{(a+b)c}{2(a-b)}$$

1.10. Write a FORTRAN program which evaluates the two functions

$$x = \frac{(a+b)(c+d)}{a - 2b}$$

$$y = \frac{(x+a)(x+b)}{(x - c)}$$

Run the program on your computer using the values

$a = -1.2; b = 3.1; c = -6.8; d = 11.4$

1.11. Write a FORTRAN program to evaluate

$$x = \frac{a + b^2 + c}{(a-b)^2 c^{1/2}}$$

Run the program on your computer using the values

$a = 1.2; \ b = 2.61; \ c = 0.100000E+2$

1.12. Repeat Exercise 1.11 for the function

$$x = \frac{\sqrt{a+b}}{(a+c)^{1/3}}$$

1.13. Write a FORTRAN program to evaluate the function

$$y = \frac{x^2 + 2x + 1}{x^2 + 3}$$

where

$$x = \frac{\sqrt{(a+b)(c-d)}}{(a+d)^3}$$

The values of both x and y should be printed. Run the program on your computer using the values

$a = 1.2; \ b = 3.6; \ c = 15.2; \ d = 11.4$

1.14. Write a FORTRAN program to evaluate the function

$x!$

Run this program on your computer using $x = 6$ [that is, $(1)(2)(3)$ $(4)(5)(6)$].

2 *Arithmetic Operations*

In this chapter we shall discuss FORTRAN statements which are used to perform arithmetic operations. In particular we shall discuss addition, subtraction, multiplication, division, and raising to a power. Here, as in the remainder of the book, we shall write FORTRAN statements using capital letters and we shall write algebraic equations, which are not part of a computer program, using lower case letters.

We shall duplicate some of the material discussed in Secs. 1.3 and 1.4 here. However, the discussion in this chapter is considerably more detailed.

2.1 ADDITION AND SUBTRACTION

The FORTRAN symbols for addition and subtraction are + and −, respectively. That is, they are the conventional plus and minus signs. Thus, a FORTRAN statement involving addition and subtraction will closely resemble an ordinary algebraic equation. For instance, suppose that we wish to add three quantiites, b, c, and d. Let us call their sum a. Then, the algebraic equation would be

$$a = b + c + d \tag{2.1}$$

The corresponding FORTRAN statement would be

$$A = B + C + D \tag{2.2}$$

Similarly, if we wish to perform an operation which corresponds to the algebraic equation

$$a = b + c + d - e - f \tag{2.3}$$

we would write the FORTRAN statement

```
A=B+C+D-E-F
```
(2.4)

Then, FORTRAN statements which involve the operations of addition and subtraction are written in essentially the same way as the corresponding algebraic expressions. (We have written the FORTRAN variables as single letters. In Sec. 2.5, we shall consider how more elaborate names can be used.)

As a final example of addition, consider the following sequence of FORTRAN statements

```
B=1.67
C=3.42
D=1.8Ø
E=Ø.95
A=B+C-D
F=A+D-E
```

In this sequence, we have set the variables B, C, D, and E equal to 1.67, 3.42, 1.80, and 0.95, respectively. Then, we calculate

$$a = b + c - d = 1.67 + 3.42 - 1.80 = 3.29$$

That is, A is equal to 3.29. This value of A is then used in conjunction with D and E to obtain F.

$$f = a + d - e = 3.29 + 1.80 - 0.95 = 4.14$$

The following should be noted. When we set a value of a variable equal to a constant (for example, B=1.67) or compute the value of a variable (for example, A=3.29) the computer remembers this value, that is, the values of the variables are stored in the memory of the computer. At a future time, these values can be obtained from the memory for use in calculations. The names of the variables are designated by the FORTRAN statement. That is, writing B=1.67 causes the value 1.67 to be stored under the name B in the memory. Similarly the statement A=B+C−D computes B+C−D and stores it under the name A.

2.2 MULTIPLICATION, DIVISION, AND EXPONENTIATION

Now let us consider FORTRAN statements which involve multiplication. The symbol for multiplication is the asterisk *. This is used because key punches did not have multiplication signs. Let us assume that we want to compute the product of b and c and set this product equal to a. That is, we wish to obtain the algebraic expression

$$a = bc \qquad\qquad\qquad\qquad (2.5)$$

The corresponding FORTRAN statement is

$$A=B*C \qquad\qquad\qquad\qquad (2.6)$$

Note that we *cannot* write multiplication as A=BC. *The asterisk must always appear between quantities which are to be multiplied.*

As a further example of multiplication, let us consider a program sequence which performs the following algebraic operation

$$a = 2.16, \qquad b = 3.42, \qquad c = a + b, \qquad d = 2ca$$

A FORTRAN program segment that would perform this operation is

```
A=2.16
B=3.42
C=A+B
D=2.*C*A
```

Now let us consider the operation of division. In FORTRAN, division is always indicated by a slash, /. Then, the algebraic expression

$$a = \frac{b}{c} = b/c = b \div c \qquad\qquad\qquad\qquad (2.7)$$

would be written as

$$A=B/C \qquad\qquad\qquad\qquad (2.8)$$

As a further example let us write a FORTRAN program segment which carries out the following algebraic operation

$$a = 1.2, \qquad b = 3.6, \qquad c = a + b, \qquad d = ca/b$$

The corresponding FORTRAN program segment is

```
A=1.2
B=3.6
C=A+B
D=C*A/B
```

The final operation that we consider in this section is exponentiation, or raising to a power. This is conventionally indicated by a superscript. For instance,

$$a^2 = aa \tag{2.9}$$
$$a^{1/2} = \sqrt{a} \tag{2.10}$$

Since superscripts cannot be typed conveniently on key punches or terminals, a special symbol for an exponent (that is, superscript) is used in FORTRAN. This is the double asterisk ** (that is, one asterisk following another). For instance, consider the following algebraic statements.

$$c = a^2 \tag{2.11a}$$
$$d = a^{1/2} \tag{2.11b}$$

The FORTRAN statements which correspond to these are, respectively,

```
C=A**2
D=A**0.5
```
$$\tag{2.12a}$$
$$\tag{2.12b}$$

Note that the exponent is the term which *follows* the double asterisk. In Eq. (2.12b), we wrote 0.5 rather than ½. In this next section we shall discuss the reason for this and indicate how ½ could be used in a statement like (2.12b).

As an example, let us write FORTRAN statements corresponding to the following algebraic equations

$$b = c + d + e, \qquad f = bd/e, \qquad g = \sqrt{f} = f^{0.5}$$

That is, we add the quantities c, d, and e. The result is then multiplied by d/e and the square root of the resultant term is taken. The corresponding FORTRAN program segment is

```
B=C+D+E
F=B*D/E
G=F**Ø.5
```

In the next section we shall consider procedures for working with more complex arithmetic expressions.

2.3 HIERARCHY—USE OF PARENTHESES

Thus far, we have considered arithmetic expressions which have a relatively small number of operations. For instance, in the last example of the previous section, we used three FORTRAN statements to compute a square root. Actually only one statement need be used. If we are to write more complicated algebraic expressions, some rules are required. These rules define the order in which operations are performed.

The rules of *hierarchy* establish the priorities of the operations. Hence, they establish the normal sequence in which the operations will be executed. Let us illustrate hierarchy by considering some algebraic expressions. Suppose that we have the equation

$$a = bc + d/e \tag{2.13}$$

We know that this means to multiply b by c and then to divide d by e and, after this is done, we take the sum of the two resultant expressions. That is,

$$a = (bc) + (d/e)$$

The parentheses clarify the operations. However, because of the usual rules of hierarchy of algebra, they are not necessary. If we did not have these rules, then Eq. (2.13) would not be clear. For instance, suppose that b is multiplied by c and the result is added to d, and *then* the resulting quantity is divided by e, then this would result in

$$a = (bc + d)/e$$

which is a very different result. Thus, the rules of hierarchy are very important if equations are to be clearly defined without using an excessive number of parentheses.

Let us now state the rules of hierarchy in FORTRAN. The FORTRAN statement is examined reading from left to right (that is, in the usual manner). Assume that this is done three times.

a. The first time, *all* exponentiation is performed moving from right to left in the expression.

b. Next, all multiplication and/or division is performed moving left to right.

c. Finally, all addition and/or subtraction is performed moving from left to right.

It is said that there are three levels of hierarchy: (1) exponentiation, (2) multiplication and division, and, last (3) addition and subtraction. If more than one operation is at the same hierarchy level, then the operations are performed in order from left to right with the exception of exponentiation which is performed from right to left. Let us illustrate hierarchy with some examples. Consider the FORTRAN statement

$$A=B+C/D+E**2 \tag{2.14a}$$

The first operation to be performed is that E is squared. Next, C is divided by D. Finally, B, C/D, and E**2 are added. Thus, statement (2.14a) is equivalent to

$$a = b + \frac{c}{d} + e^2 \tag{2.14b}$$

Let us discuss another example

$$A=B*C**3+2.\emptyset*E \tag{2.15a}$$

Here C would be raised to the power 3 first. Next B would be multiplied by C**3 and E would be multiplied by 2. Then, the sum would be taken. Thus, statement (2.15a) is equivalent to the algebraic expression

$$a = b(c^3) + 2.0e \tag{2.15b}$$

Let us consider a third example

$$A=B+C/D-E+F**G \tag{2.16a}$$

First F is raised to the G power. Next C is divided by D and, finally, the sum of all the terms is taken. Thus, statement (2.16a) is equivalent to

$$a = b + \frac{c}{d} - e + f^g \qquad\qquad (2.16b)$$

Parentheses

The rules of hierarchy are very helpful. However, there are times when additional flexibility is required. For instance, consider the algebraic expression

$$a = \frac{c + d}{e + f} \qquad\qquad (2.17a)$$

We cannot use a single FORTRAN expression to represent this equation, if we just rely on hierarchy. However, there is additional flexibility that we can use. Equation (2.17a) can be rewritten in the following way

$$a = (c + d)/(e + f) \qquad\qquad (2.17b)$$

That is, we can use parentheses to group terms. In a similar way, parentheses can be used in FORTRAN. For instance, a FORTRAN statement which is equivalent to Eqs. (2.17) is

$$A=(C+D)/(E+F) \qquad\qquad (2.18)$$

The FORTRAN rules for parentheses are essentially the same as those for algebra. Each expression within a pair of parentheses is treated as a separate expression. These subexpressions are evaluated first. The rules of hierarchy apply to this evaluation. Then each evaluated pair of parentheses is treated as a separate quantity. The resulting "statement" is then evaluated, using the rules of hierarchy. Let us consider some examples to illustrate the use of parentheses

$$A=(B+C)*(D-E)/(F+G) \qquad\qquad (2.19a)$$

Here, the value of B+C, D−E, and F+G are evaluated and *then* the indicated multiplications and divisions are performed. Hence, statement (2.19a) is equivalent to the algebraic expression

$$a = \frac{(b + c)(d - e)}{f + g} \qquad\qquad (2.19b)$$

Note that in FORTRAN, the asterisk *must always* be used to indicate multiplication: (B+C)(D−E) would be *incorrect*.

As another example, consider

$$A=(B+C)*(D-E)**\emptyset.5 \tag{2.20a}$$

Here, the quantities B+C and D−E are evaluated first. Then, according to the rules of hierarchy, D−E is raised to the 0.5 power and then this square root is multiplied by B+C. Thus, the equivalent algebraic expression is

$$a = (b + c)[(d - e)^{0.5}] \tag{2.20b}$$

In Eq. (2.20b), we have used both brackets and parentheses. It would be convenient to have this type of operation in FORTRAN. Unfortunately, parentheses are the *only* symbols used to group terms in FORTRAN. However, this is actually not a limitation since, in FORTRAN, parentheses can be enclosed within other parentheses. For instance,

$$A=(B+C)*(D+(E+F)*(G+H)) \tag{2.21a}$$

The rule used is that the expressions within the inner parentheses are evaluated first and then the evaluation moves to the expressions contained within the outer ones. The rules of hierarchy apply with all parentheses. They also apply to the overall expression within each set of parentheses. Each set of parentheses which has already been evaluated is treated as a separate quantity. Let us consider statement (2.21a). First E+F and G+H would be evaluated. These would be treated as two separate quantities. Then, B+C is evaluated and then D+(E+F)*(G+H) is evaluated. The product of this term and B+C is taken. Hence, the algebraic expression equivalent to statement (2.21a) is

$$a = (b + c)[d + (e + f)(g + h)] \tag{2.21b}$$

As another example, let us consider

$$A=(B**(C-D))/((D+E)*(F+G)) \tag{2.22a}$$

Applying the rules as before, we have the equivalent algebraic expression

$$a = \frac{b(c-d)}{(d+e)(f+g)} \qquad (2.22b)$$

We have considered pairs of parentheses nested with another pair of parentheses. Actually there may be several orders of nesting. The innermost pairs of parentheses are evaluated first. Each of these pairs of parentheses is then treated as a single quantity. Then the remaining innermost parentheses are treated, etc. For instance,

```
A=((B+C)*(D+(E+F)*(G+H)))**Ø.5
```

is equivalent to

$$a = \sqrt{(b+c)[d+(e+f)(g+h)]}$$

As a final example, let us consider the quadratic equation

$$ax^2 + bx + c = 0 \qquad (2.23)$$

A formula which gives the roots of this expression is

$$x = \frac{-b \pm \sqrt{b^2 - 4ac}}{2a} \qquad (2.24)$$

Let us assume that $b^2 - 4ac$ is positive and write two FORTRAN statements which evaluate these two roots. They are

```
X1=(-B+(B**2-4.*A*C)**(1./2.))/(2.Ø*A)   (2.25a)
X2=(-B-(B**2-4.*A*C)**(1./2.))/(2.Ø*A)   (2.25b)
```

Note that we have called our variables X1 and X2. This illustrates that variables in FORTRAN need not be only one letter. We shall discuss this further in Sec. 2.5. Note that we have used the parentheses to write the exponent as 1./2.. Actually, it could be written as Ø.5 in which case the parentheses around the exponent could be omitted.

The programmer should be careful when there are parentheses within parentheses. It is easy to accidentally omit one. A rule which can be used to partially check statements is that there must be an equal number of right and left parentheses in each statement.

Let us consider another place where parentheses are required. We have used the plus and minus signs to add or subtract two variables. The minus sign can also be used as an operator which changes the sign of a variable. For instance, suppose we want to use the negative of the value of the variable called D. We would write this in the FORTRAN statement as −D. Now let us use this in a FORTRAN statement. A simple one is

$$A=B*C*(-D)$$

Note the parentheses. They are included since it is *improper* to have two arithmetic signs follow each other. That is A=B*C*−D would be an incorrect FORTRAN statement.

Parentheses are also required when exponentiation is used twice. For instance, A**B**C is not allowed. Instead, write (A**B)**C or A**(B**C).

2.4 THE EQUALS SIGN

In FORTRAN, the equals sign has a special meaning which is different from its algebraic one. To define it let us again consider some arithmetic FORTRAN statements. For instance,

$$A=B+C*D \tag{2.26}$$

A single variable *must* be on the left-hand side of the equals sign. An arithmetic expression lies to the right of the equals sign. (This expression to the right of the equals sign can also be a single number or variable.) When the FORTRAN program is compiled and executed, the following occurs. A place in the memory is reserved for the variable to the left of the equals sign (in this case, A). Then, the value of B+C*D is computed and stored in the memory location reserved for A. If, at a subsequent time in the program, A is used again, its value will be read from the memory and used. It is important to note that the value of A remains in the memory for possible future use. For instance, consider the sequence

```
B=2.5
A=2.Ø*B
C=A+3.Ø
D=C+B
```

In this sequence, a memory location for B would be reserved and the number 2.5 would be stored in it. Then, 2.Ø*B which is in fact numerically equal to 5.0 would be calculated and stored in a memory location called A. This value of A would be used to calculate A+3.Ø which is numerically equal to 8.0 which would be stored in a memory location called C. Finally, C+B which is numerically equal to 10.5 would be calculated and stored in a memory location called D.

Thus far, the equals sign seems equivalent to the algebraic one. However, there are differences. If a FORTRAN expression calculates A, after A has already been stored in the memory, then the old value of A will be erased (that is, destroyed) and the new value will be stored in the memory. For instance, consider the following

```
A=2.5
B=2.Ø*A
A=B+3.Ø
C=3.Ø*A
```

In this case, the value of 2.5 will be stored in the memory location for A. Then 2.Ø*A which is numerically equal to 5.0 will be stored in the memory location for B. Next, B+3.Ø which is numerically equal to 8.0 will be calculated. This value will replace the previous stored value of A. Thus, 8.0 will now be stored in the memory location designated A. Finally, 3.Ø*A which is numerically equal to 24.0 will be calculated and stored in the memory location for C. Thus, the equals sign in FORTRAN means replace the value stored in the memory for the variable to the left of the equals sign by the value computed to the right of the equals sign. Note that the terms to the right of the equals sign must be such that a *numerical* value can be computed (that is, they must be numbers and/or variables which have already been stored in the memory).

Because of the definition of the equals sign in FORTRAN, there are FORTRAN statements which have no parallel in algebraic statements. For instance,

$$A=3.5 \tag{2.27a}$$

$$A=A+1.5 \tag{2.27b}$$

Statement (2.27b) would not be a valid algebraic equation. In FORTRAN it means that we must replace A by its previous value plus 1.5. Thus, after both of these statements have been executed, the stored value of A is 5.0. Note that A+1.5 is calculated and *then* the value of A is replaced in the memory.

As a final example, consider

```
A=3.0
B=2.0
C=A+B
A=C*B+A
```

Here the values 3.0 and 2.0 are stored under the names A and B, respectively. Then, A+B which is numerically equal to 5.0 is calculated and stored under the name C. Finally, C*B+A which is numerically equal to 5(2)+3 is calculated and this replaces the value stored under the name A.

The reader may ask why we bother to redefine the value of a variable and why we do not just define a new one. There are several advantages to redefining variables. For one thing, the programmer does not have to keep track of so many variables. In addition, we shall discuss in subsequent chapters that in certain calculations, it is often very helpful to redefine variable values. Finally, the number of variables that can be stored is limited by the size of the memory. When large programs are written, it is desirable to minimize the number of variables so that the available memory is not used up. Redefining variable values minimizes the amount of *storage space* required, since new variables need not be defined and stored in the memory.

2.5 INTEGER AND REAL NUMBERS—VARIABLE NAMES

In FORTRAN a distinction is made between integers and numbers with decimal points. The integers are whole numbers without fractional or decimal parts. Some typical integers are

```
1
15
236
19467
```

(Another name for an integer is a *fixed point number.* This is because the decimal point can be consider to be fixed at the extreme right of the number.)

Numbers containing decimal parts can also be used. Such decimal numbers are also called *real* numbers or *floating point numbers.* Typical decimal numbers are

        2.316
      146.57
        0.015
        1.0
        2.
      136.

Note that real numbers can have zero fractional parts (for example, 1.0, 2., or 136.). However, they all have a decimal point. The decimal point is used to indicate *to the compiler* that they are real numbers. We shall subsequently discuss, in this and in the next section, that the decimal point need not always be used to designate a real number. Other procedures will be given to designate a real number.

The reader may ask why we bother to have two types of numbers. Actually, there are several reasons. For one thing, integers require less storage space than do reals. In addition, the operations using integers are usually faster than those using real numbers. At times, the integer operations are more accurate than those using real numbers. Of course, if the calculations involve fractional numbers, then the real mode must be used. Usually, real numbers are used in scientific calculations. In addition, computers usually are such that the allowable range of real numbers is much greater than the allowable range of integers (for example, the largest allowable real number is much larger than the largest allowable integer).

There are various ways in which the programmer signifies if the value to be assigned to a variable is an integer or a real value. We shall call a variable an integer variable if it can only have integer values assigned to it. We shall call a variable a real variable if it can have real values assigned to it, and in this chapter we shall consider a basic procedure for doing this. In Chapter 10 we will indicate procedures for modifying the basic procedure given here.

The fundamental procedure for designating whether a variable is an integer or a real variable is by its name. Let us talk about a variable's name. It can consist of up to six characters. The characters can only be letters or numbers. The *first* character *must* be a letter. Thus, some allowable variable names are

        A   AMT   RATE   VOLTS
        ITEM3   NUMBER   AMT2   A3

Some names which are not allowed are 2ABC (starts with a number), MAXIMUM (too many characters), A2.3 (uses characters other than numbers and letters). There is one exception to this rule. The symbol $ can be used as the first (or other) character of a name. However, its use as a first character should be avoided in MICROSOFT FORTRAN.

Using multiple characters for variable names allows us to use more variables. Also it is somewhat helpful to keep track of the variables by giving them descriptive names. For instance,

        VOLTS=AMPS*RES

The first letter in the variable name indicates whether it is an integer (fixed point) variable or a real (floating point) variable. If the name starts with an I, J, K, L, M, or N, then it is an integer variable. If the variable name starts with any *other* letter, then it is a real variable. (This procedure can be modified and we shall discuss such modifications in Secs. 10.1 and 10.2. However, for the time being, we shall not consider such modifications.)

Some integer variable names are

        I   ITEM   JACK   K2
        KABC3   LAP4   MONEY   NUMBER

Some real variable names are

        ABLE   TIME   ANUMB   BOX
        RATE   CURRENT   ZERO

In the next section we shall discuss mixing of real and integer values. However, for the time being, let us keep them separate. Do not use integers for input or output until Chapter 3 is read.

All of the arithmetic operations that we have discussed can be used in either fixed point or floating point modes. For instance, consider

```
I=4
J=2
NUMB=I*J+3
```

This computes the value of NUMB which is equal to $4(2) + 3 = 11$. One fact should be noted: *An integer (fixed point) variable cannot contain any fractional part.* If we attempt to include such a part, it will be disregarded by the computer. For instance, consider the following

```
I=10
J=6
NUMB=I/J
```

When NUMB is calculated, the computer will take the ratio $10/6 = 1.666...$. However, since NUMB is an integer variable, the fractional part of the number will be *truncated* (i.e., disregarded). Thus, the value of NUMB will be the integer 1. Care should be taken when assigning variable names. One very common error made by programmers is to accidently give an integer name to a real variable or vice versa.

A single program can contain statements involving integer and real variables. For instance,

```
A=3.0
I=2
J=2
NUMB=I*J
B=2.0
COST=A+B
```

The exponent of a real variable can be an integer variable. For instance,

```
I=2
J=3
A=3.4
NUMB=I*J
COST=A**NUMB
```

Here, NUMB is calculated as 2(3) = 6. Then, COST is obtained by raising 3.4 to the sixth power. Note that an exponent can be a real as well as an integer value.

The magnitude of an integer or real number is limited by the computer. The integers in MICROSOFT FORTRAN can lie between –32768 and 32767. For example,

    1346,   −17698

will be acceptable integer numbers while

    12341689437123

would not be acceptable since it is too large.

Real numbers are also limited. A real number in MICROSOFT FORTRAN can contain seven significant figures. This does *not* mean that numbers larger than

    9999999

or smaller than

    .0000001

cannot be worked with. Scientific or exponential notation can be used. For instance, we can write (algebraically)

    $0.00000001230421 = .1230421 \times 10^{-7}$

Similarly, we can write some very large numbers as

    $1230421000000000 = .1230421 \times 10^{16}$

This type of notation can be used with FORTRAN. However, as we have discussed, superscripts are not used. Instead, as we have seen in the letter E is used to indicate a power of 10. That is, 1.236×10^{23} would be written as

    1.236E23

Negative exponents as well as positive ones can be utilized here. For instance, 0.967456×10^{-36} would be written as

.967456E−36

The value of the exponent is limited. In general, the exponent can vary between +38 and −38 (for example, .9999999E38 and .0000001E−38). Note that the exponent is an integer constant.

    A real variable can have seven significant figures. For instance, .1234567E30 is a very large number but it only has seven significant figures. The number of significant figures has to do with precision, and *not* with the size of the number. Seven-place precision is sufficient for many calculations. However, there are times when greater precision is required. FORTRAN compilers have a feature called DOUBLE PRECISION. This allows the use of twice the number of significant figures. In Chapter 8 we shall discuss DOUBLE PRECISION operations. For the time being we shall work with ordinary real constants. These are termed single precision constants. Unless extreme precision is required, computations should be made on a single precision basis. Double precision numbers require twice as much storage space in the memory. In addition, double precision calculations are slower than single precision ones.

    An interesting difference between the integer (fixed point) mode and the real (floating point) mode should be pointed out. An integer is stored in the computer as an exact integer. Thus, if we write

      I = 3
      J = 2
      K = I * J

we will obtain the value 6 for K. On the other hand, if we write

      A = 3 . 0
      B = 2 . 0
      C = A * B

we may obtain the value 5.999999 or 6.000001 for the answer. This has to do with the way that real numbers are handled by the computer. When real numbers are manipulated, there may be some loss of accuracy (for example, loss of the last significant figure). This is termed roundoff error since the computer automatically limits the number of significant figures. When many calculations are performed, or in certain critical calculations, this loss in accuracy due to roundoff which results when real numbers are used can be important. Of course, we cannot substitute integer calculations for real calculations in most cases, so that this is not a solution. Usually, if roundoff error becomes large, double precision is used.

Let us now assume that a real number becomes larger or smaller than the value that the computer can work with. For instance, suppose that the largest allowable exponent is 38 and that the largest allowable real number is .9999999E38. Similarly, the smallest positive real number (other than $\emptyset$) is .$\emptyset\emptyset\emptyset\emptyset\emptyset\emptyset$1E$-$38. Now consider the statement

A=B$^\times$C

Suppose that B=1.7E2$\emptyset$ and C=3.4E3$\emptyset$. The result for A should be 5.78E5$\emptyset$. The computer cannot work properly with this value. Thus, an erroneous result will be obtained for A. Such a result is said to be due to an *overflow*. An error message will be printed to indicate that an overflow has occurred. Computation will proceed and, in effect, results may be obtained. (In some circumstances, the error message may not be printed.)

Now consider that B=1.7E-2$\emptyset$ and C=3.4E-3$\emptyset$. Then, A should equal 5.78E-5$\emptyset$. This number is too small for the computer. Again, an erroneous result occurs. This is said to be due to an *underflow*. The answer will be set equal to zero. This may result in subsequent errors.

Another problem can result when division is performed. If the divisor is zero, the division is not performed and an error message will be printed. Operation will then be terminated.

2.6 MIXED MODE OPERATION

In the last section we discussed the integer (fixed point) and real (floating point) modes of operation. But we have not considered *mixed mode* operation, that is, we never used a statement containing both modes. (An exception to this is a real number raised to an integer power. This is a standard operation and is usually not termed mixed mode operation.) Actually, the FORTRAN compilers provide for mixed mode operation. For instance, suppose that we have the sequence of statements

$$I = 2 \tag{2.28a}$$
$$A = 3.5 \tag{2.28b}$$
$$B = A + I \tag{2.28c}$$

The third statement would be evaluated in the following way. Prior to taking the sum, the integer value 2 would automatically be converted into the real value 2., and then the sum would be obtained as 5.5. Note that the value of I which is stored in the memory remains as the integer 2.

Although mixed mode is allowable, sometimes it leads to unexpected results. We shall consider some of the details of mixed mode operation here so that these unexpected results can be avoided.

The general rule that covers mixed mode operation is the following: Whenever an arithmetic operation takes place involving two variables, one of which is real and the other an integer, the integer is converted to a real value and *then* the arithmetic operation takes place. In the example of statement (2.28), the integer value of 2 was converted to the real number 2. before the addition took place.

Let us consider some other examples. Suppose

    A=3*4+6.2

The first operation to be performed is 3*4. This is *not* a mixed mode operation since 3 and 4 are both integers. The product gives the integer value 12. Next 12 is added to the real number 6.2. This is a mixed mode operation. Hence, the integer 12 is converted to the real number 12. which is then added to 6.2. Then, the resulting value for A is 18.2.

Let us now consider a case where mixed mode operation can give erroneous results:

    A=5/4+6.2

The first operation is the division of 5 by 4. This is an integer operation since both 5 and 4 are integers. Algebraically 5/4 = 1.25. However, when the integer division is performed, 5/4 gives the *possibly unexpected* value of 1. since, when an integer is formed, the fractional part of the result is disregarded. This integer is *then* converted to a real number and added to 6.2. Thus, we obtain the result A=7.2 rather than 7.45 as might be expected. Even more surprising results occur if we perform the operation

A=3/4*(1.2+3.8)

The first operation to be performed is the division of the integer numbers 3 and 4. Since the fractional part is discarded, this division yields zero, which is then converted into a real number ($\emptyset$.) and multiplied by 5.$\emptyset$. Thus, the result is A=$\emptyset$. . Let us consider another statement

A=3/4.$\emptyset$*(1.2+3.8)

Here the first operation is the division of the integer 3 by the real number 4.$\emptyset$. This is a mixed mode operation. Hence, the integer is converted to 3.$\emptyset$. The division of two real numbers then proceeds. Then, the statement results in

A=$\emptyset$.75*5.

or

A=3.75

Now, consider the previous examples. A FORTRAN statement such as

A=I*J+B

will yield expected results, while one such as

A=I/J+B   (2.29)

may yield unexpected results. Note that A=I/D+B will *not* yield unexpected results since the division will not be in the real mode. One operation which can be used to eliminate the problem of working with mixed mode operation is to convert the integer numbers to real numbers. There are several procedures for doing this. We shall discuss one of them here.

Consider the sequence

I=2
AI=I

The variable AI is set equal to I. However, AI is a real variable (it starts with an A). Thus, the value stored in the memory location for AI will be the real number 2. . Then, AI can be used instead of I in all subsequent real operations. For instance,

$$
\begin{array}{l}
B=2. \\
J=4 \\
I=J-1 \\
AI=I \\
AJ=J \\
B=AI/AJ+B
\end{array}
$$
                                                                    (2.30)

When statement (2.30) is evaluated, we have the equivalent of

$$B=3./4.+2.$$

This is not a mixed mode operation and we obtain B=2.75.

A similar procedure can be used to convert real numbers into integers. For instance,

$$
\begin{array}{l}
A=3. \\
IA=A
\end{array}
$$

Since IA is an integer variable, the stored value of IA will be the integer 3. Care should be taken when real values are converted to integers. For instance,

$$
\begin{array}{l}
A=3.6 \\
IA=A
\end{array}
$$

In this case, the fractional part of 3.6 will be disregarded when it is stored as an integer and IA will be equal to 3.

Other difficulties can occur when converting from real to integer values. For instance, suppose that the value of a real variable should be 6.∅. Roundoff error can cause it to be calculated as 5.999999. If this is converted to an integer, the fractional part will be disregarded and the integer 5 will be obtained. One procedure for eliminating this problem is to add ∅.5 to the real variable before converting it to an integer. For instance, 5.999999 + .5 = 6.499999. When this is converted to an integer, 6 results, which is the desired value. This procedure will result in conversion to the integer closest to the real variable. For instance, if A is equal to 5.6, then adding $\emptyset$.5 results in the value 6.1. Conversion to an integer then yields 6, which is the integer closest to 5.6. A single statement which accomplishes this conversion is

```
IA=A+Ø.5
```

Let us consider one other example. Suppose

```
I=3*4.5+2
```

This mixed mode 3*4.5 would result in 3's being converted to the real 3. . The product then yields 13.5. Then, the addition is a mixed mode operation which results in 2's being converted to a real value. The sum is then 15.5. Since I is an integer variable, the fractional part would be disregarded and the integer value 15 would be stored in the memory for I.

EXERCISES

2.1 Assume that the following values have been assigned to variables in FORTRAN statements

A=2.$\emptyset$ B=3.$\emptyset$ C=2.5   D=1.5

Determine the numerical values that would be computed for X in the following FORTRAN statements.

(a) X=A+B   (b) X=B+C-D   (c) X=A+B-C+D

2.2 Write FORTRAN statements which are equivalent to the following algebraic statements.

(a) $x = a + b$ (b) $x = a + b - c + d$

2.3 Assume that the following values have been assigned to variables in FORTRAN statements

A=2.$\emptyset$ B=3.$\emptyset$ C=2.5   D=1.5

Determine the numerical values that would be computed for X in the following FORTRAN statements

(a) X=A*B   (b) X=B/C   (c) X=A*B/C
(d) X=A**2   (e) X=A**B

Check your results by writing a FORTRAN program and running it on your computer.

2.4 Write FORTRAN statements that are equivalent to the following algebraic statements where a and b are variables

$$x = ab \qquad x = a/2 \qquad x = a^3$$

2.5 Repeat Exercise 2.3 for the following FORTRAN statements.

(a) X=A+B/C   (b) X=A+B*C+D/A   (c) X=A+B*C**A
(d) X=A/B**A   (e) X=A/B*C

2.6 Repeat Exercise 2.3 for the following FORTRAN statements

(a) X=(A+B)*(C+D)
(b) X=(A-3.1)*C+D-2.0)
(c) X=(A+B)**(A+1.0)
(d) X=(A+B)/(C+D)
(e) X=((A+B)/(C+D))*(A+B**2.0)
(f) X=((((A+C)*(A+B))/(C+D))/(B-A))**2.0

2.7 After the following FORTRAN statements are evaluated, what will the values of A, B, and C stored in the memory be?

```
A=2.0
B=3.0
C=A+B
A=C**B
B=A+C
```

2.8 Repeat Exercise 2.7 for the following sequence.

```
A=2.0
B=3.0
C=A+B
```

```
A=A+C
B=A+B
B=+1.0
```

2.9 Identify the follow as integer or real numbers.

1236   1461.   1.679   0.0016   13275

2.10 Identify the following as integer or real variables.

ABLE   FIXED   VOLTS
INPUT   ITEM   KEE3   LAP
NUMBER   TIME   MITE2

2.11 Write a FORTRAN statement which adds two integers and multiplies this result by the integer 6.

2.12 Consider the following FORTRAN statement.

```
ITEM=KEY/JAM
```

If the values of KEY and JAM stored in the memory are 3 and 5, respectively, what will be the value of ITEM?

2.13 Consider the following FORTRAN statements

```
A=RATE**2
```
and
```
A=RATE**2.0
```

Are these both valid statements?

2.14 Write the following numbers in conventional form. Indicate how many significant figures each has.

(a) 2.357E3   (b) 2.6942E10   (c) .9164E5
(d) .1679421E−5   (e) .16793E23

2.15 Assume that the following values have been assigned to variables in FORTRAN statements.

A=2.0   B=3.0   C=2.5   I=2   J=3

Determine the numerical value that would be computed for X in each of the following FORTRAN statements.

```
X=A+B*I+I*J
X=I/J+B+C
X=I/(J+B)+C/A
X=I*A+J*B
```

2.16 Determine the value of X as a result of the evaluation of the following program sequence

```
A=3.5
B=2.5
I=2
J=3
X=I/J*(A+B)
```

To check your results, write a FORTRAN program and run it on your computer.

2.17 Repeat Exercise 2.16 for the following program sequence

```
A=3.5
B=2.5
I=2
J=3
AI=I
AJ=J
X=AI/AJ*(A+B)
```

2.18 Write a FORTRAN program which will convert a length expressed in inches to one expressed in centimeters. (1 in = 2.54 cm) Check this program by running it on your computer.

2.19 Write a FORTRAN program which will convert a length expressed in feet and inches (e.g., 12 ft 2 in) to meters. (1 in = 0.0254 m) Check this program by running it on your computer.

3 Input and Output Statements

Thus far we have discussed the programming of arithmetic operations. However, we have only briefly considered how data could be supplied to the computer or how the values calculated by the computer could be returned to the user. In this chapter we shall consider procedures for entering and extracting data. We shall also discuss two additional simple FORTRAN statements. Once this is done, we shall have discussed in detail all the statements needed to write *complete* programs that can be run on your computer.

3.1 FORMATTED INPUT STATEMENTS—FORMAT STATEMENTS

We shall now consider formatted input statements. These statements can be used with any standard compiler. This material was briefly considered in Sec. 1.4. A simple formatted READ statement is of the form

$$\text{READ}(5,4\emptyset)A,B,C \tag{3.1}$$

This will cause the value of the variables A, B, and C to be read from data entered from the terminal. The general form of the READ statement is READ followed by parentheses containing two numbers, separated by a comma. These numbers are called a device number and a FORMAT statement number, respectively. A list of variables then follows the parentheses. The variables are separated by commas. Note that there is no comma between the parenthesis and the list. In this example, we have used three variables. However, this number can vary.

Let us consider the numbers in the parentheses. The first number, in this case, 5, indicates the device from which the data is to be read. The number 5 refers to the terminal. This number is called a *logical unit number* (LUN). In MICROSOFT FORTRAN, the LUNs are given certain preassigned values. These are listed in Table 3.1.

Table 3.1 Preassigned Logical Unit Numbers in MICROSOFT FORTRAN

Device	LUN
Terminal	1, 3, 4, or 5
Line Printer	2
Disk Drives	6, 7, 8, 9, or 10

In Chapter 15 we shall discuss procedures for changing the LUNs. At that time we shall also discuss the procedures for reading from or writing on a disk.

The second number in the parentheses of the READ statement refers to a FORTRAN statement number. This statement must be of a very special kind. It is called a FORMAT statement. One purpose of the FORMAT statement is to specify how the data is supplied. A typical READ statement and its associated FORMAT statement would be

```
      READ(5,4Ø)M,J,K                          (3.2a)
4Ø    FORMAT(I4,I3,I5)                         (3.2b)
```

We shall use these statements to begin our disucssion of FORMAT statements. Consider statement (3.2b). The statement number (4Ø in this case) is only used to indicate that the READ statement refers to that particular FORMAT statement (numbered 4Ø), (A complete program may have many FORMAT statements and they are always designated by their statement numbers.) The terms in the parentheses of the FORMAT statement are specifications. There is one specification for each variable (in the next section we shall modify this statement). The letter I means that the variable in question is an integer. Thus, this is called an I-FORMAT field specifier or I-mask. Note that each specification is separated from the next by a comma. The specification for an integer is *always* the letter I followed by an integer number. The number following the I indicates the number of columns of the line allocated for typing the variable. For instance, for statements (3.2), the value of the variable M would be typed in the first four columns, the variable J would be obtained from the *next* three columns and the variable K would be typed in the *next* five columns. Thus, if

M=1234
J=123
K=12345

then the data typed on one line of the terminal would be

$$1234\ 123\ 12345 \tag{3.3}$$

$$\uparrow \qquad \uparrow \qquad \uparrow$$
column 1 | column 8
column 5

Note that the arrows and column numbers are not written on the terminal. These are only included here for purposes of explanation.

The FORMAT specification is rather rigid. For instance, if we have

M=23
J=234
K=345

and we use the FORMAT statement (3.2b) then we must enter the data in the following way

$$bb23\ 234\ bb345 \tag{3.4}$$

$$\uparrow \qquad \uparrow \qquad \uparrow$$
column 1 | column 8
column 5

Each lowercase b represents a blank space. The b's do not appear on the screen. They are only printed here so that the spaces can be represented in this book. That is, (3.4) actually appears as

$$23\ 234\quad 345 \tag{3.5}$$

$$\uparrow \qquad \uparrow \qquad \uparrow$$
column 1 | column 10
column 5

A specification of the FORMAT statement is said to designate the length of a *field*. Thus, in statements (3.2), the field for A is columns 1 to 4, the field for B is columns 5 to 7, and the field for C is columns 8 to 12.

Note that the integers are moved as far as possible to the right of their fields. They are said to be *right adjusted*. This is done for the following reason. The *blanks are interpreted as zeros*. Thus, if (3.5) represents the data corresponding to statements (3.2), the value of A would be

$$000023$$

which is the same as 23. However, if we replace the data of (3.5) by

$$23bb234bb345 \qquad\qquad (3.6)$$

$$\uparrow \qquad \uparrow \qquad \uparrow$$

column 1 | column 8

      column 5

then the value of A will be

$$2300$$

which is very different from 23. Hence, *all integers must be right adjusted*.

All the information about the integer must be included in the field specified by the FORMAT statement. In particular, if a minus sign is included, then it will occupy one of the columns. As an example, consider statements (3.2). If J is positive, it can contain up to three digits. However, if it is negative, then it can have only two digits since one of the columns of its field would be occupied by the minus sign. For instance, if

$$
\begin{aligned}
M &= -123 \\
J &= -23 \qquad\qquad\qquad (3.7)\\
K &= 345
\end{aligned}
$$

then the data card would be printed in the following way

$$b-123-23bb345$$

The b's again represent blank spaces. They are just written here to help the reader keep track of the number of blanks. Note that each integer is right adjusted.

A line contains 8∅ columns. We have used 19 of them. Thus, we can physically type numbers in the remaining columns. However, if statements (3.2) are used, then this information will be ignored by the computer, since it only "reads" in the fields indicated by the FORMAT specifications.

When the FORMAT statement is written, enough columns should be allocated for each variable. For instance, if it is known that the integer to be entered lies between −9999 and 9999 then five columns should be allocated for the field. In general, if the maximum number of digits of the data is not exactly known, then extra columns should be allocated to the field.

There are operations that we can use to modify the previous statements. The return terminates a line. For instance if, in response to statement (3.2), we entered the data

$$1234b56bbb5\emptyset \quad (\text{RETURN}) \qquad\qquad (3.8)$$

then the values assigned would be

$$\begin{aligned} M&=1234\\ J&=56 \qquad\qquad\qquad\qquad\qquad\qquad (3.9)\\ K&=5\emptyset \end{aligned}$$

That is, blanks beyond the **RETURN** would not be counted.

If the field is wider than the numbers to be entered, then blank spaces have to be entered to right adjust the data in the field. The counting of blanks can be tedious. MICROSOFT FORTRAN provides a procedure that eliminates the difficulty. If a comma is typed, then a field is ended. For instance if, in response to statement (3.2), we typed

$$12,34,5 \quad (\text{RETURN}) \qquad\qquad (3.10)$$

then the values assigned would be

$$\begin{aligned} M&=12\\ J&=34 \qquad\qquad\qquad\qquad\qquad\qquad (3.11)\\ K&=5 \end{aligned}$$

The commas and the **RETURN** have ended the field.

Note that the data for M must be typed in the first four columns, the data for J must be typed in the three columns following the first comma, and the data for K must be typed in the next five columns

following the second comma. That is, the comma terminates the field.
For instance, if we type

    bbbb5,6,7 (RETURN)   (3.12)

then the assigned values will be

    M=∅
    J=5   (3.13)
    K=6

The first four blanks constitute the field for M and, hence, M is assigned
the value ∅. The 5 is then assigned to J and the 6 to K. The value of 7
is ignored.

    The field specifier was developed when data input was on punched
cards and the saving of columns was important. When keyboard input is
accomplished with a terminal, then the counting of columns becomes
very tedious and the use of commas, as discussed, is to be encouraged.

    Now let us consider the input of real data. We shall consider the
real single precision numbers without an exponent. In this case, the
field specified in the FORMAT statement uses an F rather than an I.
This is called an F FORMAT field specifier or an F-*mask*. For instance,
consider the statements

        READ(5,11)A,B,C   (31.4a)
11   FORMAT(F6.3,F7.2,F4.1)   (3.14b)

The letter F specifies that the number in the field corresponds to a real
number. Again, the field specifications of the FORMAT statement are
separated from each other by commas and there is one for each variable.

    Now let us consider the numbers following the F. For instance,

    F6.3   (3.15)

The first number specifies the number of columns in the field. This is
the same as in the integer case. For instance, for the statement of
(3.14), A would be given in the first six columns of the line, B in the
next seven columns and C in the next four columns. The number following the decimal point indicates the number of digits following the
decimal point in the actual number. For instance, if the data card corresponding to statements (3.14) is

123456 12345671234   (3.16)

then the values for A, B, and C would be

    A=123.456
    B=12345.67   (3.17)
    C=123.4

The use of the FORMAT statement allows real data to be entered without typing the decimal point. Thus, more data can be put on a single line since a column is not needed for the decimal point. However, there are times when this is too restrictive. For instance, suppose [see statements (3.17)] that we want to enter

    A=1234.5

This can be done without changing the FORMAT statement. If a decimal point is actually typed, then it takes precedence over the decimal point specified in the FORMAT statement. Thus, if, corresponding to statements (3.14), we have the data

    1234.512345671.23

then the values of A, B, and C will be

    A=1234.5
    B=12345.67
    C=1.23

If a decimal point is included in the data then, when the F FORMAT is used, the data does not have to be right adjusted. However, where the decimal point is not included, then we must right adjust the data. Remember that blanks are interpreted as zeros. Again, let us consider some examples which illustrate this. Suppose that, corresponding to statements (3.14), we have data such as

    12bbbb1234567123b

then the values of the assigned variables would be

    A=120.000   B=12345.67   C=123.0

The blanks are interpreted as zeros. Then, all of the previous rules will apply with blanks treated as zeros. Thus, the programmer must be very careful when blanks are included. Suppose that we want A=.12∅, B=12345.67, and C=12.3. The data should appear as

    bbb12∅1234567b123   (3.18)

In this case, we have right adjusted the data.

    If a decimal point is included, then right adjustment is not required. For instance, the data of (3.18) could be replaced by

    .12bbb123456712.3

Then we have

    A=.12∅∅∅
    B=12345.67
    C=12.3

The blanks are still interpreted as zeros. However, in this case, they do not change the value of the numbers. Thus, including the decimal point when real data is entered can eliminate errors. However, each decimal point so entered does occupy an entire column and, thus, takes up space.

    If a real number is negative, then a minus sign must be typed. Of course, this occupies a column. For instance, suppose that we use the following data for statement (3.14)

    -12.3b1234567-123

The data would be

    A=-12.3∅
    B=12345.67
    C=-12.3

The same rules apply as before to obtain these values. The minus sign, when it occurs, just occupies a column.

    In preparing a FORMAT statement the number of columns allowed for a variable field should be considered carefully. For instance, if we know that the data is to consist of real numbers varying between

9999 and −9999 and that there are to be three decimal places (that is, −2163.976) then at least eight columns should be allowed for the numbers if the decimal point is not to be typed. That is, the field specification should be F8.3. The eight columns are taken up by the seven digits and the minus sign (if it is needed), If we also want to type the decimal point, then nine columns should be allowed (for example, F9.3). The programmer should always be careful that enough columns are allocated to enter the number. For instance, in the previous example, a number larger than 99999999. could not be entered. Thus, when all the data are not known when the program is written, it is desirable to allow extra columns. If possible, room should be allowed for decimal points since their inclusion eliminates a possible source of error.

Now let us consider the entering of data in exponential form. In this case, the field specifications in the FORMAT statement use an E (rather than an F or an I). Thus, it is called an E FORMAT field specifier or E *mask*. For instance, consider the FORTRAN statements

```
        READ(5,23)A,B,C,D                        (3.19a)
23      FORMAT(E12.5,E15.7,E14.7,E12.4)          (3.19b)
```

The letter E in the specifications indicates that a real number, expressed in exponential form, is to be entered. Again, the field specifications are separated by commas.

The numbers following the E have essentially the same significance as they do in the F FORMAT. For instance,

E12.5

The first number (12 in this case) specifies the *total* number of columns in the field. Thus, in the example of statements (3.19), *all* of the information concerning A would be entered in the first 12 columns, *all* of the information concerning B would be entered in columns 13 to 27 (the next 15 columns), *all* of the information concerning C would be entered in columns 28 to 41 (the next 14 columns), etc. Again, the number following the decimal point in the field specifications indicates the number of digits following the decimal point. The E FORMAT is, thus, similar to the F FORMAT. However, there are several factors which must be considered. To simplify the discussion, at the start we shall assume that the decimal point is always typed.

Let us consider some typical exponential numbers

    $-\emptyset.39657E-23$
    $-\emptyset.26417E15$
    $\emptyset.34619E-13$

Each of these has five places following the decimal point. However, many more columns of the card are required. For instance, for the first number, twelve columns are required, five columns for the five places following the decimal point, one column each for the minus sign, zero, decimal point, E, and minus sign of the exponent, and two for the two digits of the exponent. Thus, we require at least seven columns more than the maximum number of decimal places used. For instance,

    E12.5

is a satisfactory designation for this data. There can be some exceptions to this. If all the data to be entered is positive, then the space for the minus sign can be omitted. The zero preceding the decimal point can be omitted. In some cases, if it is known that all the input numbers are to be greater than one, then a column need not be saved for the sign of the exponent. However, to be most general, space should be reserved for a minus sign in front of the number and also a space should be reserved for a sign in front of the exponent.

    Let us consider some examples which will illustrate these ideas. We shall assume that the data corresponding to statements (3.19) is

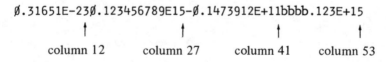

$\emptyset.31651E-23\emptyset.123456789E15-\emptyset.1473912E+11bbbb.123E+15$

   ↑   ↑   ↑   ↑

  column 12   column 27   column 41   column 53

This would cause the following values to be entered.

    $A=\emptyset.31651E-23$
    $B=\emptyset.123456789E15$
    $C=-\emptyset.1473912E11$
    $D=\emptyset.123E15$

When the E FORMAT is used, the data *must be right adjusted*. If it is not, incorrect results will occur.

We have assumed that the decimal point is always typed when real numbers are entered. Although this need not be the case, the use of the decimal point is encouraged since it helps to avoid confusion.

Actually, as in the case of the integers, commas can be used to greatly simplify real data input with either the E or F field specifier. For instance, with statement (3.14), if we enter

       12.34,45.6,81.967

then the assigned values would be

       A=12.34
       B=45.6   (3.20)
       C=81.967

Similarly, with statement (3.19), if we entered

       12.6E+∅3,-11.172E-4,15.21E6,317.2E11

then the values assigned would be

       A=0.126E+∅4
       B=-∅.1172E-2
       C=∅.1521E+∅8
       D=∅.3172E14

The use of the commas and the specification of the decimal point removes much of the tedious counting from the entering of data.

Remember that the comma terminates a field, and the next field is counted from the comma. In the FORMAT statement, you must specify enough room to enter data. For instance, using statement (3.4), the data for A must be typed in the first six columns, that for B must be in the seven columns following the comma, etc.

In MICROSOFT FORTRAN, the E and F field specifiers, when used with READ statements, actually have identical effects. Thus, E-type data can be entered using an F field specifier and vice versa. The distinction is made between the E and F field specifiers in the text to prepare the reader for the discussion of output, where a distinction between E and F *is* made.

Use of Mixed Specifications

In all of the previous examples, we did not mix FORMAT specifications. For instance, the READ statements had only integers or only real numbers, etc. Actually, the type of numbers used can be mixed. For instance, consider the statements

        READ(5,19)A,B,K   (3.21a)
19   FORMAT(F6.3,E11.3,I3)   (3.21b)

In this case, the first six columns of the card are used for entering the real variable A. The next eleven columns are used for the value of B in exponential form. Finally, the next three columns are used for the integer K. For instance, if the data used with statements (3.21) is

        123456493.656E-15326

then the values of the variables would be

        A=123.456
        B=493.656E-15
        K=326

All of the previously discussed rules apply in each field.

Use of More Than One Line for Data Entry

We have illustrated the entering of data from one line for each READ statement. Actually, more than one line can be used. *The FORMAT statement specifies the position of data on each line.* However, the list of variables in the READ statement can be greater than the number of field specifications in the FORMAT statement. In this case, and only in this case, a single READ statement requires that the data be entered on additional lines until all the required data is obtained. Let us clarify this. When all the field specifiers of the FORMAT statement are utilized, a return must be typed. That is, data is read from the first line using the FORMAT specifier. When all the field specifiers are used, a right parenthesis ")" is encountered. Any further data that is typed on the first line will be ignored. You must type **RETURN** and then the field specifiers are utilized again, starting at the left parenthesis "(". This procedure is repeated until all the required data is read. For instance, consider the following

```
        READ(5,77)A,B,C,D,E,F,G                    (3.22a)
77      FORMAT(F6.3,F7.2)                           (3.22b)
```

In this case, two variables will be read from each line. One will be typed in the first six columns while the second will be typed in the next seven columns. For instance, if we have

```
1234561234567
12.3412345678
11436122.3
11.62
```

then the values assigned to the variables would be

```
A=123.456
B=12345.67
C=12.341
D=23456.78
E=114.361
F=22.3
G=11.62
```

Note that any data typed in the 14th column or beyond, of any of the lines, will be ignored since the FORMAT statement only specifies $6 + 7 = 13$ columns of field.

As another example, consider

```
        READ(5,78)A,I,B,J,C,K
78      FORMAT(F6.3,I4)
```

Here the data will be read from three lines. On each, the first six columns would specify a real number while the next four would specify an integer. Note that if any of the first ten columns are blank, they are interpreted as zeros. Hence, the blanks specify data.

Multiple READ Statements

A program can contain more than one READ statement. *Each time a new READ statement is executed, a new data line must be used.*

Any data which has not been read from the previous line is lost. Two or more READ statements can have the same FORMAT statement or they can use different ones. For instance, consider the program sequence

```
        READ(5,43)A,B,C,D
43      FORMAT(F6.3,F7.4)
        :
        :                                                    (3.23)
        READ(5,44)E,F,G,H
44      FORMAT(F6.3,F7.4)
```

where the dots refer to other FORTRAN statements. This is equivalent to the program segment

```
        READ(5,43)A,B,C,D
43      FORMAT(F6.3,F7.4)                                    (3.24)
        :
        :
        READ(5,43)E,F,G,H
```

Since, in statement (3.23), the FORMAT statements 43 and 44 are the same, only one need be used. The FORMAT statement is not *executable*. That is, it does not in itself cause an operation to be performed. It can be placed almost *anywhere* in the program. The compiler is such that the correct FORMAT statement, using the statement number as an identifier, will be utilized each time that a READ statement is encountered. Let us consider an example. Suppose that we have

```
        READ(5,43)A,B
        READ(5,43)E,F
43      FORMAT(F6.3,F7.4)
        :
        :
```

and that the data entered is

```
    1234561234567968              (RETURN)
    1472131963486                 (RETURN)
```

The first data line will be utilized by the first READ statement while the second data line will be utilized by the second READ statement. Thus, we have

    A=123.456
    B=123.4567

C=147.213
D=196.3486

Note that the last three numbers (i.e. 968) on the first line are lost since the second READ statement requires that a return be typed before any additional data can be entered.

3.2 A FURTHER DISCUSSION OF FORMAT STATEMENTS

In the last section we discussed the basic ideas of FORMAT statements to be used in conjunction with READ statements. Here we shall discuss some extensions which can be used to simplify the writing of FORMAT and READ statements.

Often, the FORMAT statements contain repeated field specifications. For instance, consider the FORMAT statement

```
23      FORMAT(F6.3,F6.3,F6.3)
```
                                                                (3.25a)

An alternative form of this statement is

```
23      FORMAT(3F6.3)
```
                                                                (3.25b)

That is, an integer preceding the F (or I or E) in the field specifications has the same effect as if that field specification were repeated the num ber of times specified by that integer. As another example, the following two FORMAT statements are equivalent

```
27 FORMAT(F6.3,F6.3,F6.3,I4,I4,E12.2,E12.2)
```
                                                                (3.26a)
```
27 FORMAT(3F6.3,2I4,2E12.2)
```
                                                                (3.26b)

Thus, the use of the integers preceding the field specifications can, at times, make them more compact.

Another symbol which can be used to make the FORMAT statement more flexible is the slash. (This is the same symbol that is used to indicate division.) When the comma, used to separate the field specifications, is replaced by a slash, this indicates that the data is to be entered on separate lines. For instance,

```
        READ(5,36)K,ABLE
```
                                                                (3.27a)
```
36      FORMAT(I5/F6.3)
```
                                                                (3.27b)

The data for K would be obtained from the first five columns of one line while the data for ABLE would be obtained from the first six columns of the *next* line. Note that anything typed in columns 6 to 80 of the first line will be ignored. Let us consider some additional examples.

        READ(5,24)K,A,N,B   (3.28a)
  24   FORMAT(I5/F6.3)   (3.28b)

In this case, four lines of data would be required. Note that when the list of variables contains more terms than field specifications, the rules are as before (see the discussion of statements (3.22)). When all the specifications of the FORMAT statements are used, a return must be entered. Then, the field specifiers of the FORMAT statement are utilized again. Thus, K is read from the first line using an I5 specification. The slash causes a new line to be read and A is obtained from it, using an F6.3 specification. The last specification of the FORMAT statement has now been used and the complete list of variables has not been read. Thus, a return is entered and the procedure is repeated. Hence, N is read using an I5 specification. Finally, the slash requires a return to be entered and then B is read using an F6.3 specification. For instance, if the data corresponding to statements (3.28) is

    12345
    123456
    bbb21
    14.316

then the variables would be assigned the values

    K=12345
    A=123.456
    N=21
    B=14.316

As a further example, consider the statements

        READ(5,9)A,B,C,I,J,K   (3.29a)
  9   FORMAT(3F6.3/2I5,I7)   (3.29b)

In this case, the values of A, B, and C would be typed in the first 18 columns of the first line. The data for I and J would be typed in the first 10 columns of the next line, while K would be typed in the next seven columns of the same line.

If the list of variables in the READ statement contains more variables than the number of field specifiers in the corresponding FORMAT statement, then a new line (or lines) must be used and the specifications of the FORMAT statement are repeated. At times, we want only part of the specifications to be repeated. For instance, suppose that we want to enter a single integer and six real variables. The integer and two real numbers are to be typed on the first line while the second and third lines are to contain two real variables each. We can use a second set of parentheses in the FORMAT statement to accomplish this. Let us illustrate this with an example and then state the general rule.

$$\text{READ}(5,27)K,A,B,C,D,E,F \qquad (3.30a)$$
$$27 \quad \text{FORMAT}(I5,(2F6.3)) \qquad (3.30b)$$

In this case, the data could be

```
12345123456345678
142167111111
222222324123
```

The values assigned from this data are

K=12345
A=123.456
B=345.678
C=142.167
D=111.111
E=222.222
F=324.123

The general rule is the following. When data is being read, all the specifications in the FORMAT statement are utilized, until the rightmost parenthesis is encountered. If the entire list of variables in the READ statement is not completed, then type **RETURN** and enter more data. The specifications of the FORMAT statement are started again at the *rightmost* left parenthesis and continue to the *end* of the FORMAT specifications. (A left parenthesis is this one: "(".) For instance, consider

```
27        FORMAT(I5,(2F6.3))
              ↑
       rightmost left parenthesis
```

Let us consider another example

```
      READ(5,34)K,L,A,B,C,D,E,F,G,H,P,Q,R,S   (3.31a)
34    FORMAT(2I5/(2F6.3,F8.2))                 (3.31b)
```

Here, the variables K and L will be read from the first ten columns of the first line. Then, A, B and C will be obtained from the first $12 + 8 = 20$ columns of the second line. The end of the FORMAT specifications has now been reached. Thus, a return is typed. The entire set of FORMAT specifiations is *not* repeated. Control returns to the rightmost left parenthesis. Thus, the specifier 2F6.3,F8.2 will now be used for the reading of D, E, and F from the first 20 columns of the third line. After these are read, type **RETURN**. Now G, H, and P will be obtained from the first 20 columns of the next line, etc. (Note that parentheses must be used in pairs.)

A number preceding a parenthesis is equivalent to repeating the terms in the parentheses. For instance, the following FORMAT specifications are identical.

```
34    FORMAT(I3/2(F6.1,E9.3))              (3.32a)
34    FORMAT(I3/(F6.1,E9.3,F6.1,E9.3))     (3.32b)
```

As a final example, consider the statements

```
      READ(5,26)K,A1,I1,A2,I2,B,C1,J1,C2,J2,D
26    FORMAT(I3,2(F6.3,I5),F6.3)           (3.33)
```

The data would be entered on two lines. K, A1, I1, A2, I2 and B would be on the first line in that order. The end of the FORMAT specifications is then reached. Then, control would return to the 2(F6.3,I5) specifier. Hence, data for C1, J1, C2, J2, and D would be read from a second line. Note that the specifications are utilized to the end of the FORMAT statement and *not just to the end of the inner parentheses*. Some versions of MICROSOFT FORTRAN will cause the entire FORMAT specifier to be repeated, not just a part of it. That is, the parentheses can be used to repeat a specification but, when all the field descriptions are used, control returns to the start of the FORMAT statement.

3.3 FORMATTED OUTPUT STATEMENTS

We shall now consider formatted output statements which were briefly discussed in Sec. 1.3. The basic output statement is the WRITE statement. A simple example of the WRITE statement is

$$WRITE(5,41)A,B,C \tag{3.34}$$

The numbers in the parentheses have the same function as those in the READ statement. That is, the first number refers to the particular device that is to do the writing while the second number refers to a FORMAT statement number. The device number which we have used here is 5. This (see Table 3.1) refers to the terminal. We shall use the device number 2 in the remainder of this section. This will refer to the line printer. If you do not have a line printer, then use 5 for the device number. The data will be printed on the screen of your terminal.

The relationship between the WRITE statement and the FORMAT statement is similar to that between the READ statement and its FORMAT statement. Thus, the reader should be familiar with the ideas of Secs. 3.1 and 3.2 before reading the present one. We shall start with a discussion of the printing of integers. Let us consider the statements

$$
\begin{array}{lr}
K=276 & (3.35a) \\
WRITE(2,50)K & (3.35b) \\
50 \quad FORMAT('\ ',I6) & (3.35c)
\end{array}
$$

This will cause the line printer to advance one line and print

```
bbb276
```

where the b's represent blank spaces. Let us consider the FORMAT statement. It contains a new symbol, the blank space surrounded by single quote marks. This is called a *carriage control character* and it causes the line printer to advance the paper one line before printing. There are other carriage control characters. They are listed in Table 3.2.

TABLE 3.2 Carriage Control Characters

' '	Advance one line
'∅'	Advance two lines
'1'	– form feed (line printers only)
'+'	Do not advance to new line

For instance, if statement (3.35c) were replaced by

```
5Ø        FORMAT('Ø',I6)
```

then the line printer would advance two lines before printing bbb276. Note that this would be printed on the second line. That is, the line printer advances two lines and then prints the data on the second line. Thus, there will be a space of one line between the last printed line and this one. The carriage control character must be included. If it is not, serious errors can result. Hence, when WRITE statements are used, carriage control characters should not be omitted. We shall elaborate further on carriage control characters later in this section.

The field specification (I6 in this case) specifies the field in which the data is to be printed. Thus, in statement (3.35), the data is to be printed in the first six columns. Note that the data is always printed right adjusted.

Care should be taken when the field is specified. If the data contains more digits than specified by the field, then digits will be lost. For instance, if statement (3.35a) is replaced by

```
K=2763941
```

then there will not be enough room to print the data. Instead of printing the data, an error message, *FW*, will be printed. This indicates that the field width is too small to print the data.

Let us consider another example.

```
          I=3764
          J=216
          K=28Ø34
          WRITE(6,29)I,J,K
29        FORMAT('Ø',I4,I6,I8)
```

This sequence of statements will cause the line printer to advance the paper two lines and then print

```
3674bbb216bbb28Ø34
```

Again, the b's just represent blank spaces. It is desirable to make the field specifications greater than the number of digits in the data. In this way, spaces appear between the numbers and they are more easily read.

Note that when variables are printed, they are always *right adjusted* in their respective fields.

Let us now consider the printing of real data using an F FORMAT. Again, the basic ideas follow those given in Secs. 3.1 and 3.2. That is, the variables in the list of the WRITE statement are printed in accordance with the field specifications in the FORMAT statement. For instance, suppose that we have the program segment

```
        A=123.456
        B=147.
        C=-9324
        WRITE(2,6)A,B,C
6       FORMAT('Ø',F7.3,F6.3,F9.3)
```
(3.36)

This would result in the paper's being advanced two lines and then an error message would be printed because there is not enough field width to print B. The error message would again be *FW*. In addition, in place of the value of B, a number with an asterisk embedded within it would be printed. Thus, the proper data will not be printed. Let us consider the reason for the error. Six columns have been specified for the variable B and 147. appears to easily fit within six columns. However, the field specification F6.3 calls for three digits to be printed following the decimal point. These will be printed *even if they are zeros*. Thus, if 147. is to be printed in six columns, we would have to change the field specifications to F6.2. Remember that if data is negative, a column must be allocated for the minus sign. If we require three decimal places and the largest number to be printed has a magnitude of 999.999, then the specifications should be changed to F8.3, that is, room should be left for the minus sign and the decimal point.

To make the data more readable, spaces should be placed between the numbers. Thus, a more suitable FORMAT statement is

```
6       FORMAT('Ø',F8.3,F11.3,F12.3)
```

If this replaces the FORMAT statement of statements (3.36) then the data printed will be

```
b123.456bbbb147.ØØØbbb-9234.ØØØ
```

Note that the printed variables are right adjusted in their respective fields.

When data is printed using an F FORMAT specification great care should be taken. Usually, we do not know the values of the variables which are to be printed. This is to be expected since these quantities are calculated by the computer, and we do not know them beforehand. The computer works with real numbers in exponential form. Thus, it can handle a large range of numbers. Now suppose that the variable A is equal to Ø.123E15 and we attempt to print it using an F9.3 field specification. There would not be sufficient field width and the previously discussed error message would result and the correct data would not be printed. Thus, unless you are *very* sure of the number of digits in the answer, the F FORMAT specification should be avoided when the answers are to be printed. The E FORMAT specification can avoid many of these problems. Let us consider it. A typical set of statements is

```
        A=123.76
        B=Ø.23671E-15
        C=376.639
        WRITE(2,21)A,B,C                        (3.37)
21      FORMAT('Ø',E12.5,E15.7,E11.3)
```

The values of A, B, and C will be printed using exponential notation. These statements will cause the printer to advance the paper two lines and then print the following on the second line

$$b\emptyset.12376E+\emptyset3b-\emptyset.23671\emptyset\emptyset E-15bb\emptyset.377E+\emptyset3$$

Let us consider this. A is printed with an E12.5 specification. Thus, it will be printed with five digits following the decimal point. The E FORMAT specifier prints with a zero preceding the decimal point. The E12.5 specifier means that this number will be printed in the first twelve columns of the line. Remember that seven columns must be allowed for printing the sign of the number, first zero, decimal point, the letter E, the sign of the exponent, and the two digits of the exponent. If not enough columns are allowed, the previously discussed problems will result. We shall illustrate this subsequently. Then, if we want five places following the decimal point, then *at least* twelve columns should be specified for the field of the variable. Now let us consider the printing of the second variable. The value of B is printed with an E15.7 specifier. One extra column has been specified for this field. When variables are printed, they are always right adjusted. Thus, a space is placed between the values of A and B. This makes them more readable. The variable C is printed with an E11.3 FORMAT specifier. Again we have provided for a blank space before the variable.

Note that only three spaces following the decimal point are called for. This is all that will be printed. Thus, even though C has six significant figures, only three will be printed. Note that the data is rounded off (that is, if the last lost digit is 5 or higher, then the next to last digit is increased by one). Thus, if we print the number $1\emptyset.356$ using an F4.1 field specifier, the result will be $1\emptyset.4$. Note that roundoff in printing is different from roundoff error where digits are lost.

Some MICROSOFT FORTRAN compilers would allow the use of E11.5, since the $\emptyset$ preceding the decimal point is omitted. However, in general, when the E specifier is used, the number of columns should be at least seven more than the number of decimal places.

Use of Mixed Specifications

We can use a single WRITE statement to print integers, real and exponential data. For instance,

| | WRITE(2,36)A,K,BOX | (3.38a) |
| 36 | FORMAT('$\emptyset$',F7.3,I9,E15.6) | (3.38b) |

Here the printer will advance the paper two lines and then print a real number with three decimal places in the first seven columns, an integer in the next nine columns and an exponential number, with six digits following the decimal point in the next fifteen columns.

Longer Lists of Data

If the list of variables in the WRITE statement is longer than the number of specifiers in the FORMAT statement, then the complete set of specifiers is repeated. This is similar to what occurs in the case of the READ statement. Let us illustrate this with some examples

| | WRITE(2,49)A,B,K,D,E,N | (3.39a) |
| 49 | FORMAT('$\emptyset$',E15.7,E16.8,I9) | (3.39b) |

The printing then proceeds as follows. The '$\emptyset$' causes the printer to advance the paper two lines and then A, B, and K are printed with specifiers E15.7, E16.8, and I9, respectively. Since all the specifiers have been used, control then returns to the start of the FORMAT statement. The '$\emptyset$' then causes two more lines to be advanced and D, E, and N are printed using E15.7, E16.8 and I9 specifiers, respectively. Note that there will be a single blank line between the lines of data since the paper is advanced two lines but the data is printed on the second line. Thus, the basic idea here is the same as that used in the READ statement. There is one difference between input and output. On input, each line is allowed to have, at most, 8∅ columns. However, printers often have more than 8∅ columns. Thus, more columns can be utilized for printing. You should adjust the FORMAT field specifiers to account for the "width" of your printer.

A Further Discussion of Carriage Control Characters

We have indicated that the carriage control character is a symbol placed between quotes. Let us amplify this. In the next section we shall discuss the fact that symbols placed in quote marks are actually printed as text. Thus, if we have

```
        I=15
        J=1∅
        A=3.16
        WRITE(2,3∅)I,J,A
3∅      FORMAT('∅',I6,I5,F5.2)
```

then there is a total field to be printed which consists not only of the values of I, J, and A but also of the symbol ∅. Thus, the total field consists of

        ∅bbbb15bbb1∅b3.16

Note that the zero appears in the field. However, the compiler is such that the first character of every line is removed from the total field and is used as a carriage control character. Thus, in this case, the ∅ is "stolen" from the field and acts as a carriage control. This causes the printer to skip two lines (see Table 3.2) and then the line

        bbbb15bbb1∅b3.16

is printed. The first character of the total field will always be "stolen" for the carriage control character, even if it is part of a variable. For instance, consider the following

```
        I=1∅                                    (3.40a)
        J=15                                    (3.40b)
        WRITE(2,31)I,J                          (3.40c)
31      FORMAT(I5,I6)                           (3.40d)
```

We have omitted a carriage control character. Thus, in this case, the total field will be

bbb1Øbbbb15

This first character is a blank which is a single space carriage control character. This will cause the line printer to single space and print

bb1Øbbbb15

Note that the first character (a blank) is missing.

Now suppose that in statements (3.40), we change (3.40a) to

I = 1ØØØØ

The total field now is

1ØØØØbbbb15

The first character (that is, 1) is stolen as the carriage control. A 1 causes a skip to the top of the next page and then the following is printed

ØØØØbbbb15

which is in error. Thus, when FORMAT statements are written, the effect of the carriage control should always be carefully considered if errors are not to result.

In some versions of MICROSOFT FORTRAN, the loss of the carriage control character may produce results which are somewhat different from those we have indicated here. The first character may not be lost but the printing format may be changed. In any event, when you deal with WRITE statements, make sure that the associated FORMAT statement does contain a carriage control character so that the data is printed in the desired form.

Multiple WRITE Statements

A program can have more than one WRITE statement. Each WRITE statement will cause the printer (or screen) to start on a separate line unless the + carriage control character is used. (Note that not all computer systems will respond to the + carriage control character in this way.) As an example consider

```
      WRITE(2,26)A,B,C
26    FORMAT('Ø',F6.3,F8.3,F9.3)
```

```
      ·
      ·
      WRITE(2,29)D,K
29    FORMAT(' ',E16.7,I9)
```

Then the printer will advance the paper two lines and write the numerical values of A, B, and C on one line in the first 23 columns. Subsequently, the line printer will advance the paper one line and write the numerical values of D and K in the first 25 columns.

Two or more WRITE statements can use the same FORMAT statement. Remember (see Sec. 3.1) that FORMAT statements can be placed almost anywhere in the program. They are located by means of their statement numbers. Thus, the following would be a valid set of statements.

```
      ·
      ·
      WRITE(2,23)ABLE,BOY,BAKE
      ·
      ·
23    FORMAT('Ø',F5.1,F9.2,F11.4)
      ·
      ·
      WRITE(2,23)A,B,C
```

Additional FORMAT Statements

The FORMAT field specifiers given in Sec. 3.2 can also be applied to FORMAT statements associated with WRITE statements. Let us consider them here. The reader should be familiar with Sec. 3.2 before proceeding.

Multiple Field Specifications. If two or more successive field specifiers are identical, we can indicate this by placing an integer before one of the field specifiers and then omitting the others. For instance, the following FORMAT statements are equivalent

```
27 FORMAT('Ø',F6.3,F6.3,I5,I5,I5,E9.2,E9.2)(3.41a)
27 FORMAT('Ø',2F6.3,3I5,2E9.2)                (3.41b)
```

Use of the Slash in FORMAT Statements. When the slash replaces a comma in a FORMAT statement, it indicates that the line is terminated. Data printed using the field specifiers after the slash will be printed on a new line. A carriage control character is also needed to indicate the spacing of the new line. Let us consider some examples to illustrate this

```
        WRITE(2,3Ø)A,B,C                              (3.42a)
3Ø      FORMAT(' ',F6.3/'Ø',2F6.3)                    (3.42b)
```

The ' ' would cause the printer to advance the paper by one line and then print the data for A using an F6.3 specification. The slash indicates the termination of the line. The 'Ø' causes two lines to be advanced and the data for B and C are printed in the first 12 columns of the second line. Thus, there will be a single blank line between the data for A and that for B and C. Note that if a carriage control character is not printed following the slash, a character will be stolen from the total field (following the slash) to act as a carriage control.

Multiple slashes can be used to cause entire lines to be skipped. For instance, if we replace statement (3.42b) by

```
3Ø      FORMAT(' ',F6.3//'Ø',2F6.3)                   (3.42c)
```

then, after printing the data for A, the line printer will advance three lines before printing the data for B and C. The double slash causes one line to be advanced. The 'Ø' accounts for the other two. Hence, there will be two lines between the data for A and that for B and C. In general, if n slashes are put in sequence within the FORMAT statement, they will cause the line printer to advance $n-1$ lines. This is in addition to any line advances produced by carriage control characters. Note that provision for a carriage control character must always be made following a slash. Otherwise, characters will be stolen from the field.

At times, slashes are put at the *end* of a FORMAT statement to separate the data from any following printing. In this case n slashes will cause n lines (not $n-1$) to be skipped.

Use of Inner Parentheses in FORMAT Statements. When the number of terms in a list of variables in the WRITE statement is longer than the number of field specifiers, then the entire FORMAT specifications are repeated. If we only want part of the specifiers to be repeated, we can use a set of inner parentheses. This follows the rules of Sec. 3.2 and will not be repeated here. However, we will illustrate this with some examples. Consider the following

```
        WRITE(2,29)K,A,B,C,D,E,F                      (3.43a)
29      FORMAT(' ',I5/(' ',2F9.2))                     (3.43b)
```

In this case, the line printer will advance the paper by one line, print K, then advance by one line and print A and B. Control then returns to the rightmost left parenthesis which is the one following the slash. The ' ' causes the printer to advance one line and C and D are printed. Then E and F are printed on the next line. Note that there will be no blank lines between data.

   Suppose that we want a blank line between the data for I and that for A, B, C, D, E, and F. To do this the FORMAT statement can be replaced by

29   FORMAT(' ',I5//(' ',2F9.2))   (3.43c)

The double slash and the ' ' cause the paper to be advanced by two lines before A and B are printed. These values are printed on the second line. Thus, a single blank line will separate data for K from the remainder of the data. The double slash does not affect any subsequent printing since control never returns to it. Thus, the printing of the remainder of the data will be single spaced. Remember that the use of inner parentheses in this way does not work with all versions of MICROSOFT FORTRAN. Also, with some compilers, the multiple slashes may not function any differently than a single slash.

3.4 PRINTING OF TEXT IN FORMATTED OUTPUT STATEMENTS

   Very often, we want to print English text along with data. This can be used to explain or clarify the data and make it more readable. For instance, suppose that the values of A, B, and C are 123.456, 196.789, and 143.2, respectively. We could use the procedures of the previous section to print the data as

123.456   196.789   143.2   (3.44a)

However, the results would be clearer if they appeared as

A=123.456   B=196.789   C=143.2   (3.44b)

Thus, it is very desirable to include text material in the output. In this section we shall discuss procedures for the inclusion of such text.

   There is a simple procedure for printing text material. This is due to the fact that any text printed between single quote marks in the FORMAT specifications will be printed as text by the line printer. Let us illustrate this. Consider the program sequence

         A=123.45   (3.45a)
         WRITE(2,41)A   (3.45b)
41   FORMAT('ØA=',F6.2)   (3.45c)

This will cause the line printer to space two lines and to write A=123.45 on the second line. Let us discuss this. The first field specifier encountered is '∅A='. Note that information between quotation marks (and the quotation marks) are field specifications. Let us call this a *text field specifier*. In this case, the text field specification '∅A=' should cause ∅A= to be printed. However, the first character of the line (that is, ∅) is stolen for a carriage control character. Thus, only A= is printed. The next field specification F6.2 is used in the printing of the value of A. Let us call such specifiers (for example, F6.8, I9, E11.4) *data field specifiers*.

Let us now discuss some other examples. Consider the program sequence

$$A=123.45 \qquad (3.46a)$$
$$B=76.3 \qquad (3.46b)$$
$$C=\emptyset.9674E-15 \qquad (3.46c)$$
$$\text{WRITE}(2,53)A,B,C \qquad (3.46d)$$
$$53 \quad \text{FORMAT('∅A=',F6.2,'B=',F6.1,'C=',E12.4)} \qquad (3.46c)$$

This will cause the paper to be spaced twice and then the following will be printed on the second line

A=123.45B=bb76.3C=bb∅.9674E-15

where, as usual, each b represents a blank space. Let us consider this. In the FORMAT statement, the field specifiers are the text within the quote marks as well as the usual field specifiers, for example, F6.2, F6.1, E12.4. The specifiers are used in order when the WRITE statement is executed. The variables in the list of the WRITE statement are not printed until it is their "turn". Thus, in statements (3.46d and e), the first specifier encountered is '∅A='. This causes the paper to be advanced two lines and to have A= printed. Then it is the turn of the first data field specifier (F6.2). Thus, A, the first variable in the data list, is printed in the next six columns. Note that A is not printed in the first six columns, but in the six columns available after using the previous specifier(s). The next specifier is that which specifies B=. Thus, B= is printed. The next specifier encountered is the data field specifier F6.1. This is applied to the next variable in the list which is allocated the next six columns. Thus, the value of B is printed there. The next field specifier is the text field specifier 'C='. Thus, C= is printed. Finally, the third data field specifier E12.4 is applied to the third variable (that is, C) which is printed in the next twelve columns. Note that all data is right adjusted in its allocated field.

Note that a carriage control character is only included at the beginning of the line. The procedure here follows all the rules given in the last section except that the literal data is printed when called for. Remember that the carriage control character can be included with the literal data.

Printed data is always right adjusted in its specified field. This can result in data which is somewhat difficult to read. For instance, the printing that results from statement (3.46) has the form

```
A=123.45B=bb76.3C=bbØ.9674E-15
```

where, as usual, the b's represent blank spaces. It would be desirable if a space (or spaces) could be placed between the printed numerical value of A and the text B=. There are several procedures for doing this. We shall discuss some of them in Sec. 13.1. However, a simple procedure is just to insert blank spaces within the quotation marks. For instance, if we rewrite statement (3.46e) as

```
53        FORMAT('ØA=',F6.2,'bbbB=',F6.1,'bbbC=',E12.4)
```

then the resulting form of the line of data becomes

```
A=123.45bbbB=bb76.3bbbC=bbØ.9674E-15
```

This is more readable than the previous printing.

We have illustrated the printing of text and variables. Actually, we can print text material without variables if we so desire. To accomplish this, the list of variables is just omitted from the WRITE statement. For instance, consider the following statements

```
          WRITE(2,97)
97        FORMAT('ØTABLE OF NUMBERS')
```

This will result in the line printer's advancing the paper by two lines and typing

```
TABLE OF NUMBERS
```

on the second line. Text material is often printed in this way to provide headings for other information. Relatively long text material can be printed in this way by continuing the FORMAT statement over more than one line (that is, a symbol is placed in column 6 to obtain a continuation, see Sec. 1.2). Also, the number of characters on a line is limited by the line length of the printer. This number should not be exceeded or an improper printing will result.

At times, in the printing of data, we want to print a quotation mark. For instance, suppose that we want to print

NUMBER OF 'PERFECT' SAMPLES

If we just included the quotation marks in the FORMAT statement, the compiler would interpret them as specifiers for the printing of text and errors would result. To avoid this, two quotation marks are typed in sequence ''. Note that we consider a single quote, not a double quote, as a quotation mark.) The computer then recognizes that two quotation marks in sequence is just an item of text to be printed. Note that only a single quote is printed. Thus, a FORMAT statement which could be used to print the above text is

```
29       FORMAT('ØNUMBER OF ''PERFECT'' SAMPLES)
```

More complex printing of text material with or without data can be accomplished by using slashes and/or inner parentheses in the FORMAT statement. The rules here follow those given in Secs. 3.3 and 3.5. Thus, we shall not repeat them here in detail. However, we shall provide several illustrative examples. The slash is used to terminate a line. Thus, we can print on more than one line using a single pair of WRITE and FORMAT statements. Let us illustrate this with a sequence of statements.

$$A=3.5679 \qquad\qquad (3.47a)$$
$$K=276 \qquad\qquad (3.47b)$$
$$B=-\emptyset.2136E+12 \qquad\qquad (3.47c)$$
$$WRITE(2,46)A,B,K \qquad\qquad (3.47d)$$
```
46       FORMAT('ØANSWERS'/'ØA=',F6.4,
                 'B=',E11.4/'bK=',I3)       (3.47e)
```

(Note that statement (3.47e) would actually be typed on one line.) This sequence of statements will result in the following being printed

blank line

ANSWERS

blank line

```
A=3.5679B=-Ø.2136E+12
K=276
```

Note that each time a new line is started, a carriage control character must be included. If this is not done, the first character will be stolen and improper printing and line spacing can result.

Inner parentheses can be used as before when the number of terms in the list of variables is larger than the number of field specifiers. The inclusion of these parentheses prevents the entire set of FORMAT specifications from being repeated. (Remember that this will not work with all MICROSOFT FORTRAN compilers.) As an example, consider the following statements

```
         A=1.23
         B=3.46
         C=9.73                                             (3.48)
         D=11.48
         WRITE(2,93)A,B,C,D
93       FORMAT('ØANSWERS'//(' ',F6.2)
```

This will result in the printing of the following

                              blank line
         ANSWERS
                              blank line
         bb1.23
         bb3.46
         bb9.73
         b11.48

If the inner set of parentheses were not included, then the entire set of FORMAT specifications would be repeated for each variable. In this case, we would have

         ANSWERS

         bb1.23

         ANSWERS

         bb3.46

         ANSWERS

         bb9.73

         ANSWERS

         b11.48

Hollerith Field Specifer

We have discussed the inclusion of text material by means of quotation marks in the FORMAT specifications. There is another procedure which makes use of an H as a field specifier. This is called a Hollerith field specifier, and is named after Herman Hollerith, an early developer of punched cards. This form of specification of text material preceded the use of quotation marks in the development of FORTRAN. However, as we shall see, quotes are often far more convenient to use. The H field specifier has the form of an integer followed by an H. For instance,

14H

This indicates that the next 14 characters are text material. That is, it is equivalent to enclosing the 14 characters following the H in quotation marks and eliminating the 14H. As an example, the following two FORMAT statements are equivalent.

```
23      FORMAT(14HØTHE ANSWER IS,F6.3)
23      FORMAT'ØTHE ANSWER IS',F6.3
```

The Ø acts as a carriage control character and is not printed.

The primary disadvantage of the H specification is that it requires the programmer to count *exactly* the number of characters (including the blanks) which are to be printed. This is why quotes have replaced the H specifier in most applications. As a final example, consider the FORMAT statement (3.47e). An equivalent form using H specifiers is

```
46      FORMAT(8HØANSWERS/3HØA=,F6.4,2HB=,
                           E11.4/3HbK=,I3)
```

3.5 STOP AND END STATEMENTS

We shall now consider two statements which are not related to input or output statements. However, we include them in this chapter since, after we discuss them, we shall have considered enough statements to write complete FORTRAN programs.

The STOP Statement

When the computer is executing a program, some indication must be given to it that the program is completed and that the execution should cease. This is accomplished by means of the statement

    STOP

Once the STOP statement is encountered, no further computation, printing, etc. can occur.

A simple program (unformatted) sequence is

    A=2.Ø
    B=A**2   (3.49)
    PRINT,B
    STOP

Thus, the computer would print

    4.ØØØ STOP

Then, computation would cease.

Remember that, in simple programs such as the type that we have considered, which are run in the MICROSOFT FORTRAN system, it is not necessary to use the STOP statement. However, we indicate it since it is required in almost all other FORTRAN systems.

In the next chapter we will discuss programs that have several branches and a STOP statement which terminates each branch. At times, it is desirable to know which STOP statement is the one that has terminated evaluation. If we type up to six characters following the STOP statement, then these characters will be printed when the STOP statement is reached. For instance, if we have

    STOP ABC

then, when this STOP statement is executed, STOP ABC will be printed on the screen of your terminal. If each STOP statement has a different label, then we can determine which branch was used.

The END Statement

When a FORTRAN program is supplied to the computer, it must be compiled into machine language before the program can be executed (see Sec.1.1). Some indication must be provided to the compiler that the end of the program has been reached so that compilation should cease. This is accomplished by means of the statement

    END

Thus, in order to make the statements (3.49) into a complete simple, FORTRAN program, we need only append the statement END. The program then is

```
A=2.Ø
B=A**2
PRINT,B
STOP
END
```

The END statement must be the last statement in the program. Compilation ceases at the END statement. In Chapter 7 we shall discuss subprograms. When these are used, a complete program can have more than one END statement. However, for the time being, let us state that each program can have only one END statement and that it must be the last statement of the program.

It may appear as though there can only be one STOP statement. However, in the next chapter, we shall demonstrate conditions when a program can have more than one STOP statement.

3.6 SOME SIMPLE COMPLETE PROGRAMS

Let us now write some complete programs. This does not mean that we have finished our study of FORTRAN. Indeed, some of its most interesting aspects are yet to be considered. However, there are many simple programs that we can write using previously discussed statements. We shall consider several such programs in this section. This will supplement the material in Chapter 1.

We shall write a simple program that computes quantities in a right triangle. We shall assume that the lengths of two of its sides are entered as data and that the program computes the length of the hypotenuse and the tangent of one angle. The program is

```
      READ(5,1)A,B
1     FORMAT(2F8.3)
      HYP=(A**2+B**2)**Ø.5
      TANTH=A/B
      SINTH=A/HYP
      WRITE(2,2)HYP,TANTH,SINTH
2     FORMAT('ØHYP=',E1Ø.3,'TAN=',E1Ø.3
                             'SIN=',E1Ø.3)
      STOP
      END
```

The first statement calls for the values of A and B to be read from the data. A will be typed in the first eight columns and B in the next eight columns. The third to fifth statements call for the calculation of the hypotenuse, tangent, and sine, respectively. The WRITE statement and its approprite FORMAT statement cause the computed values and the appropriate text to be printed on a line. The STOP statement ends the execution of the program. Again, when the program was compiled, the END statement stopped the compilation. We have included text material with the output.

An another example, let us compute the distance traveled and final velocity of an object which has been started from rest and has been accelerated, at a constant acceleration a for t seconds. To obtain the final velocity, we use the relation

$$v = at \tag{3.50}$$

and for the distance traveled, we have the equation

$$d = \tfrac{1}{2}at^2 \tag{3.51}$$

We shall write the program so that the values of the acceleration and total time are entered on separate lines. The program is then

```
C PROGRAM TO CALCULATE VELOCITY AND DISTANCE
        READ(5,1)A,T
1       FORMAT(F8.3/F8.3)
        VEL=A*T
        DIST=0.5*A*T**2
        WRITE(5,2)VEL,DIST
2       FORMAT('0VELOCITY=',E10.3/' DISTANCE=',
                                          E10.3)
        STOP
        END
```

The first statement is a *comment* (see Sec. 1.2) which is ignored by the compiler. Note that we only require one READ statement since the slash in the FORMAT statement indicates that two lines must be used. We have also written the FORMAT statement numbered 2 in such a way that the results, with appropriate text, are printed on separate lines.

Let us now consider an example of the output that results when this program is run. Suppose that when the program was entered, the data cards supplied the values of 6.2 and 3.21 for A and T, respectively. In this case, the output would appear as

```
VELOCITY=∅.199E+∅2
DISTANCE=∅.319E+∅2
```

Note that the actual answers for VELOCITY and DISTANCE have been rounded off to three significant figures as called for by the FORMAT statement (i.e., statement number 2).

We have considered some simple programs here. In subsequent chapters we shall discuss procedures which make programming more versatile.

EXERCISES

3.1   The following represent statements in a FORTRAN program and the data. All the READ statements and all the data are shown. Determine the values assigned to all the variables.

```
        READ(5,37)L,J,K
37      FORMAT(I6,I4,I7)
        .
        12345612349671289
```

Check you results by writing a FORTRAN program and running it on your computer.

3.2   Repeat Exercise 3.1 if the data is replaced by

123bbbbb8417694

where the b's represent blank spaces.

3.3   Repeat Exercise 3.1 for

```
        READ(5,37)A,B,C,D
37      FORMAT(F6.3,F8.3,F6.1,F5.1)
        .
        196317-1211921621.31-.21
```

3.4   Repeat Exercise 3.2 for the data

196bbb-12.3bbb12bbbb15

3.5 Repeat Exercise 3.2 for the data

    bbb196bbb-12.3bbbb1215

3.6 Repeat Exercise 3.1 for

```
         READ(5,41)A,B,C,D
41       FORMAT(E11.4,E12.5,E11.4,E14.7)
bØ.1234E-15-Ø.12117E-Ø3+1.ØØ17E+Ø4
                           -Ø.1234567E-23
```

3.7 Repeat Exercise 3.6 for the data

    bbb1234E-15bb-12117E-Ø3+1ØØ17EØ4bbb-1234567E-23

3.8 Repeat Exercise 3.1 for

```
         READ(5,1)A,I,J,B,C
1        FORMAT(F6.3,I4,I4,E11.4,E12.5)
              .
1234569672-123-Ø.4162E+Ø3bØ.11721E+Ø9
```

3.9 Repeat Exercise 3.1 for

```
         READ(5,2)A,I,B,J,C,K
5        FORMAT(F6.3,I4)
              .
12.6171294
-192134773
b221611262
```

3.10 Repeat Exercise 3.9 for the data

```
12.6171294687532
12913477
b22161126
```

3.11 Repeat Exercise 3.1 for

```
         READ(5,1)A,B,C
         READ(5,2)I,J,D
1        FORMAT(F6.3,F6.3,F6.3)
2        FORMAT(I4,I4,F6.3)
              .
121467-12149-14689
1234779421.6
```

3.12 Repeat Exercise 3.11 for the data

```
121467-12119-14689-123456-14.163
1231779421.6
```

3.13 Repeat Exercise 3.1 for

```
          READ(5,1)A,B,C,D
1         FORMAT(4F6.3)
          .
          .
116719-12151-163.1-1.1
```

3.14 Repeat Exercise 3.1 for

```
          READ(5,9)A,B,C,I,J
9         FORMAT(3E11.4,2I4)
          .
          .
-Ø.1367E-Ø111.2345E+15-Ø.1234E-2112345678
```

3.15 Repeat Exercise 3.1 for

```
          READ(5,1Ø)A,B,C,D
1Ø        FORMAT(2F6.3/2E8.2)
          .
123456194.23789416
1234567861691423
```

3.16 Repeat Exercise 3.1 for

```
          READ(5,11)A,I,B,J,C,K
11        FORMAT(F6.3,I4,(F7.1,I3))
          .
-1234519171234567123
1963111208
```

3.17 Repeat Exercise 3.16 using the data

```
-12.3619176196.3128Ø1
bb14321Ø6417
```

3.18 Write a set of READ and FORMAT statements to read the values of the variables I, J, and K. I is to range between −999 and +999, J between −999999 and 999999 and K between 1 and 999. All the variables are to be placed on one line.

3.19 Repeat Exercise 3.18 putting the variables on three separate lines.

3.20 Repeat Exercise 3.18 but now use the variables A, B, and C instead of I, J, and K, where A is to range between −999.99 and 999.99, B is to range between −1537.14 and 960.99, and C is to lie between −9999.99 and +9999.99. Only one data line is to be used.

3.21 Repeat Exercise 3.20 but now use three lines.

3.22 Repeat Exercise 3.20 but now use exponential notation.

3.23 Repeat Exercise 3.26 but now use three lines.

3.24 Repeat Exercise 3.22 but now assume that A and B are to be entered on one line and C on another.

3.25 Write a set of READ and FORMAT statements to read in order A, B, I, C, D, and J where A and C are to be real numbers and B and D are to be in exponential notation. A and C are to range between −999.99 and 999.99 while B and D are to have a large range but only four significant figures are required to represent them (for example, 0.1236E+17) and I and J are to have at most three digits. All values can be positive or negative. Two lines, with three variables each, are to be used.

3.26 Determine the output that will be printed as a result of the following program sequence.

```
        I=116
        J=196
        K=1476
        WRITE(2,41)I,J,K
41      FORMAT('0',I9,I5,I4)
```

3.27 How would the results of Exercise 3.26 be changed if the FORMAT statement were changed to

```
41      FORMAT(' ',I3,I4,I3)
```

3.28 Determine the output that would be printed as a result of the following program sequence.

```
          A=123.67
          B=-196.26
          C=137.49
          WRITE(2,98)A,B,C
98        FORMAT(' ',F6.2,F7.2,F11.2)
```

Check your result by writing a FORTRAN program and running it on your computer.

3.29 Repeat Exercise 3.28 for the FORMAT statement

```
98        FORMAT(' ',F6.3,F7.4,F11.4)
```

3.30 Repeat Exercise 3.28 if the first statement becomes

```
          A=Ø.12367E+15
```

3.31 Repeat Exercise 3.28 for the program sequence

```
          A=123.67
          B=-Ø.1942E+15
          C=-199.672
          WRITE(2,1Ø3)A,B,C
1Ø3       FORMAT(' ',E12.5,E12.5,E14.7)
```

3.32 Repeat Exercise 3.31 if the FORMAT statement is replaced by

```
1Ø3       FORMAT(' ',E12.7,E14.7,E16.11)
```

3.33 Why is it desirable to print real data using an E FORMAT rather than an F FORMAT?

3.34 Repeat Exercise 3.28 for the program sequence

```
          I=116
          A=123.67
          B=Ø.1697E+15
          C=141.36
          WRITE(2,19)I,A,B,C
19        FORMAT(' ',I4,F7.3,E12.5,E15.7)
```

3.35 Write a pair of WRITE and FORMAT statements which will print the variables A, B, C, I, and J, allocating eight columns and three decimal places to each of the real variables and four columns to each of the integers. What range of values can be printed for each variable?

3.36 Repeat Exercise 3.35 but use exponential notation for the noninteger values. Allow for printing six significant figures.

3.37 Write a pair of WRITE and FORMAT statements which will print the values of A, B, I, C, D, J, E, F, and K in that order on three lines. There should be a blank line between each line. Use exponential notation allowing four significant figures and a sign for the real data and four figures and a sign for the integers.

3.38 Discuss the importance of including carriage control characters in FORMAT statements.

3.39 Discuss the output that would be produced by the following statements.

```
        WRITE(2,24)A,B,C,D,E,F
24      FORMAT('Ø',E11.4/' ',E11.3)
```

3.40 Repeat Exercise 3.39 if the single slash is replaced by three slashes in the FORMAT statement.

3.41 Repeat Exercise 3.39 for the statements

```
        WRITE(2,98)A,B,C,I,J,K
98      FORMAT(' ',3E11.4/(' ',I4)
```

3.42 Repeat Exercise 3.35 but now identify each variable (for example, print A=, B=, etc.) before the numerical value of the variable is printed.

3.43 Repeat Exercise 3.42 using the specifications of Exercise 3.36.

3.44 Write a pair of WRITE and FORMAT statements which will head a page with the statement TABLE OF DATA.

3.45 Repeat Exercise 3.42 but have the printed data preceded by the printed statement ANSWERS.

3.46 Illustrate the use of inner parentheses in the printing of text and data.

3.47 Repeat Exercise 3.42 but now use Hollerith field specifications rather than quotation marks in the FORMAT statement.

3.48 Discuss and compare the STOP and END statements.

3.49 Write a complete FORTRAN program which accepts the values of a, b, c, and k and then computes the following

$$d = a + b + c^2, \qquad e = d^k, \qquad f = d + e$$

The values of e and f should be printed.

4 *Control Statements*

In this chapter we shall consider FORTRAN statements which can make our programs much more versatile. Some of these statements will cause the computer to follow different branches of the program. We shall demonstrate that such branching can be very helpful at times.

The statements that we shall discuss here are called *control statements*. They are used to control the execution of the program in some way. The concept of this type of control is different from that which we have discussed previously.

4.1 THE ARITHMETIC IF STATEMENT

There are many times in a program when we wish to vary the type of calculation depending upon the sign of a variable. For instance, suppose that we enter two variables, a and b, and then wish to compute $\sqrt{a-b}$. If a is greater than b, then $a-b$ will be positive and we can determine the square root. On the other hand, if b is greater than a, then the square root is an imaginary number (note $\sqrt{-1}$ is an imaginary number). However, $\sqrt{a-b} = \sqrt{-1} \sqrt{b-a}$. Thus, in such cases, we are able to compute $\sqrt{b-a}$ and then, when the answer is printed, we must indicate that the result is an imaginary number. Finally, if $a = b$, we could indicate that the result is zero. Thus, we would like the computer to follow one of three possible branches depending on whether $a-b$ is positive, negative, or zero.

One statement which allows such branching to be made is the arithmetic IF statement. Its form is

        IF(C)1Ø,2Ø,3Ø   (4.1)

That is, it consists of the word IF followed by a set of parentheses containing a variable which is followed by three integer numbers, separated by commas. (Note that there is *no* comma between the parenthesis and the first integer.) The numbers are FORTRAN statement numbers. If the variable, C in this case, is negative, the next statement executed is the one which has been numbered 1∅. Each step in the program is then executed in order starting with the statement numbered 1∅. We state that the *control* is transferred to statement 1∅, which is one of the branches of the program. If C were zero, then control would go to the statement numbered 2∅. Finally, if C were positive, then control would go to the statement numbered 3∅. Thus, if the variable within the parentheses of the IF statement is negative, control is transferred to the statement numbered with the first number. If the variable within the parentheses is zero, then control proceeds to the statement numbered with the second number. Finally, if the variable within the parentheses is positive, control is transferred to the statement numbered with the third number. One fact should be observed. The IF statement should always transfer control to an executable statement (that is, arithmetic statement). Control should *never* be transferred to a nonexecutable statement such as a FORMAT statement. Improper operation results if this is done. Let us now illustrate the use of the arithmetic IF statement. Consider the following program, which computes $\sqrt{a-b}$.

```
         READ(5,1)A,B
1        FORMAT(2F6.3)
         C=A-B
         IF(C)25,15,5
5        ROOT=(A-B)**∅.5
         WRITE(5,2)ROOT
2        FORMAT('∅ROOT=',E12.5)
         STOP
15       WRITE(5,3)
3        FORMAT('∅ROOT=∅')
         STOP
25       ROOT=(B-A)**∅.5
         WRITE(5,4)ROOT
4        FORMAT('∅ROOT=I',E12.5)
         STOP
         END
```

$$(4.2)$$

The values of A and B are entered from data. Then, C=A−B is computed. If C is positive, then control is transferred to the statement numbers 5 and $\sqrt{a-b}$ is calculated and printed with the appropriate text (that is, ROOT=). The first STOP statement then terminates execution of the program.

If $a-b = \emptyset$, then the IF statement transfers control to statement 15. This causes ROOT=$\emptyset$ to be printed. The second STOP statement causes execution to be terminated.

Finally, if $a-b$ is negative, control is transferred to the statement numbered 25 and $b-a$ is calculated and printed. Note that I appears before the square root in the printed output. We have used $\sqrt{-1} = $ I here. Thus, I indicates that the number is imaginary. The third STOP statement then terminates execution of the program.

Note that there are three STOP statements in program (4.2). There are three branches to the program. Since we wish only one of them to be executed, the operation must terminate at the end of each branch. We accomplish this by adding the appropriate STOP statement. If the two STOP statements were removed from the ends of the branches, execution would continue, proceeding through other branches. This would produce improper operation and output which would be in error. Note that there is only one END statement and that it is the last statement in the program.

We have considered that the quantity within the parentheses is a single variable. Actually, it may be an arithmetic expression. For instance, the IF statement of program (4.2) could be replaced by

$$IF(A-B)25,15,5 \qquad\qquad (4.3)$$

It often proves convenient to include such arithmetic expressions within the parentheses of the IF statement. For instance, in the program just discussed, we would not have to define the variable C if this were done.

The IF statement provides a three-way choice, that is, the quantity within the parentheses is positive, negative, or zero. Often, we wish only to make a two-way choice. For instance, if X is positive or zero, we would want the program to take one branch, while if X is negative, we would want the program to take the second branch. This can be accomplished by making two of the statement numbers the same, for instance,

$$IF(X)7,21,21 \qquad\qquad (4.4)$$

Here, if X is negative, control is transferred to statement number 7, while if X is positive or zero, control is transferred to statement 21.

We have illustrated examples where control was transferred to statements which occurred after the IF statement. Actually, this need not be the case. For instance, consider the following program sequence

```
        .
        .
7       A=A+1.∅
        IF(A)7,15,15                                    (4.5)
15      D=2.*A
        .
        .
```

If A is negative, then control is returned to statement number 7. This causes the value of A to be increased by 1. This new value of A is tested by the IF statement. If it is still negative, control is again transferred to statement number 7. Eventually, the value of A will become nonnegative, and then control is transferred to statement number 15.

Care should be taken when control is transferred to a statement preceding the IF statement. For instance, suppose that we change the sequence of (4.5) to

```
7       A=2.*A
        IF(A)7,15,15                                    (4.6)
15      D=2.*A
```

If A is negative, the IF statement will transfer control to statement number 7. However, if A is negative, then 2.*A will also be negative. Thus, the program will cycle between the IF statement and statement number 7 indefinitely. You should always know how to stop the computation in such cases.

The statement immediately following an IF statement must have a statement number, otherwise it will *never* be executed. For instance, consider

```
        IF(B)2∅,3∅,7∅                                   (4.7)
        B=B+3                                           (4.8)
```

Statement (4.8) will never be executed since the IF statement will always direct control elsewhere. If statement (4.8) were numbered, then the IF statement could direct control to it. In subsequent sections of this chapter, we shall consider other statements which can direct control to numbered statements.

4.2 THE CONTINUE STATEMENT

We now shall discuss a statement which causes no operation to be performed. It is the statement

```
CONTINUE
```
(4.9)

When the program is executed and a CONTINUE statement is encountered, control just passes to the next statement with no operation being performed. The reader may question the inclusion of the statement in the FORTRAN language. It can be used as a numbered statement. Thus, it can be used in conjunction with IF statements to transfer control. In the remainder of this chapter, and the next, we shall see other occasions where the CONTINUE statement could be used.

Let us consider a simple example here. Suppose that we wish to enter a number X and then form the product

$$y = x(x-1)(x-2) \ldots (x-j)$$
(4.10)

where j is the largest whole number which is less than x. That is, each of the factors of Eq. (4.10) must be positive (*not* negative or zero). For instance, if $x = 5.3$, then

$$y = 5.3 \, (4.3) \, (3.3) \, (2.3) \, (1.3) \, (0.3)$$

Consider the following program sequence

```
        :
        Y=1.Ø
5       Y=Y*X
        X=X-1
        IF(X)1Ø,1Ø,5
1Ø      CONTINUE
        C=Y+1
        :
```
(4.11)

We assume that the value of X has been entered. In statement number 5 we replace Y by Y*X. (Note that the initial value of Y is 1.Ø.) Next X is reduced by 1. The IF statement tests X. If it is positive, control is returned to statement 5. The value of Y is then multiplied by X−1. The value of X is then reduced by 1 and the operation is repeated. As long as the IF statement tests a positive value of X, control is returned to statement 5 and the value of Y is multiplied by the new factor of X diminished by 1. If the value of X tested by the IF statement is negative or zero, then control goes to the CONTINUE statement and the remainder of the program, indicated by the statement C=Y+1 and the dots, is executed. The same results could be achieved if the statement C=Y+1 were numbered as 1∅. However, it is often convenient for the programmer to use the CONTINUE statement since it serves to isolate parts of the program for him. In the next chapter we shall discuss those cases where the CONTINUE statement must be used. However, for the time being, let us consider that its use is just a matter of convenience.

4.3 THE LOGICAL IF STATEMENT

There is another form of IF statement called the *logical* IF statement. At times, it is much more convenient and powerful to use than the arithmetic IF statement.

Let us consider an example of the logical IF statement.

```
D=1∅.5                                              (4.12a)
IF(A.GT.B)D=2∅.3                                    (4.12b)
B=D+1∅.5                                            (4.12c)
```

Here we assume that A and B are values that have been entered and/or computed earlier in the program. The symbol .GT. means greater than. Operation proceeds in this way. If the statement enclosed in the parentheses of the IF statement is true, in a logical sense, then the FORTRAN statement outside of the parentheses (that is, D=2∅.3) is executed as if it were the next statement in the program. Control then proceeds to the next statement in the program (that is, B=D+1∅.5). On the other hand, if the statement enclosed in the parentheses is false, then the FORTRAN statement outside of the parentheses is ignored and control proceeds to the next statement (that is, B=D+1∅.5). For instance if, prior to executing statement (4.12), we had A=11.6 and B=3.2, then A is greater than B. Thus, the statement in the parentheses is true and the value of D becomes 2∅.3. Hence, B=3∅.8. On the other hand, if A is equal to or less than B, then D remains at 1∅.5 and the value of B is 21.∅.

The general form of the logical IF statement is

```
IF (logical expression 1) FORTRAN statement a          (4.13a)
FORTRAN statement b                                    (4.13b)
```

The *logical expression* enclosed in parentheses is one which can either be true or false. If logical expression 1 is true, then FORTRAN statement *a* is executed. After this, FORTRAN statement *b* is executed. If logical expression 1 is false, then FORTRAN statement *a* is ignored. FORTRAN statement *b* is the next one executed. FORTRAN statement *a* must be an executable statement (e.g. not a FORMAT statement). It cannot be another logical IF statement or a DO statement. (DO statements will be discussed in Chapter 5.)

In order to utilize the logical IF statement, we must be able to write logical expressions, that is, expressions which can be either true or false. To do this we make use of a set of symbols called *relational operators*. The relational operators and their meanings are given in Table 4.1.

Table 4.1 Relational Operators

Operator	Meaning
.GT.	greater than
.GE.	greater than or equal to
.LT.	less than
.LE.	less than or equal to
.EQ.	equal to
.NE.	not equal

Note that all the relational operators are enclosed by periods.

Let us consider another example of the logical IF statement.

```
:
A=2.*B
IF(C.LT.D)A=A+B**2                                    (4.14)
C=B**2
G=A+C
:
```

We assume that B, C, and D have been entered and/or computed earlier in the program. Then, A is computed to have the value 2.*B. If the value of C is less than the value of D, then the statement

$$A=A+B**2 \qquad\qquad (4.15)$$

is executed. This value of A is the one that is used subsequently in the program (for example, where G=A+C is computed). On the other hand, if C is *not* less than the value of D, then statement (4.15) is ignored and A=2.*B is the value that is used in subsequent parts of the program

We have just used single variables in the logical expressions. This need not be the case with some compilers and arithmetic expressions can be included here. For instance, the following is a valid logical IF statement

        IF(A**2-B.GT.C+2.*A*D)B=C**2

In this case, the statement is true if $a^2 - b$ is greater than $c + 2ad$.

The logical IF statement can be more versatile than we have thus far indicated. For instance, consider the statement

        IF(C.LT.D.AND.I.EQ.J)A=B+C**2   (4.16)

The statement contained in the parentheses is only true if both C is less than D *and also* if I is equal to J. Several conditions can be included in the logical IF statement. At times, this can prove very convenient.

The expression .AND. is called a *logical operator*. We can use it if we want to write a logical expression which is true if, and only if, several subexpressions are true. In addition, there are other logical operators which can be very helpful. We shall list them in Table 4.2. In that table, S_1 and S_2 refer to simple logical expressions which can be true or false. For instance, they could represent

        C.LT.D
        A.NE.B

Table 4.2 Logical Operators

Operation	Meaning
S_1.AND.S_2	True if S_1 and S_2 are both true
	False if either S_1 or S_2 (or S_1 and S_2) are false
S_1.OR.S_2	True if either S_1 or S_2 are true (or both are true)
	False only if both S_1 and S_2 are false
.NOT.S_1	True if S_1 is false; false if S_1 is true
S_1.XOR.S_2	True if either S_1 or S_2 are true
	False if both S_1 and S_2 are true or if both S_1 and S_2 are false

Note that the logical operators are enclosed by periods. Let us consider some examples of the use of logical operators.

$$IF(A.LT.B.OR.C.GT.B)A=2\emptyset. \qquad (4.17)$$

The expression in the parentheses is true if any of the following three expressions is true: (1) if A is less than B *or* (2) if C is greater than B *or* (3) if both A is less than B and C is greater than B. The expression in parentheses is false only if both B is equal to or less than A *and* B is equal to or greater than C. Parentheses can be used to clarify operations if several logical operators are to be used. The rules for the use of parentheses in logical expressions are basically the same as those for arithmetic expressions. For instance, we could write statement (4.17) as

$$IF((A.LT.B).OR.(C.GT.B))A=2\emptyset. \qquad (4.18)$$

Each inner set of parentheses is considered as a single logical expression which is either true or false. All of the "single" logical expressions are then considered in conjunction with the logical operators to determine if the overall logical expression is true or false. Note that the overall logical expression determines the operation of the IF statement.

As a second example of the use of parentheses, consider the statement

$$IF(((A.LT.B).OR.(C.GT.B)).AND.(I.EQ.K))A=2\emptyset$$

$$(4.19a)$$

The logical expression of the IF statement is true if either or both of the logical expressions

```
A.LT.B
C.GT.B
```

are true and, *in addition*, if

```
I.EQ.K
```

is true.

Just as the hierarchy of arithmetic operators can reduce the number of parentheses required in arithmetic statements, there is a hierarchy in logical operations that can reduce the need for parentheses. Let us consider the hierarchy. The logical statement is examined reading from left to right (that is, in the usual manner). Assuming that this is done several times.

   a. The first time, all arithmetic expressions contained in the logical
      statement are evaluated according to the rules of hierarchy.
   b. Next, all the relational operations (that is, .GT., .GE., .LT.,
      .LE., .EQ., and .NE.) are performed.
   c. Next, all .NOT. operations are performed.
   d. Next, all .AND. operations are performed.
   e. Finally, all .OR. and .XOR. operations are performed.

Note that there are five (*a, b, c, d* and *e*) levels of hierarchy. A single
logical statement can have more than one operation at the same hierarchy level. In this case, they are performed in order from left to right.
Let us illustrate this hierarchy with some examples. Consider statements
(4.17) and (4.18). They are equivalent. The inner parentheses of statement (4.18) cause expressions A.LT.B and C.GT.B to be evaluated
before the .OR. operation is performed. However, the rules of hierarchy
would cause the same order of evaluation since the relational operations
are performed before the logical ones. Now let us consider statement
(4.19a). Some, but not all of the inner parentheses can be eliminated.
An equivalent statement is

      IF((A.LT.B.OR.C.GT.B).AND.I.EQ.K)A=2∅.   (4.19b)

Note that the parentheses can be removed from the expressions A.LT.B,
C.GT.B, and I.EQ.K, since they will be evaluated first according to the
rules of hierarchy. The one pair of inner parentheses is required in statement (4.19b) since we want the .OR. operation performed before the
.AND. operation. However, this violates the rules of hierarchy and,
hence, parentheses are required.
      Let us consider the following statement as a third example.

      IF(A.GT.B.AND.C.GT.E.OR.I.EQ.K)A=1.5

This is equivalent to

      IF((A.GT.B.AND.C.GT.E).OR.I.EQ.K)A=1.5

The set of inner parentheses is not required here since, according to the
rules of hierarchy, the .AND. operation is performed before the .OR.
operation.
      There are times when parentheses must be used. If two logical
operators follow one another directly, and the *second* one is not
.NOT., then parentheses must be used, for instance

```
IF(A.NOT.(.GT.)B)
```

The parentheses must enclose .GT. . In addition, parentheses must also be used if the expression following a .NOT. has more than a single element, for instance

```
.NOT.(A.GT.B)
```

Two of the relational operators are .EQ. and .NE., meaning equal to and not equal to, respectively. As a practical matter these should only be used with integers. When real numbers are stored or used in calculations, there can be some loss of low significant figures. For instance, suppose that we should have calculated the following exact values: A=2.∅, and B=2.∅. However, after calculations, we may actually have the following stored.

```
A=2.∅∅∅∅∅1
B=1.999999
```

We want A and B to be considered equal when they are compared. However, the logical expression

```
A.EQ.B
```

will be false since they are not exactly equal. Thus, .EQ. and .NE. should only be used with integers where such roundoff errors do not occur. We can use an equivalent of .EQ. or .NE. with real numbers. For instance, suppose that we want A.EQ.B. Actually, because of roundoff, we want the logical statement to be true if the magnitude of A−B is less than some small number. For instance, if the magnitude of A−B is less than ∅.∅∅1, we say that A and B are "essentially" equal. Thus, we want to write a logical expression which is true if A−B is sufficiently small. The following can be used

```
C=A-B                          (4.20a)
IF(C.LT.∅)C=-C                 (4.20b)
IF(C.LT.∅.∅∅1)G=3.∅           (4.20c)
```

Let us consider this. We set C equal to A−B. After statement (4.20b) is executed, C will be positive. If (4.20a) results in a negative C, then (4.20b) causes its sign to be changed. Note that we shall determine if the magnitude of C is less than ∅.∅∅1. However, any negative C is less than ∅.∅∅1 (for example, − 15∅∅ is less than ∅.∅∅1). Thus, we must test the magnitude of C. This is why (4.20b) is included. In statement

(4.20c), the logical statement is only true if the magnitude of A−B is less than $\emptyset.\emptyset\emptyset 1$. If this is true, then we set G=3.$\emptyset$. (Note that this is an arbitrary statement which could be replaced by any valid FORTRAN statement.) If C is greater than $\emptyset.\emptyset\emptyset 1$, the statement G=3.$\emptyset$ is ignored. Then, we do not require that A be exactly equal to B, but only that their difference be smaller than some value specified by the programmer ($\emptyset.\emptyset\emptyset 1$ in this case). In this way, the error due to roundoff can be essentially eliminated from this logical operation. Note that the three statements (4.20) can be replaced by the single one

```
IF((A-B)*(A-B).GE..ØØØØØ1)G=3.Ø
```

Note that the square of a number is always positive. This is an example of more efficient programming.

4.4 THE UNCONDITIONAL GO TO STATEMENT

In Section 4.1 we demonstrated that an IF statement could be used to transfer control from one portion of a program to another. There are other procedures for transferring control. We shall consider them in the next three sections. In this section we shall discuss the unconditional GO TO statement. An example of this is

```
GO TO 3
```
                                                                                    (4.21)

When this statement is encountered, the computer stops executing statements in order and control is transferred to the statement that is numbered 3. Execution then proceeds in order starting with that statement. There must be a statement which is numbered 3. This statement must be an executable statement. The general form of the unconditional GO TO statement is

```
GO TO N
```

where N is an integer *number*. Then, the statement numbered N is the one which is executed next. The program *must* contain an executable statement numbered N.

Let us consider an example using the unconditional GO TO statement. Suppose that we want to calculate $\sqrt{|a-b|}$ and then use this in some calculations. That is, suppose that a and b are entered or calculated. We then want to calculate $\sqrt{a-b}$ if a is equal to or greater than b and $\sqrt{b-a}$ if b is greater than a. This value is then used in future calculations. Let us consider a program segment which accomplishes this.

```
        IF(A-B)1∅,2∅,3∅
1∅      ROOT=(B-A)**∅.5
        GO TO 4∅
2∅      ROOT=∅.                              (4.22)
        GO TO 4∅
3∅      ROOT=(A-B)**∅.5
4∅      ANS=ROOT*2.*(B+A)**2
```

The arithmetic IF statement directs control to the appropriate statement so that $\sqrt{|a-b|}$ is calculated. The last statement of each branch causes control to pass to the statement numbered 4∅. Control then skips over any intermediate statements. Hence, only one of the three branches is executed. The remainder of the program proceeds using the value of ROOT which was calculated in the appropriate branch.

It is often convenient to use unconditional GO TO statements in conjunction with logical IF statements. For instance, a valid statement is

```
    IF(A.GE.B)GO TO 6∅                        (4.23)
```

In this case, if A is greater than or equal to B, then the next statement executed is the one numbered 6∅.

The statement following a GO TO statement should always be numbered, otherwise it will never be executed (see the discussion at the end of Sec. 4.1.)

4.5 THE COMPUTED GO TO STATEMENT

The unconditional GO TO statement directs the control to a specific statement which is determined by the programmer when he writes the program. However, we often want such branching to be a function of some numerical value which has either been entered as data or been calculated by the computer. One form of such branching is that which is controlled by the arithmetic IF statement. Let us now consider a GO TO *statement*. Its general form is

$$\text{GO TO } (N_1, N_2, \ldots, N_j), K \qquad (4.24)$$

That is, it consists of the words GO TO, followed by a pair of parentheses. The parentheses contain a sequence of integer numbers (not variables), separated by commas. An integer *variable* is outside of the parentheses. (Note that there is a comma between the parentheses and the variable.) The variable, K in this case, is an integer determined earlier in the program. If K=1, then the statement numbered N_1 is the next one that will be executed. If K=2, then the statement numbered N_2 is the next that will be executed. If K=3, then the statement numbered N_3 is the next one that is executed, etc. For instance, consider the following program segment

```
K=3                                    (4.25a)
GO TO (5,7,15,24,9),K                  (4.25b)
```

In this case, control will be transferred to statement number 15, since 15 is the third number in the list.

If statement (4.25a) were changed to

```
K=5
```

then control would be transferred to the statement numbered 9 since it is the fifth number on the list.

If the value of K is less than 1 or greater than the number of terms in the list, 5 in this case, then the computed GO TO statement will be ignored. There must be executable statements numbered with each number in the list of the computed GO TO statement.

The example of statement (4.25) is very simple. Usually, the branching is based on some computed value, for instance

```
K=2+I*J                                (4.26a)
GO TO(1,2,6,4,9,7),K                   (4.26b)
```

Here the program can take one of six possible branches.

The arithmetic IF statement can cause the program to take one of three possible branches, based on values of variables. The computed GO TO statement can allow the programmer to select a larger number of branches if desired.

Let us consider a sample program which illustrates some of the ideas of the chapter. We shall write a program that computes a salesman's commission. Suppose that his total sales are entered as data. His commission is to be the following: if the sales are $1000.00 or less, the commission is one percent; if the sales are greater than $1000.00 but equal to or less than $5000.00, the commission is to be two percent;

if the sales are greater than $5000.00, the commission is to be three percent on the first $5000.00, and four percent on any amounts over $5000.00. We shall write a program sequence which performs the required calculation. The input and output statements will be omitted. SALES represents the total sales. It is entered as data (that is, the appropriate input statements are assumed to be represented by the dotted lines).

```
C IF STATEMENTS TO DETERMINE SALES RANGE
      IF(SALES.LE.1ØØØ.ØØ)K=1
      IF(SALES.GT.1ØØØ.ØØ.AND.SALES.LE.5ØØØ.ØØ)K=2
      IF(SALES.GT.5ØØØ.ØØ)K=3
      GO TO (5,1Ø,15),K
C COMMISSION IF SALES LESS THAN 1ØØØ.Ø1
5     COMM=SALES*.Ø1
       .
       .
       .
      STOP
C COMMISSION IF SALES BETWEEN 1ØØØ.Ø1 AND 5ØØØ.ØØ
1Ø    COMM=SALES*.Ø2
       .
       .
       .
      STOP
C COMMISSION IF SALES GREATER THAN 5ØØØ.ØØ
15    ADJSAL=SALES-5ØØØ.ØØ
      COMM=15Ø.ØØ+ADJSAL*.Ø4
       .
       .
       .
      STOP
```

(Note the comments, which are ignored by the compiler. However, they are often included as an aid to the programmers who must read the program.)

The logical statement of the first IF statement is true if the sales are less than or equal to $1000.00. In this case, K=1. If the sales are greater than $1000.00 but less than or equal to $5000.00, then the second IF statement causes the value of K to be set equal to 2. The third IF statement causes the value of K to be set equal to 3 if sales are greater than $5000.00. The computed GO TO statement then directs the program to one of three branches. In the first, we calculate COMM=SALES*Ø.Ø1. The results would be printed. This print statement (or statements) is indicated by the dotted line. Execution then stops. The second branch, starting with statement number 1Ø is similar to the first except that SALES are multiplied by Ø.Ø2, corresponding to the two percent commission.

In the third branch, ADJSAL, which are the sales in excess of
$5000.00, is calculated. Then the commission is calculated in the next
line. (Note that three percent of $5000.00 is $150.00.)

This program illustrates the use of both computed GO TO statements and logical IF statements. We could have used alternative forms.
However, the ones used were presented for illustrative purposes.

4.6 THE ASSIGNED GO TO STATEMENT

A statement which is similar to the computed GO TO statement is
the assigned GO TO statement. It has the form

$$\text{GO TO K,}(N_1,N_2,N_3,\ldots,N_j) \tag{4.27}$$

Here, N_1, N_2, ... represent statement numbers. K is an integer which
must be equal to one of N_1, N_2, . . . , N_j. When the GO TO statement
is encountered, control proceeds to the statement whose number is the
value of K. Note that the value of K must equal the actual statement
number. (This is different from the computed GO TO case.)

The value of K cannot be computed. This is different from the
case of the computed GO TO. In this case, it is assigned by a statement
called an ASSIGN statement whose form is

$$\text{ASSIGN 3}\emptyset\text{ TO K} \tag{4.28}$$

For instance, a sequence of statements could be

```
  :
ASSIGN 2Ø TO NUMB
  :                                              (4.29)
GO TO NUMB,(15,2Ø,3Ø,55)
  :
```

In this case, after the assigned GO TO statement is encountered, control
goes to the statement numbered 2Ø. Note that there must be a numbered, executable statement corresponding to each number in the GO
TO statement.

There may be more than one ASSIGN statement in a program.
The last one executed, prior to encountering the assigned GO TO statement is the one which is used.

Consider the following program segment.

```
ASSIGN 4Ø TO KEE
IF (G-A.GT.X)ASSIGN 2Ø TO KEE
GO TO KEE,(4Ø,2Ø)
```

If G−A is greater than X, then the value 2Ø will be assigned to KEE. On the other hand, if G−A is not greater than X, then 4Ø is the value assigned to KEE. Thus, the program branches, depending upon the values of G−A and X.

Note that, if there are IF or GO TO statements present, the control does not always proceed in the order in which the program was written. For instance, the ASSIGN statement can actually appear after the GO TO statement in the listing of the program. Of course, the ASSIGN statement must be *executed* before the GO TO statement.

The list of numbers in the parentheses of the assigned GO TO statement limits the values that can be assigned. For instance, in (4.29), if NUMB is not assigned the value 15, 2Ø, 3Ø or 55, then an error will result and the execution of the program will be terminated. It is often desirable to do this to avoid improper results. However, it is not necessary. For instance, in (4.29) we could write

```
GO TO NUMB                                          (4.30)
```

and the program would function in the same way as (4.29) except that now NUMB could be any valid statement number. A valid statement number is one that is specified for an executable statement. If an invalid number were assigned to NUMB, then operation would terminate (e.g. if there were no executable statement with the label in question).

The assigned GO TO statement is an alternative to the computed GO TO statement. The computed GO TO is somewhat more versatile since the desired statement number can either be assigned, by a simple statement such as K=3 (see statements (4.25)), or computed (see statements (4.26)). The assigned GO TO can make it easier for the programmer if there is a long list of statement numbers, since he does not have to count the list to determine the number that corresponds to the statement number. However, the computed GO TO is usually used rather than the assigned GO TO because of its greater versatility.

4.7 ALGORITHMS—PSEUDOLANGUAGES

If we are to compute anything, we must develop the ideas that are to be used to direct the computation. The complete collection of these ideas that lead to the final program is called an *algorithm*. After the algorithm is determined, then its ideas are implemented by actually writing the program. If a program is simple, it may seem as though the first step can be skipped and that we can immediately write the program. In such simple cases, we have the algorithm " in our mind." When we deal with more complex programs, it is a good idea to write out the algorithm before getting involved with the details of programming. The algorithm is described in English (or whatever your native tongue is). In writing it we can concentrate on the ideas of the program without having to worry about where the commas and parentheses have to be placed.

Let us use the computation of velocity and distance given in Sec. 3.8 as our first illustration of the writing of an algorithm. Here we are called upon to perform the following calculations. A body is accelerated with acceleration a for t seconds. Find the distance that the body travels and its final velocity. The algorithm could be listed as follows

READ A AND T
COMPUTE VELOCITY = A*T
COMPUTE DISTANCE TRAVELED = ½A*T**2   (4.31)
WRITE VELOCITY AND DISTANCE
STOP

Note that this is not a program but simply a collection of ideas. We can now take these ideas and write a FORTRAN program. Actually, these ideas could now be used to write a program in any one of several programming languages. The algorithm is not written in any particular programming language. We say that it is written in a *pseudolanguage*. This is a description that can be understood by any programmer reading it. Once the algorithm is written we can then worry about the details of the program, for instance, do we want to write it in FORTRAN. The actual programs were given in Sec. 3.6 and will not be repeated here.

Now let us calculate a somewhat more complex program. Let us calculate $\sqrt{a - b}$. The ideas of the program were discussed in Sec. 4.1. It is assumed that the reader is familiar with them. Let us now write the algorithm using pseudolanguage.

PROGRAM WHICH CALCULATES $\sqrt{A - B}$
READ A AND B
IF A IS GREATER THAN B   (4.32)

```
    COMPUTE A−B
    WRITE A−B
    IF A=B WRITE ROOT=∅
    IF A IS LESS THAN B
       COMPUTE B−A
       WRITE B−A AND INDICATE THAT RESULT IS IMAGINARY
    STOP
```

We have indented the pseudolanguage program to indicate the different branches of the program. This is called *paragraphing*. We can also indent in the actual program to separate the branches. For instance, we will not rewrite program (4.2) to indicate paragraphing. We shall also add comments to make the program more understandable. These techniques are often used when complex programs are written.

```
C PROGRAM TO TAKE SQUARE ROOT OF DIFFERENCE
OF TWO NUMBERS
        READ(5,1)A,B
1       FORMAT(2F6.3)
C BRANCH IF POSITIVE NEGATIVE OR ZERO
        IF(A-B)25,15,5
C       POSITIVE BRANCH
5         ROOT=(A-B)**∅.5
          WRITE(5,2)ROOT
2         FORMAT('∅ROOT=',E12.5)                    (4.33)
        STOP
C       ZERO BRANCH
15        WRITE(5,3)
3         FORMAT('∅ROOT=∅')
        STOP
C       NEGATIVE BRANCH
25        ROOT=(B-A)**∅.5
          WRITE(5,4)ROOT
4         FORMAT('∅ROOT=I',E12.5)
        STOP
        END
```

The comments can be related to the pseudolanguage algorithm.

4.8 FLOWCHARTS

At times, a pictorial representation of an algorithm or programs aids in the understanding of it. Such a pictorial representation is called a *flowchart*. A typical one representing algorithm (4.31) is given in Fig. 4.1. There are different shaped boxes which represent different operations. Some commonly used symbols are shown in Fig. 4.2. The *terminal point* is used to indicate the starting and stopping point in the algorithm. It can also be used to indicate other operations which shall be subsequently discussed. The *process* typically represents arithmetic operations which can be carried out by one or more FORTRAN statements. The *decision* represents, as the name implies, a decision-making process. IF statements are decision-making processes. The input and/or output of data is represented by one of the input/output blocks. The *punched card, document,* and *magnetic tape* blocks represent specific forms of input/output.

As is illustrated in Fig.4.1, the various blocks of the flowchart are interconnected by lines with arrowheads which indicate the "flow of the process." At times, it is awkward to draw the lines (e.g., they would cut across other lines or through blocks). In this case, the *connector* symbol can be used. Letters or numbers are placed within the connector circle. All connectors with the same letter or number are considered to be connected together.

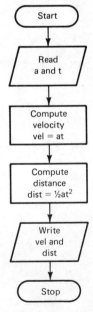

Fig. 4.1 A flowchart of the algorithm (4.31) to calculate velocity and distance. This program is given in Sec. 3.6.

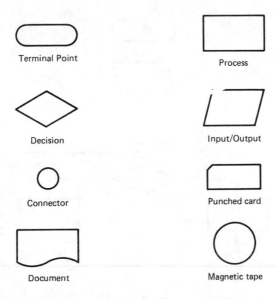

Fig. 4.2 Some symbols used in the preparation of flowcharts

We have illustrated a flowchart in this section. Some programmers make extensive use of flowcharts in obtaining algorithms and writing programs. Other programmers find flowcharts to be more trouble than they are worth and do not use them. In general, the use of flowcharts is decreasing.

4.9 INTRODUCTION TO STRUCTURED PROGRAMMING

We shall now discuss a procedure for writing algorithms which has been shown to result in programs with fewer errors (bugs). In general, when complex algorithms are written, they (almost) always contain some logical errors. That is, the programs do compute something, but not the answer to the given problem. When there is indiscriminate use of branching, programs with bugs often result. Let us illustrate good and bad programming with some flowcharts. We will not consider actual programs here. In fact, the process and decision boxes will not be labeled. We shall just use the flowchart to illustrate the flow of control.

We start with the flowchart of Fig. 4.3. Note how the control loops back around various parts of the program. Looping back in a program is often very useful, as we shall see. However, as we have

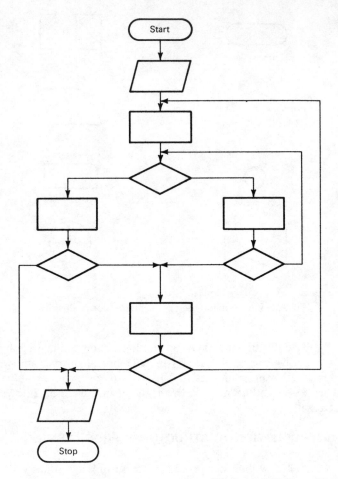

Fig. 4.3 Flowchart for the unstructured algorithm that is difficult to debug

illustrated it here, the looping can be confusing and make the program hard to debug. For instance, suppose that there is an error in the program and that wrong answers are produced. In order to debug the program we must study the entire program. Almost every part of the program affects all the other parts because of the looping back. Thus, when the program is debugged, we cannot consider small parts of the program to see if they are correct. Instead, we must work with the entire program which is a very tedious procedure.

Now look at the flowchart of Fig. 4.5. The program is divided into two main branches. Each of these branches is divided into two branches. One of the remaining four branches is again divided. The program can be divided into five paths. Each branch is clearly defined and can be easily studied and debugged since it does not interact with the re-

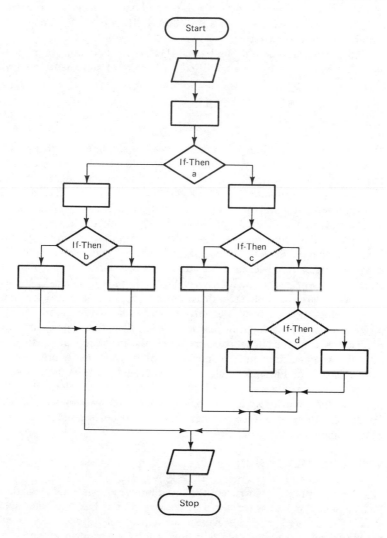

Fig. 4.4 Flowchart for a structured algorithm

mainder of the program. Programs such as those of Fig. 4.4, where the flow of control is through clearly marked paths or modules are said to be *structured*. Techniques of *structured programming* will be discussed further in subsequent parts of this book.

We have drawn the flowcharts that illustrate decision processes that branch into two paths. If an arithmetic IF is used, the branching can also result in three paths.

It is often desirable to use logical IF statements to control branching. This can be easily accomplished with pairs of statements such as

```
IF(A.GT.B)GO TO 100
GO TO 50
```
(4.34)

Now, if A is greater than B, control moves to the branch starting with statement number 100, while if A is equal to or less than B, control moves to the branch that starts with the statement numbered 50.

The indescriminate use of GO TO statements can lead to the unstructured form shown in Fig. 4.3. If the GO TO statement is used *carefully*, then a structured program form will be obtained.

Structured programming also makes use of paragraphed forms and pseudolanguages. Structured programming techniques not only make programs easier to write, understand, and debug, but they also make it easier for *teams* of programmers to write complex programs. That is, when very large complicated programs are written, one programmer usually does not perform the entire job. It is divided, and several programmers are each given specific tasks. Structured programming is ideally suited for such programs, since the program can be divided into subprograms that have a minimum of interaction. A program as simple as that of Fig. 4.5 would not be written by a team. However, it can be used to illustrate the ideas we have discussed. Here the task could be divided into two tasks corresponding to the two main branches. Of course, there could be further subdivision corresponding to the other branches of the program.

4.10   DOCUMENTATION

When a program is written, the programmer knows what algorithm he has used, why he has written it in the way that he has, and what data should be entered, etc. However, after a relatively short time, many people forget these details. In addition, a program written by one programmer is often used by others. Thus, it is desirable to keep complete records about a program. Such record keeping is called *documentation*.

The documentation should contain the following information about the program.

1. The name of the program.
2. Its purpose (i.e., what problem is solved).
3. The name and address of the programmer. This allows the programmer to be contacted if any problem arises.
4. The input information that must be supplied, for instance, descriptions of what data is needed and how it is to be supplied (e.g., the FORMAT of the data cards).
5. A description of the output data and how it is to be listed.
6. Any auxilliary equipment that is required, for instance, some programs require a floppy disk and disk drive (see Chapter 15).
7. The type of FORTRAN used to write the program (e.g. MICROSOFT FORTRAN).

All of this information allows people, even if they are inexperienced in FORTRAN programming, to run the program.

In addition, documentation should be useful to programmers. Thus, it should provide a description of the program itself. Hence, the algorithm used and the actual FORTRAN program should be listed. This material would include

8. A pseudolanguage description of the algorithm.
9. A flowchart of the algorithm (optional).
10. A complete listing of the program.
11. Test data

Items 8-10 enable a programmer to understand the computer program. Item 11 allows the user to determine if the program runs properly on his computer. That is, the programmer can run the program and check it to see that the correct answers are computed.

In general, good documentation provides the reader with a complete description of how to run the program and explains the program and the algorithm. Documentation can be of great help to programmers and to others who run programs and should be considered as an essential part of programming.

4.11 THE PAUSE STATEMENT

At times, we want to cause the computer to pause in its computations so that we can perform some functions. For instance, some data could be stored on a floppy disk. You might have to load the disk on the disk drive. At times, the data may be stored on several disks. Thus, you may have to load and unload disks at different times during the execution of the program. A FORTRAN statement which causes such pauses in the program is the

     PAUSE   (4.35)

statement. When it occurs, computation ceases until you reinitiate operation. You will be aware of the occurrence of a pause because

     PAUSE

will appear on the screen. The PAUSE statement can also be modified so that text can be printed in addition to the word PAUSE. In this case it is written as

     PAUSETEXT   (4.36)

TEXT represents any text material containing up to six characters. For instance, suppose that we have the statement

     PAUSEDSK156

When this is executed, PAUSEDSK156 will appear on the screen and execution will pause. This indicates that disk number 156 should be placed in the disk drive.

     Once the disk is put in the drive, you must cause the execution of the program to continue. Typing any letter *except* T will cause the execution to continue. If you type T, then execution will be terminated.

EXERCISES

4.1 Describe the consequences of the following statement.

     IF(ANS)5,7,2

4.2 Repeat Exercise 4.1 for the statement

     IF(A-B**2)1Ø,2Ø,3Ø

4.3 Consider the program segment

```
           .
           .
           B=A**2
           IF(B-A)1Ø,2Ø,3Ø
1Ø         C=B+A
           .
           .
           STOP
2Ø         C=2.*B+3.*A
           .
           .
           STOP
3Ø         C=B-A
           .
           .
           STOP
```

If the value of A=3.Ø has been previously entered, detemine the value of C.

4.4 Repeat Exercise 4.3 for A=Ø.5.

4.5 Repeat Exercise 4.3 for A=1.Ø. What problem, due to roundoff error, can arise here?

4.6 A quadratic equation is of the form

$$ax^2 + bx + c = \emptyset.$$

The roots of this equation are given by

$$x = \frac{-b \pm \sqrt{b^2 - 4ac}}{2a}$$

Write a program to evaluate these two roots. Use arithmetic IF statements to aid in the evaluation of the square root.

4.7 Illustrate the use of the CONTINUE statement.

4.8 Describe the consequences of the following program sequence.

```
A=4.Ø
B=3.Ø
IF(A.GT.B)B=6.Ø
C=B+A
```

4.9 Repeat Exercise 4.8 for the program sequence

```
A=4.Ø
B=3.Ø
K=2
IF(A-2.*B.LT.2.)K=3
I=3
ANS=1.Ø
IF(I.EQ.K)ANS=Ø
:
```

4.10 Repeat Exercise 4.9 but change the second statement to

```
B=-3.Ø
```

4.11 Consider the program sequence

```
B=A*2
C=B+A
IF(B.GT.A)C=2.*B+3.*A
STOP
```

If A=3.Ø has been previously entered, what is the final value of C?

4.12 Repeat Exercise 4.11 for A=−3.Ø.

4.13 Why is it undesirable to use the logical statement A.EQ.B?

4.14 Why is it proper to use the logical statement I.EQ.K?

4.15 Discuss the final value of A which will be obtained for the following program sequence. Assume that all listed variables have been entered or calculated previously. The discussion should be in terms of these values.

```
A-3.Ø
IF(A.GT.B.OR.C.GT.D)A=4.Ø
```

4.16 Repeat Exercise 4.15 for

```
A=3.Ø
IF((A.GT.B.OR.C.GT.D).AND.A-B.GT.Ø.)A=4.Ø
```

4.17 Repeat Exercise 4.15 for

```
A=3.0
IF((A.LE.B-C.AND.D.LE.ANS).OR.(I.EQ.K.AND.K.
                               NE.N))A=4.0
```

(Assume that this IF statement is typed on a single line.)

4.18 Describe the consequences of the following statements

```
      A=3.0
      GO TO 30
20    A=4.0
30    CONTINUE
      B=A+7.0
```

4.19 Repeat Exercise 4.18 for the program sequence

```
      B=6.5
      A=3.0
      IF(A.LE.B)GO TO 30
      A=4.0
30    CONTINUE
```

4.20 Repeat Exercise 4.6 but use unconditional GO TO statements in your program.

4.21 Determine the final value of A in the following program sequence.

```
      K=3
      GO TO (1,15,9,17)K
1     A=1.0
      STOP
9     CONTINUE
      A=2.0
      STOP
15    A=3.6
      STOP
17    A=0.0
      STOP
```

4.22 Repeat Exercise 4.21 if the first statement is replaced by the following two statements.

```
        J=1
        K=2*J+2
```

4.23 Repeat Exercise 4.22 if the first statement is replaced by

```
        J=Ø
```

4.24 Repeat Exercise 4.22 if the first statement is replaced by

```
        J=3
```

4.25 Determine the final value of A in the following program sequence.

```
        ASSIGN 6 TO KEE
        A=3.Ø
        GO TO KEE,(1,4,6)
1       A=4.Ø
        STOP
4       A=9.Ø
        STOP
6       CONTINUE
        STOP
        END
```

4.26 Repeat Exercise 4.25 if the first statement is replaced by

```
        ASSIGN 1 TO KEE
```

4.27 Repeat Exercise 4.25 if the first statement is replaced by the following four statements.

```
        B=4.
        C=3.
        ASSIGN 6 TO KEE
        IF(B.LT.C)ASSIGN 4 TO KEE
```

4.28 Repeat Exercise 4.27 if the first statement is replaced by

```
        B=2
```

4.29 Discuss the uses of the PAUSE statement.

4.30 Apply the procedures you have learned (all need not be used) to write a structured program to perform the following: A student's grades on five tests are to be entered. If the average is less than 60 percent, a warning message is to be printed. The following are also to be determined and printed: the average, the highest grade, the lowest grade. The grades are to be entered in the order in which the tests were taken. First write out the algorithm in pseudo-language and then use this to write the program.

4.31 Apply the procedures you have learned (all need not be used) to write a structured program to perform to perform the following: A store uses a discount system which deducts an amount from the bill to encourage buying. The following is the amount to be deducted from the bill. If, during a month, a customer purchases up to $10.00 worth of goods, then 0 percent is deducted. For total purchases between $10.01 and $15.00, 5 percent will be deducted from the amount in excess of $10.00. For total purchases between $15.01 and $20.00, 5 percent will be deducted from the amount in excess of $10.00 but less than $15.01 and 8 percent is deducted from the amount in excess of $15.00. For any purchases above $20.01, 5 percent is deducted from the amount in excess of $10.01 but equal to or less than $15.00, 8 percent is deducted from the amount in excess of $15.00 but equal to or less than $20.00, and 10 percent is deducted from the amount in excess of $20.00. Write a program which can be used to compute the final monthly bill if the total purchases are entered. First write the algorithm in pseudolanguage and then use it to write the program.

4.32 Write a structured program to compute the function

$$f(x) = x^3 + 2x^2 + g$$

where

$$g = 1 \text{ if } x^3 - x^2 - 3x \geq 0$$
$$0 \text{ if } x^3 - x^2 - 3x < 0$$

The value of x is to be entered as data. First write the program in pseudolanguage and then use it to write the program.

5 Looping—DO Loops

In this chapter, we shall discuss procedures that use single statements to cause control in a program to loop back on itself a specified number of times. This is often extremely useful and it simplifies many calculations. We shall describe and illustrate this operation in this chapter. The looping that we shall present here can be used when structured programs are written. In the next chapter, we shall discuss a procedure which, when coupled with this looping procedure, results in a very powerful mode of operation.

5.1 BASIC LOOPING—FUNDAMENTALS OF DO LOOPS

Often, in making computations, we want to perform the same type of calculation many times. In such cases, rather than writing a program which has many steps repeated, it is convenient to cause the control to loop back on itself. We shall also see that such looping not only is more convenient than simply repeating steps in the program, but also allows us to enter data or compute variables which vary the number of times that the looping occurs.

Let us illustrate such looping. Suppose that we want to compute factorial K ($K!$). That is

$$K! = K(K-1)(K-2)\ldots \quad (1)$$

Thus,

$$5! = 5 \times 4 \times 3 \times 2 \times 1 = 120$$

Let us write a program that computes $K!$ We shall not write the input and output statements. However, we assume that there are input statements which allow the value of K to be entered and that there are output statements which result in the printing of KFACT. (Note that we start the variable name with a K since it is an integer.)

```
              ⋮
         I=1
         KFACT=1
1∅       CONTINUE
            KFACT=KFACT*I
            I=I+1                                              (5.1)
         IF(I.LE.K)GO TO 1∅
2∅       CONTINUE
              ⋮
```

Let us consider the program segment. The value of K has been entered and KFACT and I are set equal to 1. Then KFACT is multiplied by I. This new value is then stored as KFACT. The first time that this is done, I=1 so that KFACT is unchanged. However, the next time, I is increased by 1. If I is less than or equal to K then control is returned to the statement numbered 1∅ and the process is repeated using the new value of I, i.e., next KFACT is multiplied by 2. This looping is repeated until I becomes greater than K. Now, when the logical expression is executed, the logical statement is false. Hence, control is transferred to the statement numbered 2∅. Thus, the final value of KFACT will be the desired factorial.

The maximum size of the integer with which we can work is limited to 32768. However, K! increases very rapidly with K. Thus, this program is limited to values of K which are less than eight.

The two CONTINUE statements are not necessary. We could omit the first one and number the KFACT=KFACT*I statement as number 1∅. The second CONTINUE statement, numbered 2∅, is just included to show you where this end of the loop is.

We have demonstrated looping using three statements. These are the first CONTINUE, the statement I=I+1, which increases the variable by 1, and the IF and GO TO statement. This is a satisfactory procedure. However, this type of looping is encountered so often, that a special notation, called a DO statement is used. Then, only one statement is required to establish looping. This is usually more convenient than using the three statements and the loop is now called a DO *loop*.

Let us illustrate the use of the DO statement by using it to obtain a program segment which is equivalent to (5.1). (The constant K which is used in this program has a fixed numerical value which we assume has been entered earlier in the program.) After seeing this and another simple example, we shall discuss the DO statement in general. The segment is

```
        .
        .
        .
C ILLUSTRATION OF A DO LOOP
        KFACT=1
        DO 2∅ I=1,K                    (5.2)
          KFACT=KFACT*I
2∅      CONTINUE
        .
        .
        .
```

The statement DO 2∅ I=1,K has the following effect. The statements between the DO statement up to and including the statement numbered 2∅ are executed using I=1. Then, I is increased by 1 (now I=2). Control is transferred back to the DO statement. If I is equal to or less than K, then the statements up to and including the statement numbered 2∅ are executed again, now using I=2. Now I is again incremented (I=3). Control is returned to the DO statement and the process is repeated. Eventually the incremented value of I will exceed K. In this case, control is given to the statement following statement number 2∅ and the looping ceases.

Note that we have paragraphed the program to "set off" the DO loop. Thus, the reader can easily locate it. When a DO loop is paragraphed, it is conventional not to indent the DO statement and the last statement of the loop.

Let us consider another example containing a DO loop.

```
        B=∅.
        DO 3∅ I=2,4
          AI=I
          B=AI/2.+B                    (5.3a)
3∅      CONTINUE
        C=2.*B
```

In this case, the first value of I used is 2. Then, AI=I establishes a real variable equal to the integer I. Then, evaluation of the next statement results in B being set equal to 2./2.+0 = 1. The CONTINUE statement is then "executed." I is then incremented. Control then returns to the

DO statement. Now, AI is set equal to 3.. Then B is set equal to 3./2.+1 =2.5. The CONTINUE is again "executed," I is incremented, and control returns to the DO statement. Now I is set equal to 4. Then, we have AI set equal to 4.. Then, B is set equal to 4./2.+2.5=4.5. After I is set equal to 5., control returns to the DO statement since I is greater than 4. Control is transferred to the statement following statement 3∅. The "final" value stored for B is 4.5. Hence,

$$C = 9$$

We have illustrated DO loops as ending with a CONTINUE statement. Actually, this is not necessary. The last statement can be one of many executable statements. We shall discuss which executable statements are allowable later in this section. Thus program segment (5.3a) could be written as

```
      B=∅.
      DO 3∅ I=2,4
         AI=I                                     (5.3b)
3∅       B=AI/2.+B
         C=2.*B
```

Let us now write the DO statement in a general form. (Later in this section we shall further generalize this form somewhat.) Let us now consider

$$DO\ n\ INT=N_1,N_2 \tag{5.4}$$

Here, n, N_1, and N_2 stand for integers, n must be an integer *constant* which must be the same as the statement number of some statement following the DO statement, N_1 and N_2 must be integers, but they can be either *constants or variables*. Then, the general form is

```
      DO n INT = N₁,N₂
      :                                           (5.5)
n     CONTINUE
```

The program then loops between the DO statement and the statement numbered n. Let us consider some terminology. The statement numbered n is called the *object* or *terminal statement* of the DO loop. In (5.5) the object of the DO loop is the CONTINUE statement. INT is called the *index* or DO *variable* of the DO loop. It must be an *integer* variable (for example, I, K, KEY, etc.). N_1 is called the *inital value* and N_2 is called the *final value, test value,* or the *limit value.* These must be integer constants or integer variables. When the DO statement is encountered, the index is set equal to the initial value N_1. Then, control passes through the program until the object statement is executed. At that time, the value of the index (that is, INT) is increased by 1. The new value of the index is then tested. If it is equal to or less than the test value N_2, then control returns to the statement immediately following the DO statement and the statements of the DO loop are executed again using the new value of the index. This procedure is repeated. Control is cycled through the DO loop over and over again. Each cycle uses a new index which is one greater than the old one. At the end of each cycle the object statement is executed, then the index is increased by 1, and tested. If the new index is greater than the test value, control then proceeds to the statement following the object statement and the DO loop is ended.

Before considering some rules that must be observed when DO loops are used, let us further generalize the DO statement somewhat. For the DO statements that we have discussed, the index is increased by 1 each time that the DO loop is cycled. However, there are times when we want this increment to be an integer greater than 1. The general rules for writing the DO statement provide for this. A third number can be added. In this case, the DO statement has the form

$$DO \ n \ INT = N_1, N_2, N_3 \qquad (5.6)$$

This is the same as statement (5.4) except that a third integer, N_3, has been added. It may be a constant or a variable. The third integer, N_3, is called the *increment*. After the object is executed, the index is increased by the increment. If the increment is omitted, it is assumed to be 1. Thus, the following two statements are equivalent

```
DO 20  I=1,10,1                                            (5.7)
DO 20  I=1,10
```

As an example, consider the program segment

```
      I=0
      DO 20  KEE=1,5,2                                     (5.8)
        I=KEE+I
20    CONTINUE
```

In this case, the first time through the DO loop, the value of KEE=1. then I=1. On the second cycle of the DO loop, KEE=3. Then, I=4. On the third cycle, KEE=5. Then the value of I becomes 9. The cycling of the DO loop then ends. Note that it is *not* cycled using KEE=7.

Let us now consider some formal rules for DO loops. The first of these is the rule for writing a DO statement. This must consist of the word DO followed by a blank space followed by an unsigned integer which refers to a statement number (that is, 10 is an unsigned integer, -10 or $+10$ have signs). This is followed by a blank space and then an integer variable (name) which defines the index of the DO loop. The index is followed by an equals sign. This is followed by two or three unsigned integers. These can be constants or variables. These are the initial value, test value, and increment. (The increment may be omitted.) Commas separate these two or three integers. (If the increment is omitted, then the second comma *must* be omitted.)

The second rule concerns the positiveness or negativeness of the parameters of the DO loop. The statement number (*n* of statement (5.6)) *must be an unsigned integer*. In MICROSOFT FORTRAN, the initial value and test value (N_1 and N_2) can be either positive or negative. (If they are negative, then they should be variables rather than constants.) The increment should be positive. For instance, the following is a valid set of statements

```
N1=-1∅
N2=-2
N3=1
DO  15  I=N1,N2,N3
```
(5.9)

When the object statement is reached, the index is incremented and tested to see if it is greater than the test value. If it is, then looping terminates. (Note that -6 is less than -2.) If a negative increment is used, for instance,

```
DO  15  I=1∅,2,N
```
(5.10a)

where $N=-1$, then the index will be greater than the test value and the loop will only cycle once. If we have

```
N1=-1∅
N2=-2
N3=-1
DO  15  I=N1,N2,N3
```
(5.10b)

then the loop will cycle with the index values −10, −11, −12... and
never terminate. Future versions of MICROSOFT FORTRAN may be
such that negative increments can be used. For instance, statement
(5.10a) will result in index values of 10, 9, 8, 7, 6, 5, 4, 3, and 2. Note
that *negative* constants cannot be used for the initial or test values on
some versions of MICROSOFT FORTRAN.

The following sequence is also valid.

$$I = 2+M$$
$$J = 2\emptyset * I$$
$$K = 3+I \qquad\qquad (5.11)$$
$$DO\ \ 2\emptyset\ \ KEE = I, J, K$$

Care should be taken when a variable is used to define the increment.
It should never become zero. If it does, the loop will cycle indefinitely
with the initial value of the index.

The third rule to be observed is that the DO loop parameters (that
is, the index, initial values, test value, or increment) *cannot* be altered
by a statement within the DO loop. That is, statements within the DO
loop *cannot* change the value of the index, initial value, test value, or
increment. For instance, the following is an *invalid* program segment.

```
C AN INVALID PROGRAM SEGMENT
      DO 3Ø I=1,N
        I=I+1
        N=N+2
        A=I+A
3Ø      CONTINUE
```

This is invalid because the statement I=I+1 and N=N+2 change parameters of the DO loop. On the other hand, the following is a valid
program segment.

```
C A VALID PROGRAM SEQUENCE
      DO 3Ø I=1,N
        K=I+K
        J=K*N
3Ø      CONTINUE
```

Note that here the parameters of the DO loop are used within the DO
loop. However, their values are not changed by these statements. Thus,

the parameters of the DO loop *cannot* appear to the left of the equals sign in any statement within the DO loop, but they can appear to the right of the equals sign.

The fourth rule concerns the object of a DO loop. It must be an executable statement. However, there are certain executable statements which *cannot* be the terminal statement (object) of a DO loop. These are STOP, PAUSE, GO TO, arithmetic IF, another DO, or RETURN statements. (We have not yet discussed the RETURN statement. It will be covered in Chapter 7.) Under certain circumstances, a logical IF statement can be the terminal statement of a DO loop. However, to avoid confusion, we shall not use an IF statement as the terminal statement of a DO loop. We can always add a CONTINUE statement to be used as a terminal statement of a DO loop. It is not always necessary that the terminal statement of a DO loop be a CONTINUE statement. However, it often clarifies the program for the programmer if a CONTINUE statement is used for this purpose.

We have presented some basic rules here. In the next section we shall consider behavior of DO loops when they are used in conjunction with control statements. However, before doing this, we shall discuss some additional aspects of the rules discussed here.

It may be possible that the index of the DO loop never equals the test value. For instance, consider

$$\text{DO } 3\emptyset \quad I = 1, 1\emptyset, 2 \qquad\qquad (5.12)$$

In this case, the values taken by the index I during each evaluation of the DO loop are 1, 3, 5, 7, and 9. Note that when the terminal statement (object) of the DO loop is reached, the index is increased by the increment and then it is tested. If the new index is greater than the test value, the DO loop is terminated. If the new value is equal to or less than the test value, then the DO loop is cycled once again. Now let us consider statement (5.12). After I=9 is cycled through the DO loop and statement $3\emptyset$ is reached and executed, then the index is set equal to 11. However, this is greater than the test value. Thus, the DO loop is terminated (i.e., it is not cycled again). Now consider the statement

$$\text{DO } 25 \quad I = 3, 1 \qquad\qquad (5.13)$$

Here the DO loop will cycle only once. You may ask why we write such statements. Actually, such statements would not be written explicitly. However, a similar situation can arise since the initial value, test value, and/or increment can be variables. For instance, consider

$$DO \ 35 \ I=M,N,2 \qquad\qquad (5.14)$$

where M and N are values which have been calculated earlier in the program. It could be that these calculated values cause M to be greater than N. In such cases, the DO loop will always cycle at least once. That is, testing of the index does not take place until the end of each loop.

Use of Flowcharts with DO Loops

Flowcharts can, of course, be used to illustrate algorithms which contain loops. In addition to representing algorithms, we can also use flowcharts to give us a pictorial representation of the program itself. Let us call this a *program flowchart*. The notation used in the program flowchart will be that given in Fig. 4.2. In addition, we shall introduce some additional symbolism.

To indicate a DO statement, we shall use a modified diamond, that is, a box whose horizontal sides are parallel but which has diamond-shaped ends. This is indicated in Fig. 5.1. Here we have drawn a flowchart for the program segment (5.2) where we have just calculated the factorial. Note that we have put statement numbers just outside of the boxes where desirable. Of course, in such cases, such a labeled box can contain only one statement.

5.2 ADDITIONAL ASPECTS OF DO LOOPS

In this section we shall discuss some additional aspects of DO loops.

Use of Branching in Conjunction with DO Loops

We shall discuss some aspects of branching in conjunction with DO statements. Let us consider a program segment which uses branching statements within a DO loop.

```
    :
    :
    D=Ø.
    DO 35 I=1,5
       AI=I
       B=AI+C
       IF(B.GT.Ø.)TO TO 1Ø              (5.15)
       B=-B
1Ø        CONTINUE
          D=D+B
35        CONTINUE
    :
    :
```

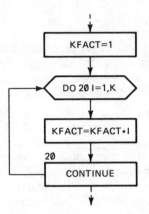

Fig. 5.1 A program flowchart for the program segment (5.2)

A program flowchart for this program segment is shown in Fig. 5.2. It is assumed here that C has been previously calculated. In this case, the IF statement and the two statements following it result in the final value of B being positive (that is, the magnitude of B is the value computed). Thus, when the DO loop is completed, D will equal the sum of the magnitudes of all the values of B. When control reaches statement 35, the value of I is increased by 1 and control is returned to the DO statement and the index is tested. If the new I is equal to or less than 5, the DO loop is cycled again. If the new I is greater than 5, control passes from the DO loop.

It is possible to use branching statements which remove control from the DO loop. For instance,

```
        .
        .
        I=Ø
        DO 1Ø K=1,1Ø,2
          J=K+NUMB
          IF(J.GE.4)GO TO 2Ø                (5.16)
          I=I+J
1Ø      CONTINUE
2Ø      CONTINUE
        N=2*J+I
        .
        .
```

A flowchart for this program is shown in Fig. 5.3. Here we assume that NUMB has been entered or computed earlier. Now we cycle through the

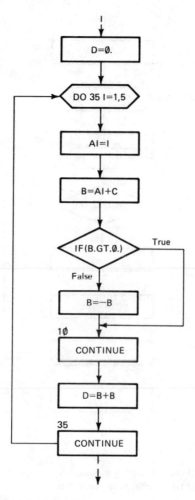

Fig. 5.2 A program flowchart for the program segment (5.15). It is assumed that C is calculated earlier in the program

DO loop. If J is less than 4, the GO TO 2∅ statement is ignored and the operation of the DO loop is the normal one. On the other hand, if J becomes equal to or greater than 4, control is transferred to statement 2∅. This is outside of the range of the DO loop. In this case, execution of the DO loop ceases. Then, the next statement evaluated is N=2*J+I which uses the last calculated values of I and J. For instance, suppose that NUMB=2 has been calculated previously. Then, the first time

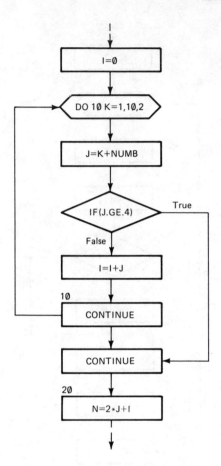

Fig. 5.3 A program flowchart for the program segment (5.16). It is assumed that NUMB is calculated earlier in the program

through the DO loop, K is set equal to 1 and J is set equal to 3, and the logical statement is false. Then, I is set equal to 3 and then the terminal (object) statement is "executed." The DO loop is cycled again. Now K is set equal to 3 and J is set equal to 3 + 2 = 5. The IF statement causes the next statement to be executed to be statement 2∅, which terminates the looping. Then, the final values of J and I are 5 and 3, respectively. Note that the statement J=K+NUMB was evaluated during the partial run (i.e., last run) through the DO loop while I=I+J is not, since it occurs after the IF statement.

The value of the index is stored in memory and can be used in future calculations if desired. For instance, in the example just discussed, the value of K stored (after the IF statement causes the operation of the DO loop to cease) was 3. This can be used in future calculations. A word of caution is required with compilers other than the MICROSOFT FORTRAN compiler. If the DO loop is terminated in the ordinary way (that is, the value of the index which is tested is greater than the test value), then the value of the index will vary from compiler to compiler. For instance, the stored value may be the last used value of the index, or it may be the last used value of the index plus the increment, or it could be another value. If we want to use the index value later in the program, and it is possible that the DO loop may terminate normally, then a new variable can be defined equal to the index. For instance, in (5.15) the statement after the DO statement could be

$$KA=K \hspace{8cm} (5.17)$$

In this case, each time that the DO loop is *repeated*, we set KA=K. Thus, when operation of the DO loop is terminated by any means, KA will be equal to the last used value of the index K. Hence, the value of KA can be used in subsequent calculations.

In program sequence (5.16), the logical expression of the IF statement used integer variables. However, this need not be the case. For instance, the following is a valid program sequence using an arithmetic IF statement

```
          :
          :
          DO 5 I=1,1Ø
            AI=I
            B=AI*C-3.
            IF(B)1Ø,2Ø,2Ø                          (5.18)
1Ø          CONTINUE
5         CONTINUE
2Ø        CONTINUE
          :
          :
```

(It is assumed that C was established earlier in the program.) In this case, the DO loop will be terminated before the tenth cycle if B becomes positive or zero, otherwise it will terminate after the tenth cycle.

We have illustrated that it is permissible to use branching statements to transfer control out of the range of a DO loop. The converse is *never* allowed. Thus, *it is improper to use a branching statement to transfer control into the range of a DO loop from outside of the range.*

That is, a DO loop can only be entered when the control passes through the DO statement itself.

Required Use of CONTINUE

We have often used the CONTINUE statement as the object of a DO loop. It is often convenient, but not necessary, to do so. However, it is sometimes *necessary* to use the CONTINUE statement as the object of a DO loop. Consider the following program segment.

```
        :
        :
     J=M
     DO 1Ø I=1,N
        J=J+1
     IF(J)1Ø.1Ø,6Ø
1Ø      CONTINUE
     DO 5Ø K=1,1Ø
        J=J+K*M
5Ø      CONTINUE
6Ø      CONTINUE
        :
        :
```
                                                                (5.19)

where we have assumed that M has been defined earlier in the program. If the first CONTINUE statement were omitted, then either the IF statement or the DO 5Ø K=1,1Ø statement would have to be the terminal statement (object) of the first DO loop. This is *not* allowed. Thus, there are circumstances when the CONTINUE statement must be used. Of course, this never presents a problem since the CONTINUE statement can be added easily.

5.3 NESTED DO LOOPS

It is permissible, and at times very desirable, to include one DO loop within the range of another one. (The range runs from the DO statement to the terminal statement (object).) All of the previous rules are followed in this case. Let us illustrate this with a program segment

```
        :
     J=Ø
     M=Ø
     DO 5Ø I=1,1Ø
        J=J+I
        DO 2Ø K=1,5,2
```

$$M=M+J+K \hspace{3cm} (5.20)$$
```
2Ø        CONTINUE
          J=J+1
5Ø        CONTINUE
          .
          .
```

Let us consider the operation of this segment. The outer DO loop is encountered first. Then, we start by calculating J which is equal to $0 + 1 = 1$. The second DO loop is then encountered. This is then completely evaluated. (Note that we are still in the first cycle of the outer DO loop and that the inner DO loop lies completely within the range of the outer DO loop.) Then, on the first cycle, K is equal to 1. Hence, M is equal to $0 + 1 + 1 = 2$. On the second cycle of the inner DO loop, K is equal to 3. Hence, now M is equal to $2 + 1 + 3 = 6$. On the third cycle of the inner DO loop, K is equal to 5. Hence, M is equal to $6 + 1 + 5 = 12$. The operation of the inner DO loop then terminates since its index equals its test value. Then, we evaluate J=J+1 which is equal to 2. Note that this is done in the first cycle of the outer DO loop. The value of I is increased by one and since I is less than the test value, control is returned to the statement following the first DO statement. The outer DO loop is now cycled with I equal to 2. Then, J is set equal to $2 + 2 = 4$. The inner DO loop is again encountered. It is now cycled using J equal to 4. Thus, on the first cycle, M is set equal to $12 + 4 + 1 = 17$, on the second cycle of the inner DO loop, M is set equal to $17 + 4 + 3 = 24$. On the third cycle of the inner DO loop M is set equal to $24 + 4 + 5 = 33$. Operation of the inner DO loop then terminates. We then compute J=J+1 which is equal to 5 as part of the second cycle of the outer DO loop. K is increased by 1 and control then returns to the statement following the first DO statement. The operation repeats itself until the tenth execution of the outer DO loop. A program flowchart for the program segment of (5.20) is given in Fig. 5.4.

A nested DO loop may have the same object as its outer DO loop. For instance, the following two program segments are equivalent

```
          DO 2Ø J=1,1Ø,2
          .
          DO 15 K=1,6,3                              (5.21)
          .
15        CONTINUE
2Ø        CONTINUE
```

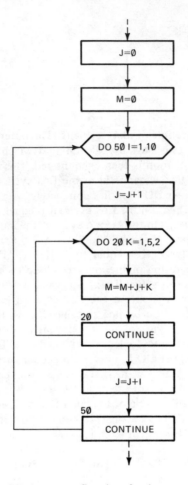

Fig. 5.4 A program flowchart for the program segment (5.20)

and

```
DO 20 J=1,10,2
    :
DO 20 K=1,6,3                                              (5.22)
    :
20      CONTINUE
```

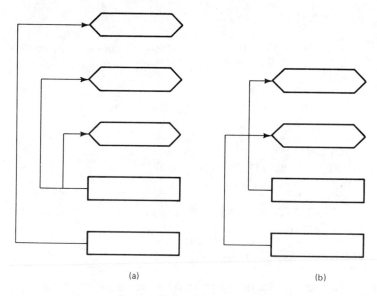

(a)   (b)

Fig. 5.5 (a) A valid nesting of DO loops; (b) an invalid nesting of DO loops

When nested DO loops are written, the object of the inner DO loop *must not occur after* the object of the outer DO loop.

We have illustrated one DO loop nested within another. Actually, this nesting can be carried further. A DO loop can be nested within a second DO loop which, in turn, is nested within a third DO loop. Remember that the object of each inner DO loop cannot occur after the object of its outer DO loop. Figure 5.5 illustrates the (a) proper and (b) improper nesting of DO loops. Each inner DO loop must lie within the range of its outer DO loop. They can share the same object statement.

Branching can be used in conjunction with nested DO loops, if the rules and discussion of Sec. 5.2 are applied. IF and GO TO statements can be used to transfer control out of the range of the DO loop and also to statements *within* a given DO loop. However, *we cannot transfer control into* the range of a DO loop. Thus, control can be transferred from an inner DO loop to *its* outer one, but we cannot transfer control from an outer DO loop into an inner one. Of course, we can always transfer control completely outside of the range of the DO loop.

As as example of nested DO loops, let us evaluate the following equation.

$$z = x^2 + 2x + y^3$$

for values of x = 0.0, 0.1, 0.2, 0.3, . . . , 1.0 and for values of y = 0.0, 0.1, 0.2, 0.3, . . . , 1.0. First let us write the algorithm in pseudolangauge, see Sec. 4.5.

ALGORITHM FOR EVALUATION OF $x^2 + 2x + y^3$
OBTAIN X BY LOOPING (LOOP 1)
LOOP 1 FOR I=1 to 11
   SET X=(I−1)*.1
   OBTAIN Y BY LOOPING (LOOP 2)
   LOOP 2 FOR J=1 TO 11
     SET Y=(J−1)*.1
     EVALUATE Z=X**2+2.*X+Y**3   (5.23)
     WRITE Z
   TERMINAL STATEMENT OF LOOP 2
TERMINAL STATEMENT OF LOOP 1

In the outer loop I ranges from 1 to 11. Then we establish a real variable X which is 0.1*(I−1). Hence, X ranges from 0.0 to 1.0. In the inner loop we do the same for Y. As part of the inner loop we also calculate Z and print it. For the first cycle of the inner loop, Z is calculated using the values X=0.0, Y=0.0. The inner loop cycles again and Z is evaluated using X=0.0, Y=0.1. For each value of X, the inner loop cycles completely. Thus, after the first complete cycling of the inner loop, i.e., the index J has taken on the values 1, 2, . . . , 11, Z has been calculated for X=0.0 and Y = 0.0, 0.1, . . . , 1.0. Now the outer loop goes through its second cycle. The value of X is now computed to be 0.1. The inner loop goes through 11 cycles. This results in the calculation of Z for X=0.1 and Y = 0.0, 0.1, . . . , 1.0. This operation continues until all the desired values are used in the calculation of Z.

Let us write the actual FORTRAN programs.

```
C PROGRAM THAT EVALUATES X**2+2.*X+Y**3
C       OUTER DO LOOP TO OBTAIN X
        DO 1ØØ I=1,11
          X=(I-1)*.1
C         INNER DO LOOP TO OBTAIN Y AND Z
          DO 1ØØ J=1,11                        (5.24b)
          Y=(J-1)*.1
          Z=X**2+2.*X+Y**3
          WRITE(2,1)X,Y,Z
```

```
1ØØ      CONTINUE
1        FORMAT('ØX=',F4.2,'Y=',F4.2,'Z=',E12.5)
         STOP
         END
```

The flowchart for the algorithm used to calculate $z = x^2 + 2x + y^3$ is shown in Fig. 5.6. Normally, if a flowchart is drawn, it is done before the program is written since it is actually an aid in writing the algorithm. We did not do it in this case since our primary purpose was to illustrate nested DO loops.

As a further example of the use of nested DO loops, let us consider the following. Suppose that we have two functions

$$z_1 = x^2 + 2x + 1 + .5y \qquad (5.25a)$$

and

$$z_2 = y^2 - 4y + 3 \qquad (5.25b)$$

We allow x and y to take on the values $x = 0.0, 0.1, \ldots, 1.0$ and $y = 0.0, 0.1, \ldots, 1.0$. We want to find the values of x and y for which the magnitude of $z_1 - z_2$, $|z_1 - z_2|$, is a maximum. We also want to know this maximum value. An algorithm for this program is

```
ALGORITHM TO CALCULATE MAX |Z₁ - Z₂|
INITIALIZE BIG=0
SET UP LOOP TO ESTABLISH X
LOOP 1 FOR I=1, 11
    X=(I-1)*.1
    SET UP LOOP 2 TO OBTAIN Y, Z, DIF, AND BIG
    LOOP 2 FOR J=1,11
        Y=(J 1)*.1
        Z1=X**2+2.*X+1+0.5*Y                        (5.26)
        Z2=Y**2-4.*Y+3
        DIF=Z1 - Z2
        MAKE DIF POSITIVE
        IF(DIF.LT.Ø)DIF=-DIF
        COMPARE DIF WITH BIG SET BIG=LARGEST DIF
        IF(BIG.GE.DIF)GO TO 1Ø
            BIG=DIF
            X1=X
            Y1=Y
            (1Ø)CONTINUE
```

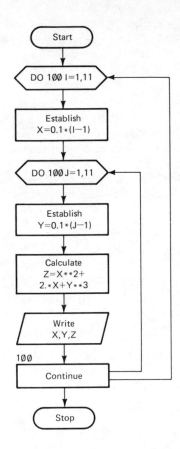

Fig. 5.6 A program flowchart for the algorithm to evaluate $x^2 + 2x + y^3$ for $x = 0.0, 0.1, 0.2, \ldots 1.0$ and $y = 0.0, 0.1, 0.2, \ldots , 1.0$. Looping symbolism is used here.

```
END LOOPS 1 AND 2
WRITE BIG,X1,Y1
STOP
```

A flowchart for this algorithm is given in Fig. 5.7.

We start by setting a variable BIG=0. Eventually, this will equal the maximum difference between Z1 and Z2. The outer DO loop causes the value of X to be varied through the desired range. In the inner DO loop Y, Z1 and Z2 are calculated for each X. Now, still in the inner DO loop, the difference DIF=Z1−Z2 is obtained. If DIF is negative, then the logical expression of the IF statement is true. Then, DIF is replaced by its negative. Thus, DIF will equal the magnitude of the difference between Z1 and Z2.

Next, BIG and DIF are compared. If BIG is less than DIF, then we set BIG=DIF and record the corresponding values of X and Y as X1 and Y1, respectively. If BIG is not less than DIF, then the last three operations are skipped. Thus, when the cycling of the DO loop is complete, the final value of BIG will be equal to the largest DIF computed and the corresponding values of X and Y will be stored as X1 and Y1, respectively. These values are then printed.

A FORTRAN program which implements this algorithm is

```
C CALCULATION OF MAX Z1-Z2
C INITIALIZE BIG
         BIG=Ø
C OUTER DO LOOP TO ESTABLISH X
         DO 1ØØ I=1,11
           X=(I-1)*.1
C        INNER LOOP TO OBTAIN Y,Z1,Z2,DIF AND BIG
           DO 1ØØ J=1,11
           Y=(J-1)*.1
           Z1=X**2+2.*X+1.+Ø.5*Y
           Z2=Y**2-4.*Y+3.
           DIF=Z1-Z2
C        MAKE DIF POSITIVE
           IF(DIF.LT.Ø)DIF=-DIF                       (5.27)
C        COMPARE DIF WITH BIG
           IF(BIG.GE.DIF)GO TO 1ØØ
             BIG=DIF
             X1=X
             Y1=Y
1ØØ      CONTINUE
         WRITE(2,1)X1,Y1,BIG
1        FORMAT('ØX=',F3.1,'Y=',F3.1,'BIG=',E9.2)
         STOP
         END
```

EXERCISES

5.1 Determine the final value of K when the following program segment is evaluated.

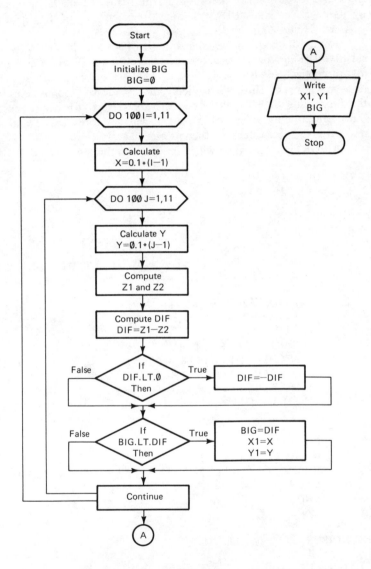

Fig. 5.7 A program flowchart for the algorithm to evaluate $(Z1 - Z2)_{max}$

```
       K=1
       DO 1Ø I=1,1Ø
         K=K+I*3
1Ø     CONTINUE
```

Check your result by writing a FORTRAN program and running it on your computer.

5.2 Repeat Exercise 5.1 for the program segment

```
       K=1
       DO 1Ø I=1,1Ø
         K=I*3
1Ø     CONTINUE
```

5.3 Repeat Exercise 5.1 for the following program segment. Determine the final value of M here.

```
       N=2
       NJ=N*3+1
       M=N
         DO 25 K=N,NJ
       M=M+M*K
25     CONTINUE
```

5.4 Write a program that computes the sum

$$KSUM=1+2+3+\ldots+N$$

where N is an integer to be entered from data. Start by writing an algorithm in pseudolanguage. Check your program by running it on your computer.

5.5 Write a program which evaluates and prints the function

$$y = x^3 + 2x^2 + x + 1$$

for values of x between 0 and 10. Vary x in steps of 0.1. Start by writing an algorithm in pseudolanguage, draw a flowchart. Check your program by running it on your computer.

5.6 Repeat Exercise 5.5 for the function

$$y = -x^3 + 2x^2 + 20x + 1$$

5.7 Determine the final value of K when the following program segment is evaluated.

```
K=1
DO 1Ø,I=1,1Ø,2
   K=K+I*3
1Ø    CONTINUE
```

Check your result by writing a FORTRAN program and running it on your computer.

5.8 Determine the final value of A when the following program segment is evaluated

```
A=1.Ø
DO 1Ø I=1,1Ø,3
   AI=(I-1)*2
1Ø    A=AI+A
```

Check your result by writing a FORTRAN program and running it on your computer.

5.9 Repeat Exercise 5.7 for the program segment

```
N=2
M=5*N-1
K=Ø
DO 25 I=N,M,2
   K=K+I
25    CONTINUE
```

Check your result by writing a FORTRAN program and running it on your computer.

5.10 Draw a flowchart for the program segment of Exercise 5.1

5.11 Repeat Exercise for the program of Exercise 5.5.

5.12 Repeat Exercise 5.10 for the program of Exercise 5.6.

5.13 Discuss the operation of the following program segment. What is the final value of A?

```
K=Ø
DO 25 I=1,1ØØ,2
K=K+I
```

```
           A=2.Ø*K
           IF(A.GT.18.)GO TO 3Ø
25         CONTINUE
3Ø         CONTINUE
```

5.14 Repeat Exercise 5.13 if the IF statement is replaced by

```
IF(A-18.)25,25,3Ø
```

5.15 Repeat Exercise 5.5 but now write a program which determines the values of x which yield values of y which are less than 3.

5.16 Repeat Exercise 5.5 but now write a program which determines the values of x which yield values of y which are equal to or greater than 10 but less than 200.

5.17 Repeat Exercise 5.5 but now write a program which finds the largest value of y and its corresponding x.

5.18 Discuss valid and invalid uses of control statements in conjunction with DO loops.

5.19 Draw a flowchart for the program of Exercise 5.13.

5.20 Repeat Exercise 5.19 for the program of Exercise 5.15.

5.21 Determine the final value of X when the following program segment is evaluated.

```
           X=Ø
           DO 1Ø I=1,1Ø
           AI=Ø.1*I
           DO 5 J=1,5
           AJ=J
           X=X+AI*AJ
5          CONTINUE
1Ø         CONTINUE
```

5.22 Write a program which will calculate and print the values of z and the corresponding values of x and y for the function given. Use values of x between Ø and 1Ø and values of y between 1 and 5. Vary x and y in steps of Ø.1.

$$z = -3x^3 + 2x^2 + x + y^3 + y$$

Start by writing a program in pseudolanguage. Draw a flowchart. Check your program by running it on your computer.

5.23 Repeat Exercise 5.22 for

$$z = -x^3 + x^2 + 10x - y^3 + 20y$$

5.24 Discuss legal and illegal use of control statements in conjunction with nested DO loops.

5.25 Modify the program of Exercise 5.22 to obtain the largest value of z and the corresponding values of x and y.

5.26 Write a computer program which will calculate and print the values of z and the corresponding values of x, y and d for the function given. Use values of x between $\emptyset$ and 5, and values of d between $\emptyset$ and $1\emptyset$, using increments of $\emptyset$.1 in each case.

$$z = x^3 + 2x + y^2 - 2y - d^3 + d$$

Also obtain the largest and smallest values of z and the corresponding values of x, y, and d.

5.27 If a, b, and c represent the lengths of the sides of a right triangle, where c is the hypotenuse, then

$$c^2 = a^2 + b^2$$

Write an algorithm, draw a flowchart, and write a FORTRAN program which will determine all the integers between 1 and 100 that can be the lengths of the sides of a right triangle.

5.28 Consider the two simultaneous equations

$$y = 1 - x^3$$
$$y = x$$

They have a solution in the range $0 \leqslant x \leqslant 1$. Write an algorithm, draw a flowchart, and write a computer program that determines one solution to within 0.0001. (Note that we must solve for the value of x.) The program should be in structured form. Hint: $1 - x^3 - x = 0$ at the solution. A value of x which satisfies this equation can be found by varying x in steps of 0.0001. $1 - x^3 - x$ will change sign when the root lies between two successive steps. Of course, if one of the steps falls on the root, then $1 - x^3 - x = 0$. In general, implementation of this procedure will involve many steps. Let us consider how the number of steps can be reduced. If x_0 is the root, then, if $x < x_0$, $1 - x^3 - x$ will be positive while if $x > x_0$, $1 - x^3 - x$ will be negative. Thus, if larger steps are taken (e.g., 0.1 at the start) an approximate value for x_0 can be found by noting when the sign of $1 - x^3 - x$ changes. For instance, we know that it lies between x_1 and $x_1 + 0.1$ if the sign changes for the step after x_1. The procedure can then be repeated but now the increment can be halved (0.1/2 = 0.05). (Now start at x_1.) This will further refine the location of the root. Continue this process until the root is located to the desired accuracy.

6 Subscripted Variables—Arrays

Very often, a program must be written which causes the same calculations to be performed on each one of a list of variables. For instance, suppose that we write a simple computer program which is used to obtain a student's average grade over five tests. If there are 40 students in the class, then we could define 40 different variables and repeat the program segment 40 times. However, this is not necessary. We can make use of something called a *subscripted variable* or an *array* which eliminates the need for both defining 40 different variables and for writing 40 repetitive program segments. In this chapter, we shall study subscripted variables and arrays.

There are many other examples of the use of arrays. For instance, if a class has 1000 students, then subscripted variables will almost certainly be used in a program for computing grades. In addition, most programs which make use of mathematical calculations make use of arrays. We shall illustrate such programs in this chapter. Thus, this topic is an important one which can be of great help to the programmer.

6.1 SINGLE SUBSCRIPTED VARIABLES—ONE-DIMENSIONAL ARRAYS

Let us consider a simple, but very useful form of subscripted variable in this section. In Sec. 6.3 we shall generalize our discussions. Mathematically, when we have subscripted variables, we write them in the following way

$$b_1, b_2, b_3$$

Here, the b's represent variables, which are usually related in some way. For instance, they could represent grades in a test: b_1 would be the grade of student 1; b_2 would be the grade of student 2, etc. In FORTRAN, we must place all the symbols on a single line. Thus, we cannot use subscripts. Subscripted variables are indicated in the following way,

$$B(1),B(2),B(3),\ldots$$

That is, a subscripted variable consists of the variable name followed by a pair of parentheses containing an integer. Note that B(2) does *not* indicate B times 2 since there is no asterisk present.

The entire set of subscripted variables is termed an *array*. Actually, it is called a one-dimensional array since each variable has only one subscript. In Sec. 6.3 we shall discuss variables with more than one subscript. Each term in the array [for example, B(1)] is called an *element* of the array.

Let us consider some FORTRAN statements using subscripted variables

$$
\begin{aligned}
&A(1)=B*C \\
&A(2)=A(1)+B \qquad\qquad (6.1) \\
&A(3)=2.*A(2)+C
\end{aligned}
$$

That is, the subscripted variables are treated just as any other variable. Each variable in the array is *independent* of the others.

The rules for naming subscripted variables are the same as those for naming nonsubscripted variables, that is, the name should have up to six alphanumeric characters. The first character must be either a letter (or possibly a $) which indicates whether the variable is a real or an integer variable. (An exception to this will be discussed in Secs. 10.1 and 10.2.) All of the variables in an array must be of the same type (that is, all must be real variables or all must be integer variables). Let us consider some examples:

```
ABLE(1)
BOX(3)
BOY(2)
ZEBRA(14)
```

all represent real variables. In addition,

```
KEE(3)
ITEM(4)
NUMB(3)
```

all represent integer variables.

The subscript should be an integer. However, it can be an integer *variable*. For instance, the following is a valid program sequence

$$
\begin{aligned}
&\text{ITEM=1} \\
&\text{JIG=2*ITEM} \\
&\text{A(ITEM)=6.0} \\
&\text{A(JIG)=A(ITEM)+4.5}
\end{aligned}
\tag{6.2}
$$

In this case, ITEM=1 and JIG=2. Thus, the third and fourth statements result in A(1)=6.0 and A(2)=10.5.

The subscript can also be a simple FORTRAN expression. For instance,

$$
\text{A(ITEM+2)}
\tag{6.3}
$$

The FORTRAN manual should be checked to determine which expressions are allowed.

The DIMENSION Statement

Each variable is stored in the main storage memory at the time of the program execution. When the program is compiled, the compiler reserves the appropriate storage space. In the case of unsubscripted variables, each time a new variable is encountered by the compiler, storage space is reserved for it in the memory. For instance, if we have the statement

$$
\text{A=3.0}
\tag{6.4}
$$

and this is the first statement containing the variable A, then the compiler would reserve a storage location for a real variable called A. In the case of subscripted variables, the task is not as easy. For instance, consider the statement

$$
\text{A(ITEM)=3.0}
\tag{6.5}
$$

This could lie in a DO loop whose range is a variable. Consequently, the compiler would have no means of determining how many subscripted variables were present. The *programmer* must indicate how many storage locations must be reserved for each subscripted variable. A FORTRAN statement which accomplishes this is called a DIMENSION statement. A typical one is

$$\text{DIMENSION A(2\emptyset)} \tag{6.6}$$

This statement indicates that there is an array called A and that it has 20 terms. In this case, 20 storage locations for A(1), A(2), . . . , A(2∅) are set aside for this variable. It is very important that the dimensions of the array be large enough. If, for instance, there are 21 terms in the A array [that is, A(21) is used] and statement (6.6) is used for the DIMENSION statement, then erroneous results may be produced with no indication that an error has resulted. At times it may not be possible to execute such a program. Note that an array can have fewer elements than indicated in the DIMENSION statement. Storage locations in this case will be reserved, but not used, and the program will be executed properly. Note that this is wasteful of storage since part of the main storage memory is devoted to doing nothing.

More than one array can be dimensioned in a single DIMENSION statement. For instance,

$$\text{DIMENSION A(2\emptyset),BOX(25),ITEM(15),NUMB(6)} \tag{6.7}$$

Note that this consists of the word DIMENSION followed by a blank which is followed by the first array and its dimension. Each subsequent array and dimension is separated by a comma. In this case, four arrays have been dimensioned; A, with 20 elements, BOX with 25 elements, ITEM with 15 elements, and NUMB with 6 elements.

The DIMENSION statement must precede *any executable* statement as well as any FORMAT statement. The subscripts *must* be positive integers, i.e., 1, 2, 3, ...

6.2 USE OF ONE-DIMENSIONAL ARRAYS

In this section we shall illustrate the use of one dimensional arrays. We shall start by writing a program that obtains the mean or average value of a set of numbers. We shall assume that there are N numbers in the set where N is a variable that can be entered from data and can range from 1 to 100. We shall start by writing a program with unformatted input and output.

```
C PROGRAM TO OBTAIN AVERAGE
        DIMENSION A(1ØØ)
        READ(5,1)N
1       FORMAT(I4)
C       LOOP TO ENTER DATA
        DO 2Ø I=1,N
          READ(5,2)A(I)
2         FORMAT(F8.1)
2Ø      CONTINUE
C       TAKE SUM
        SUM=Ø.
        DO 3Ø I+1,N
          SUM=SUM+A(I)
3Ø      CONTINUE
        TAKE AVERAGE
        AVE=SUM/N
        WRITE(5,3)AVE
3       FORMAT('ØAVE=',F8.3)
        STOP
        END
```

Let us consider this program. In the first statement we dimension the array. It can have up to 100 terms. The next statement causes a data card to be read which supplies the actual number of terms. This must be an integer which lies between 1 and 100. Note that information for the DIMENSION statement *cannot* be supplied from data. This is because the DIMENSION statement supplies information to the compiler.

The first DO loop (whose object is statement 2Ø) causes N cards to be read. Only one number, corresponding to a value of A(I) will be read from each line. Note that each time that the DO loop is cycled, a READ statement is executed. Thus, in effect, there are N READ statements, and each one requires a line feed.

Next, we define a variable called SUM and set it equal to zero. Now consider the next DO loop. Each time that it is cycled, SUM is increased by A(I). Thus, after the first cycle, SUM=A(1) and after the second cycle of the DO loop SUM=A(1)+A(2). Hence, after the DO loop is cycled N times, SUM will be the sum of all the A(N). To obtain the average, SUM must be divided by the number of terms. This is done in the statement following the DO loop. This statement is

$$AVE=SUM/N$$

This is a mixed mode operation. Thus, when it is executed, N will be converted to a real variable. Finally, the average AVE is printed and execution is terminated. Note that the CONTINUE statements are not necessary. The statements immediately preceding them could have been numbered 2∅ to 3∅, respectively. However, we have included the CONTINUE statements here because they help to clarify the program for the reader. Let us consider the statement SUM=∅. The MICRO-SOFT FORTRAN compiler does not set all variables equal to zero before the execution is begun. Note that all the other variables are defined, possibly as data, so that there is no need to initialize them.

As an additional example, let us consider a program which obtains the average of 3 tests in a class containing N students. We shall assume that there shall be no more than 100 students in the class. Each student will be indentified by an integer. The student's average will be entered into an array called AVE. We shall again use unformatted input and output statements.

```
C PROGRAM TO OBTAIN AVERAGE
        DIMENSION T1(1∅∅),T2(1∅∅),T3(1∅∅),AVE(1∅∅)
        READ(5,1)N
1       FORMAT(I4)
        DO 1∅ I=1,N
        READ(5,2)K,T1(K),T2(K),T3(K)
2       FORMAT(I4,3F8.1)                              (6.9)
1∅      CONTINUE
        DO 2∅ I=1,N
        AVE(I)=(T1(I)+T2(I)+T3(I))/3.
        WRITE(5,3)I,AVE(I)
3       FORMAT(' ',I4,F9.1)
2∅      CONTINUE
        STOP
        END
```

The first statement dimensions the arrays T1, T2, T3, and AVE. These will contain the grades of test 1, test 2, and test 3, and the average of the three tests, respectively. Then N, the number of students, is read. Each of the remaining lines contains four numbers, an integer representing the student's "ID number" and three others, which represent his grades on the three tests. These lines are read in the first DO loop (whose object is statement number 1∅). Note that I, the index of the DO loop, is *not* used in any of the statements. This DO loop just calls for the reading of N lines of data. These each supply K, T1(K), T2(K), and T3(K). Note that it would be *improper* to write READ(5,2)T1(K),

T2(K),T3(K),K, since T1(K),T2(K), and T3(K) would be read using the last used value of K. Thus, errors would result. Let us discuss this further. When the READ statement is executed, the values are "read" from left to right. As soon as a value is read, it is made available for subsequent use. Thus, in the statement

$$\text{READ}(5,2)\text{K},\text{T1}(\text{K}),\text{T2}(\text{K}),\text{T3}(\text{K}) \qquad (6.10)$$

the value of K read from the data is available for use *before* T1(K), T2(K), and T3(K) are read.

In this program N lines of data will be read for students 1 to N. Their test grades will be entered in the appropriate arrays with the appropriate subscript. Note that writing the DO loop in this way *does not* require that the data be entered in the order of the ID numbers. As long as the student's identifying number and grades are entered properly on the data line, it does not matter in what order the lines are entered.

Suppose, as a further example, that we want to determine the highest average. We could insert the following program sequence after statement 2∅.

```
        HIGH=AVE(1)
        DO 3∅ I=2,N
          IF(AVE(I).GT.HIGH)HIGH=AVE(I)       (6.11)
3∅      CONTINUE
        WRITE(5,4)HIGH
4       FORMAT('∅HIGHEST AVERAGE=',F6.1)
```

In this case, we start with HIGH=AVE(1). We then enter the DO loop. If A(2) is greater than HIGH, then HIGH is replaced by A(2), otherwise HIGH is unchanged. Each time that the DO loop is cycled, HIGH is compared with the next AVE(I). If AVE(I) is greater than HIGH, then the previous numerical value of HIGH is replaced by the value of that AVE(I). Then, after the DO loop is completed, the final value of HIGH will be the largest element of the AVE array. This operation is equivalent to that of algorithm (5.26) where BIG is obtained.

As a final example of this section, let us evaluate the equation

$$z = a_n x^n + a_{n-1} x^{n-1} + \ldots + a_1 x + a_0 \qquad (6.12)$$

where the a's, n, and x are known constants. For instance,

$$z = 6x^4 + 3x^3 + 7x^2 + 2x + 1$$

Before we consider the complete program, let us consider the evaluation of the function. A straightforward program sequence which would accomplish this is

```
         .
         .
         .
      NN=N+1
      Z=A(1)
      DO 2Ø I=2,NN
         Z=Z+A(I)**X**(I-1)              (6.13)
2Ø       CONTINUE
         .
         .
         .
```

where the coefficients a_i are contained in the A array. Note that it is mathematically conventional to call the subscript of the first coefficient 0, i.e., a_0. However, the lowest subscript commonly allowed in FOR-TRAN is 1. Thus, we have

$$A(1) = a_0$$
$$A(2) = a_1$$

etc. Note that there are a total of $n+1$ coefficients. In the above program it is assumed that the values of these coefficients, N, the highest power, and X, the value of x, have been read in. The DO loop then adds each successive term to Z until the entire function is calculated.

The above is a straightforward procedure for calculating the function. However, it represents very inefficient FORTRAN since x has to be raised to a power many times. This is a relatively slow computer operation. Hence, if N is large, this program will use a great deal of computer time. Efficient programming is not a topic that should be discussed in an elementary FORTRAN text. However, this program is so inefficient that some discussion of efficiency should be made here. A much more efficient program segment would be

```
         .
         .
         .
      NN=N+1
      Z=A(NN)
      DO 2Ø I=1,N
         Z=Z*X+A(NN-I)
2Ø       CONTINUE
         .
         .
         .
```

Let us explain this. The first step sets

$$z = a_n$$

When the DO loop is cycled the first time, we have

$$z = a_n x + a_{n-1} \tag{6.14}$$

After the second cycle we have

$$z = a_n x^2 + a_{n-1} x + a_{n-2} \tag{6.15}$$

Then, after N cycles, we obtain

$$z = a_n x^n + a_{n-1} x^{n-1} + \ldots + a_0 \tag{6.16}$$

Thus, this procedure evaluates the function but, at no time does X have to be raised to a power. Therefore, this program segment is much more efficient than the first one.

Now let us consider the complete program.

```
C PROGRAM THAT OBTAINS A FUNCTION
        DIMENSION A(2Ø)
C ENTER HIGHEST POWER
        READ(5,1)N
1       FORMAT(I4)
C ENTER X
        READ(5,2)X
        NN=N+1
C ENTER COEFICIENTS
        DO 1Ø I=1,NN
        READ(5,2)A(I)
2       FORMAT(F9.3)
1Ø      CONTINUE                                    (6.17)
C EVALUATE FUNCTION
        Z=A(NN)
        DO 2Ø J=1,N
        N1=NN-J
        Z=Z*X+A(N1)
2Ø      CONTINUE
        WRITE(5,3)Z
3       FORMAT('ØVALUE IS',E15.7)
        STOP
        END
```

We have dimensioned the A array to have $2\emptyset$ terms. Thus, as it stands, this program can be used for values of n equal to or less than 19.

Subscripts

In the previous examples, the subscripts were integer constants or integer variables. This is required in MICROSOFT FORTRAN.

6.3 MULTIDIMENSIONAL ARRAYS

The single dimensional arrays that we have considered are used to represent lists of numbers or variables which have only a single subscript. However, there are many circumstances in which we wish to represent such things as tables of numbers with several columns or variables with multiple subscripts. FORTRAN provides a means for doing this. Now multiple dimensional arrays are used. For instance, consider program (6.9) where we calculate the student's average in three tests. Four arrays were used there, one for each of the tests and one for the average. Actually, we could store all this information in a single array or table. Let us illustrate this.

Student number	Test 1	Test 2	Test 3	Ave.
1	100	100	100	100
2	80	60	70	70
3	100	70	80	83.3
.	.	.	.	. (6.18)
.	.	.	.	.
.	.	.	.	.

(Note that the student's number is not part of the array. We do not need that number since it is the same as the row number.)

At times we work with mathematical expressions where the variables have multiple subscripts such as x_{32}, $y_{1,2,3}$, etc. In mathematics, we often work with arrays of numbers called *matrices*. These can be represented by multidimensional arrays. Let us consider such a matrix.

$$\begin{bmatrix} x_{11} & x_{12} & x_{13} & \cdots & x_{1m} \\ x_{21} & x_{22} & x_{23} & \cdots & x_{2m} \\ \cdot & \cdot & \cdot & & \cdot \\ \cdot & \cdot & \cdot & & \cdot \\ x_{n1} & x_{n2} & x_{n3} & \cdots & x_{nm} \end{bmatrix} \qquad (6.19)$$

Here the array has two dimensions. There are n rows and m columns. It is conventional in such two-dimensional arrays for the subscripts to indicate the position of the element in the array. The first subscript indicates the row and the second the column. For instance, x_{23} lies in the second row and in the third column.

In FORTRAN we must place all symbols on one line. We indicate multiple subscript variables in the following way

$$X(1,2)$$

This represents $x_{1,2}$. Note that the subscripts are placed in parentheses and are separated by a comma. In MICROSOFT FORTRAN, we can represent up to three subscripts in this way. For instance,

$$A(3,6,7)$$

Just as in the case of single subscripted variables, DIMENSION statements must be provided for multiple subscripted variables. A typical DIMENSION statement is

$$DIMENSION \ A(2,3) \tag{6.20}$$

This means that there is an array called A and that 6 storage locations will be required for it. The allowed subscripts of the elements of the A array are then

$$
\begin{aligned}
&A(1,1)A(1,2)A(1,3)\\
&A(2,1)A(2,2)A(2,3)
\end{aligned}
\tag{6.21}
$$

More than one array can be dimensioned in a single DIMENSION statement. For instance,

$$DIMENSION \ A(6,3)BOX(6), ITEM(3,3,1\emptyset) \tag{6.22}$$

In this case, we have the A array with double subscripts and 18 terms, the BOX array with a single subscript and 6 terms, the ITEM array with triple subscripts and 90 terms.

Remember that it is extremely important to provide enough storage space in the DIMENSION statement. For instance, if we have DIMENSION $A(6,2\emptyset)$, and $A(7,3)$ appears in the program, very serious errors can result and an error message may not be given.

Now consider the array of (6.18). It actually consists of four columns since the student's identifying number is not an element of the array. Let us use this array to illustrate the use of multidimensional arrays by writing a program which obtains the average of three tests in a class containing N students. This is similar to the program of (6.9) except that now a multidimensional array will be used.

```
C PROGRAM TO AVERAGE THREE TESTS
        DIMENSION TEST(1ØØ,4)
C ENTER DATA
        READ(5,1)N
1       FORMAT(I6)
        DO 1Ø I=1,N
          READ(5,2)K,TEST(K,1),TEST(K,2),TEST(K,3)
2         FORMAT(I4,3F8.1)
1Ø      CONTINUE                                    (6.23)
C OBTAIN AVERAGE
        DO 2Ø I=1,N
          TEST(I,4)=Ø
          DO 15 J=1,3
            TEST(I,4)=TEST(I,4)+TEST(I,J)
15        CONTINUE
          TEST(I,4)=TEST(I,4)/3.
          WRITE(5,3)I,TEST(I,4)
3         FORMAT(' ',I4,F9.1)
2Ø      CONTINUE
        STOP
        END
```

The discussion of this program is similar to that of (6.9). We shall consider its differences here. Note that the fourth column of the TEST array, i.e., TEST(I,4), now takes the place of the AVE array. The second DO loop (that is, the one whose object is 2Ø) cycles N times. Each cycle results in the computation of one student's average. The statement

TEST(I,4)=Ø.

sets the value of TEST(I,4), which will become the average of student I, to zero each time that the outer DO loop is cycled. The third (inner) DO loop takes the place of the following statement which occurred in (6.9).

AVE(I)=(T1(I)+T2(I)+T3(I))/3.   (6.24)

Note that after the inner DO loop is cycled, the memory location called

TEST(I,4) stores the sum of student I's three tests. Subsequently, this is divided by 3 and stored back in memory location TEST(I,4). Thus, this memory location now stores the average of student I's grades. This program is convenient since the programmer does not have to write all the arrays and we can easily change the number of tests. We shall demonstrate this in the next section. For clarification, this program was deliberately written to parallel that of (6.9). The FORTRAN is some-what inefficient here. However, in Sec. 15.1, procedures for making the program more efficient will be considered.

In the next section we shall discuss a procedure which will sim-plify entering of data into an array. Once this is done we shall generalize this program and also discuss additional examples of multidimensional arrays.

6.4 SPECIAL FORMS OF INPUT AND OUTPUT STATEMENTS WITH ARRAYS

There are special forms of input and output statements, that can be used with arrays to simplify the reading of and printing of data. Suppose that we want to enter data into an array. We could use a DO loop, with an unformatted READ statement, in the following way

```
      DO 1Ø I=1,2Ø
1Ø    READ(5,1)A(I)
1     FORMAT(F8.3)
```

Each time that the DO loop is cycled, a "new" READ statement is executed. Thus, each numerical value of A(I) must be placed on a separate data line.

There is another FORTRAN statement which can be used with arrays and which does not require separate data lines for each element in the array. This statement replaces those of (6.25). It is

```
      READ(5,1)(A(I),I=1,2Ø)                          (6.26)
1     FORMAT(5F6.3)
```

Now the data will be entered five items to a line. Statement (6.26) is called an *implied DO loop*.

The implied DO loop has several advantages. The obvious one is that only one, rather than two, statements need be written by the pro-grammer. However, there are others. The implied DO loop, in contrast to (6.25) does not require that each value of A(I) be placed on a separate line.

Note, in (6.26), the location of the three commas in the READ statement and also that there is no comma after (5,1). This FORMAT statement specifies that each data line will contain five numbers, each occupying six columns. Anything printed beyond column 30 of each data line will be ignored.

The READ statement can contain more than just one array. For instance, we can have

$$\text{READ}(5,27)X,(A(I),I=1,2\emptyset) \qquad\qquad (6.27)$$
$$27 \qquad \text{FORMAT}(F6.3/(4F8.2))$$

In this case, X will be read from the first line and the A(I) will be read from the next five lines, four numbers to a line. Remember that not all MICROSOFT FORTRAN compilers work in this way with inner parentheses in FORMAT statements.

$$\text{READ}(5,1)N \qquad\qquad (6.28)$$
$$\text{READ}(5,2)(A(I),I=1,N)$$

In this case, N is entered on one data line and then the next READ statement causes N values of A(I) to be read in accordance with FORMAT statement 2. The two statements of (6.30) can be combined in a single one in the following way

$$\text{READ}(5,3)N,(A(I),I=1,N) \qquad\qquad (6.29)$$

The value of N is read *first*. This is then used in the implied DO loop. Note that the statement

$$\text{READ}(5,3)(A(I),I=1,N),N$$

must not be used since the test value N of the implied DO loop would not be known until after the implied DO loop is completed. The implied DO loop requires the value of N. Thus, a previously used value of N, or some value determined by the compiler (if N had not been previously determined) would be used. Such operation should only be attempted by experienced programmers.

We have considered implied DO loops with an increment of 1 [for example, in (6.27), I increases in increments of 1 from 1 to 20]. Actually, this need not be the case. We can specify the increment just as in the case of an ordinary DO loop (see Sec. 5.1). For instance,

$$READ(5,6)(A(I),I=1,21,2) \qquad (6.30)$$

In this case, A(I) will be read for

$$I=1,3,5, \quad . \quad . \quad . \quad ,21$$

We have illustrated the implied DO loop with input statements. It can also be applied to output statements. For instance, consider the following output statement

```
      WRITE(2,2)X,(A(I),I=1,2Ø)
2     FORMAT(' X=',E1Ø.3/(' ',4E1Ø.3)          (6.31)
```

(Remember that not all MICROSOFT FORTRAN compilers function in this way with inner parentheses.) Here, X= and the value of X will be printed on one line. Then, under this, the A array will be printed, four values to a line.

To illustrate the use of an implied DO loop, we shall modify program (6.17) which becomes

```
C PROGRAM THAT OBTAINS A FUNCTION
      DIMENSION A(9)
C ENTER DATA
      READ(5,1)N,(A(I),I=1,N),X
1     FORMAT(I3,1ØF6.1)
C EVALUATE FUNCTION
      Z=A(N)                                    (6.32)
      NN=N-1
      DO 2Ø I=1,NN
      Z=Z*X+A(N-1)
2Ø    CONTINUE
      WRITE(5,2)Z
2     FORMAT('ØFUNCTION IS',E15.7)
      STOP
      END
```

In this case, N must be the total number of coefficients (i.e. one more than the highest power). This is a shorter program than (6.17). Note that we have arbitrarily dimensioned the A array to have nine elements so that we could fit all the data on one line.

Implied DO loops can be used with multiple dimensional arrays. For instance, consider the following statement

$$\text{READ}(5,1)((A(I,J),J=1,4),I=1,3) \qquad (6.33)$$

Note that there are six commas in the expression. This is like a nested DO loop. The index of the inner DO loop is cycled completely for each increment of index of the outer DO loop. That is, A(I,J) will be read in the following order

$$A(1,1),A(1,2),A(1,3),A(1,4),A(2,1),A(2,2)$$
$$A(2,3),A(2,4),A(3,1),A(3,2),A(3,3),A(3,4) \qquad (6.34)$$

The converse order would occur if the statement had been written as

$$\text{READ}(5,1)((A(I,J),I-1,3),J=1,4) \qquad (6.35)$$

Formatted input statements can also be used.

Nested implied DO loops can also be used for printing data. For instance,

```
      WRITE(2,23)((A(I,J),J=1,4)I=1,3)        (6.36)
23    FORMAT(' ',4E10.3)
```

This will result in the array's being printed, four items to a line, since the FORMAT statement specifies four values to a line.

As an example of an implied DO loop, and of arrays in general, we shall now consider a complete program. In Sec. 6.3 we considered the program (6.23) which obtained a student's average for three tests. We shall now modify that program so that a variable number of tests can be averaged. The program is as follows.

```
C A PROGRAM TO AVERAGE TESTS
      DIMENSION TEST(100,6)
C ENTER DATA
      READ(5,1)N,M
1     FORMAT(2I5)
      DO 10 JJ=1,N
        READ(5,2)K,(TEST(K,J),J=1,M)        (6.37)
2       FORMAT(I4,5F6.1)
10    CONTINUE
```

```
C AVERAGE TESTS
        DO 2Ø  I=1,N
          TEST(I,MM)=Ø
          DO 15  J=1,M
            TEST(I,MM)=TEST(I,MM)+TEST(I,J)
15        CONTINUE
          TEST(I,MM)=TEST(I,MM)/M
          WRITE(5,3)I,TEST(I,MM)
3         FORMAT(' ',I6,F9.1)
2Ø      CONTINUE
        STOP
        END
```

We have written the DIMENSION statement so that the program can be used with up to 100 students and up to 5 tests. The first READ statement provides for entering N and M, the number of students and the number of tests, respectively. As before, we assume that each data card contains the student's identification number and his grades on all the tests. The READ statement in the first DO loop (whose object is statement number 1Ø) causes K, the student's number, to be read. The implied DO loop enters the student's grade into the K row and appropriate column of the TEST array. The outer DO loop then cycles again. Note that JJ is a dummy variable which just causes this (first) DO loop to cycle N times. Thus, data will be read for each student. Each time that the statement READ(5,2)K,(TEST(K,J),J=1,M) is executed, new values are read in for K and the elements of the TEST array. The value of K is written over the old value (that is, it replaces it in the main storage memory). Remember that we use this type of procedure for entering data since it eliminates the need for keeping the students' data in order. The program after statement number 1Ø is very similar to the program (6.23).

Now suppose that we want to grade the students on the basis of their test average. The instructor must enter the grade limits (for example, 90 or better is an A grade, less than 90 but equal to or greater than 80 is a B grade, etc.). We then want the student's number and grade printed. We shall now consider a program segment that does this. Let us use a numerical code for the grades. This is

$$
\begin{aligned}
A &= 4 \\
B &= 3 \\
C &= 2 \\
D &= 1 \\
F &= \emptyset
\end{aligned}
\qquad (6.38)
$$

Thus we want to print out the student's number and his grade code. The program segment which we shall discuss should be placed after statement number 2∅ and before the STOP statement in program (6.37). This segment is

```
C  PROGRAM SEGMENT TO OBTAIN GRADES
       READ(5,6)MINA,MINB,MINC,MIND
6      FORMAT(4F8.1)
       DO 3∅ I=1,N
       L=∅
       IF(TEST(I,M+1).GE.MIND)L=L+1              (6.39)
       IF(TEST(I,M+1).GE.MINC)L=L+1
       IF(TEST(I,M+1).GE.MINB)L=L+1
       IF(TEST(I,M+1).GE.MINA)L=L+1
       PRINT,I,L
3∅     CONTINUE
```

The first statement causes the reading of the data which supplies the minimum average for the grades of A, B, C, and D, respectively. Each cycle of the DO loop evaluates the grade for one student. Note that I is the row of the TEST array. Hence, I is equal to the student's identifying number. TEST(I,M+1) is the student's average.

Let us consider one cycle of the DO loop. We start with L=0. If the student's average is greater than MIND, then the first IF statement causes L=1. Similarly, the value of L is increased by 1 each time that the logical expression of an IF statement is true. Thus, the value of L corresponding to the student's grade will be obtained. Thus, each time that the DO loop is cycled, a student's grade is evaluated and printed. We can shorten this program segment somewhat. A separate DO loop need not be written to compute the grades. The five IF statements could be placed before the WRITE statement in (6.37) and the WRITE statement could be modified to

$$WRITE(5,3)I,TEST,(I,M+1),L$$

Now all the data would be printed at once. The FORMAT statement would have to be modified appropriately. The statement

$$READ(5,6)MINA,MINB,MINC,MIND$$

would have to be inserted earlier in the program.

The above discussion illustrates a shorter and more efficient program. However, if we use the original scheme and put (6.39) between

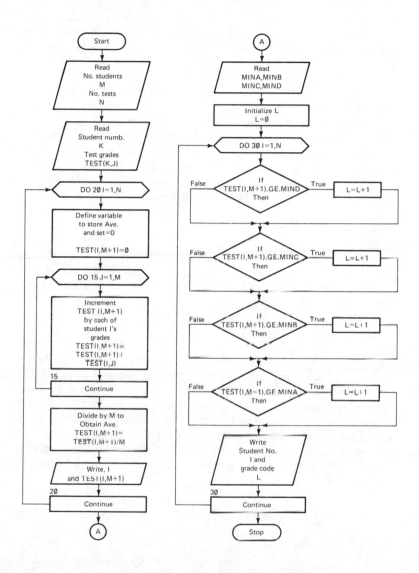

Fig. 6.3 A program flowchart for the combined programs (6.37) and (6.39).

statement number 2Ø1 and the STOP statement, then the program is somewhat more understandable since the program segments are kept separate. In addition, it is desirable to use a separate DO loop for the grades. In this way, the averages will be printed out and execution pauses. The instruction can then decide on the limits for the grades A, B, C, D, and F and enter them. The remainder of the program is then executed. The final grades will then be printed. A flowchart for this program is given in Fig. 6.1.

We could print the grades directly, rather than use the numerical codes. For instance, we could define LL=L+1 and then use a computed GO TO in conjunction with LL to direct control to one of five different WRITE statements and FORMAT statements. Each would print the student number I together with the correct letter grade which would be incorporated as text in the FORMAT statement.

Storage Order of Arrays

There is another procedure that we can use to read or print arrays. However, before discussion this we must consider something about the storage of arrays. Consider a single dimensional array. Suppose that it is dimensioned using the statement

        DIMENSION A(6)

Then, six consecutive storage spaces are reserved for A(1), A(2), A(3), A(4), A(5), and A(6), respectively, in the core memory. The DIMEN—SION statement of a *multidimensional* array also reserves a *list* of consecutive storage spaces. Let us consider the order in which the elements of the array are stored. The following rule is used. All subscripts start with their lowest values, the first (leftmost) subscript is cycled to its maximum value, then the second subscript from the left is increased by one and the first is recycled, etc. For instance, if the DIMENSION statement is

        DIMENSION A(2,2,2)   (6.40)

then the order of storage is

            A(1,1,1)
            A(2,1,1)
            A(1,2,1)   (6.41)
            A(2,2,1)

```
A(1,1,2)
A(2,1,2)
A(1,2,2)
A(2,2,2)
```

If the array is two dimensional, then this rule results in a storage order which is based on the columns. That is, first the first column is stored, then the second, etc.

There are some short forms of statements which could be used for reading data into or out of an array, using their storage order. Suppose that we have the following program sequence:

```
     DIMENSION A(5,2∅)
     :                                              (6.42)
     WRITE(6,26)A
26   FORMAT(6E1∅.3)
```

Note that the WRITE statement contains the array name *without* subscripts. In this case, the A array will be written, six values to a line, using an E1∅.3 specification. The storage order will be used.

We can use a similar statement to enter data:

```
   DIMENSION A(2,3)
        READ(5,1)A
1       FORMAT(6F4.1)
```

In this case, if the data were

```
1.∅,2.3,4.5,6.2,7.1,8.6
```

then we would have A(1,1)=1, A(2,1)=2.3, A(1,2)=4.5, A(2,2)=6.2, A(1,3)=7.1, and A(2,3)=8.6.

This short form is very convenient. It does have some drawbacks. The entire array as specified by the DIMENSION statement must be printed out or entered. Often, we do not want to do this. (Consider (6.23). The array is dimensioned to have 100 rows; however, N might only be 20.) In addition, the storage order must be used. This may be very inconvenient. For instance, consider the array (6.18). We would have to enter the grades for test 1 in order, and then those for test 2, and then those for test 3. Thus, the short form is often awkward when used with multiple dimensional arrays.

Let us consider an additional item about arrays. When entered as data it is often desirable to have them subsequently printed out to check to see if the data was entered properly. Indeed, it is good practice to check all data entered this way, and not just array data. Having the entered data printed back is called *echo checking*.

EXERCISES

6.1 Consider the program segment

```
I=2
J=I**3+1
A(I*J)=4.3
A(I+J)=6.8
```

What is the value of A(11)?

6.2 Discuss the need for DIMENSION statements.

6.3 An array is to be used to store the grades of 100 students in a class. Write a suitable DIMENSION statement for this array.

6.4 Describe the operation of the following program

```
      DIMENSION B(200)
      READ(5,1)N
1     FORMAT(I4)
      DO 10 I=1,N
10    READ(5,2)B(I)
2     FORMAT(F8.1)
      ANS=1.0
      DO 20 I=1,N
20    ANS=ANS*B(I)
      WRITE(5.3)ANS
3     FORMAT('0',E14.3)
      STOP
      END
```

Check your result by running the program on your computer.

6.5 Describe the operation of the following program

```
      DIMENSION A(100)
      READ(5,1)N
1     FORMAT(I4)
```

```
        DO 1Ø I=1,N
1Ø        READ(5,2)A(I)
        BIG=Ø.
        K=Ø.
15      DO 2Ø I=1,N
          IF(BIG.GE.A(I))GO TO 2Ø
          BIG=A(I)
          K=I
2Ø      CONTINUE
        WRITE(5,3)K,A(K)
3       FORMAT('Ø',I6,E15.3)
        GO TO 15
        STØP
        END
```

6.6 Modify the program (6.11) which averages student's grades so that the data is printed in order of descending averages. That is, the highest average and corresponding student identification number are printed first, then the next highest average and corresponding student indentification number are printed, etc. [Hint: see Exercise 6.5.]

6.7 Write a program for the evaluation of the equation

$$z = a_n x^n + a_{n-1} x^{n-1} + \ldots + a_1 x + a_0$$
$$+ b_m y^m + b_{m-1} y^{m-1} + \ldots + b_1 y + b_0$$

where the a's, b's, n, m, x, and y are to be entered by the user. Use only one-dimensional arrays.

6.8 Discuss the need for multidimensional arrays.

6.9 An array is dimensioned in the following way

DIMENSION A(3,4)

Discuss the consequences of the DIMENSION statement.

6.10 Repeat Exercise 6.9 for the DIMENSION statements

DIMENSION A(6,15,4)
DIMENSION B(-1:6,15,-4:3)

6.11 Describe the operation of the following program

```
        DIMENSION C(2Ø,11)
        DO 1Ø I=1,2Ø
        DO 1Ø J=1,1Ø
1Ø         READ(5,1)C,(I,J)
1          FORMAT(F8.1)
        DO 2Ø I=1,2Ø
        C(I,11)=Ø.
        DO 2Ø J=1,1Ø
           C(I,11)=C(I,11)+C(I,J)
2Ø         CONTINUE
        ANS=Ø.
        DO 3Ø I=1,2Ø
        ANS=ANS+C(I,11)*I
3Ø         CONTINUE
        WRITE(5,2)ANS
2          FORMAT('Ø',E15.4)
        STOP
        END
```

6.12 Repeat Exercise 6.6 but now modify program (6.23).

6.13 Write a program which is to be used for the evaluation of the equation

$$z = a_{1,n}x_1{}^n + a_{1,n-1}x_1{}^{n-1} + \ldots + a_{1,1}x_1 + a_{1,0}$$
$$+ a_{2,n}x_2{}^n + a_{2,n-1}x_2{}^{n-1} + \ldots + a_{2,1}x_2 + a_{2,0}$$
$$+ a_{3,n}x_3{}^n + a_{3,n-1}x_3{}^{n-1} + \ldots + a_{3,1}x_3 + a_{3,0}$$

where the a's, n, and the variables x_1, x_2, and x_3 are to be entered by the user. First write the algorithm in pseudolanguage and draw the flowchart. Then write the program. Check it by running it on your computer.

6.14 Repeat Exercise 6.13 but now assume that the number of variables $(x_1, x_2, \ldots, x_m)$ is arbitrary but less than 10.

6.15 Repeat Exercise 4.31 but now assume that the store has 10,000 customers. Write the program so that the correct bill will be obtained for each of them.

6.16 Modify the program of Exercise 6.4 so that implied DO loops are used for the input statements.

6.17 Repeat Exercise 6.21 for the program of Exercise 6.5.

6.18 Repeat Exercise 6.21 for the program of Exercise 6.6.

6.19 Repeat Exercise 6.21 for the program of Exercise 6.7.

6.20 Modify the program of Exercise 6.6. Use the form of statement given in (6.42) so that the user can check to see if the data was entered properly.

6.21 Repeat Exercise 6.20 for the program of Exercise 6.7.

6.22 Repeat Exercise 6.20 for the program of Exercise 6.13.

6.23 A certain store stocks 1000 items. Each one has a separate item number. Every time that one is sold, the item is listed. Once a week the inventory is checked. Write a program to do this. Assume that the inventory at the start of the week is to be printed. Each line contains an item number and the inventory of that item. Start by writing an algorithm in pseudolanguage and draw a flowchart. Then write the program. Check the program by running it on your computer.

6.24 Modify the program of Exercise 6.23 so that a warning message is printed if the inventory of an item drops below a specified value. The value that initiates the warning is different for each item. Assume that this information is stored on a set of punch cards.

6.25 Write a computer program using arrays to solve the set of simultaneous equations

$$3x_1 + x_2 - x_3 = 2$$

$$x_1 + 3x_2 + x_3 = 10$$

$$x_1 + 2x_2 + 5x_3 = 20$$

Hint: if we multiply the third equation by -3, and add it to the first and then multiply the third equation by -1 and add it to the second, we obtain

$$0x_1 - 5x_2 - 16x_3 = -58$$

$$0x_1 + x_2 - 4x_3 = -10$$

$$x_1 + 2x_2 + 5x_3 = 20$$

If we multiply the second equation by 5 and add it to the first, we have

$$0x_1 - 0x_2 - 36x_3 = -108$$
$$0 + x_2 - 4x_3 = -10$$
$$x_1 + 2x_2 + 5x_3 = 20$$

Now we can divide the first equation by -36

$$0x_1 + 0x_2 + x_3 = 3$$
$$0x_1 + x_2 - 4x_3 = -10$$
$$x_1 + 2x_2 + 5x_3 = 20$$

Repeating this procedure, we can finally obtain

$$0x_1 + 0x_2 + x_3 = 3$$
$$0x_1 + x_2 + 0x_3 = 2$$
$$x_1 + 0x_2 + 0x_3 = 1$$

Then,

$$x_3 = 3$$
$$x_2 = 2$$
$$x_1 = 1$$

The procedure here is called the Gauss reduction technique. Note: First write an algorithm in pseudolanguage, and draw a flowchart and then write the program. Check your program by running it on your computer.

6.26 Generalize the procedure of Exercise 6.39 to n simultaneous equations. (Note that the solution of high order simultaneous equations can lead to inaccurate results unless special procedures, which are beyond the scope of this book, are used.)

7 *Subprograms*

In this chapter we shall discuss ways of greatly simplifying some programs. We shall also see how these procedures can aid in structuring programs and how they can aid in team programming.

There are many times when the same sequence of calculations are repeated several times in a program. In fact, the program segment could be repeated using different variable names and statement numbers. However, this involves extra effort on the part of the programmer. FORTRAN provides a means of avoiding this. The repeated program segment is written in a special program called a *subprogram*. This (single) subprogram can be used with the proper variables each time that the program segment is needed. The program which *uses* the subprogram is called the *main program*. When subprograms are used, statements are written into the main program which *call* the subprogram when it is needed. (Sometimes subprograms call other subprograms.) The subprogram then directs the computation. When the desired results are obtained, control reverts to the main program and computation continues using the values calculated by the subprogram. In this chapter, we shall discuss the procedures for writing subprograms and how they are used in conjunction with main programs.

Subprograms are often written by the programmer and are included in the same terminal input as the main program. However, there are certain subprograms that are used over and over again in very many programs. For instance, at some point in many thousands of programs, the calculation of the sine of an angle is called for. Each programmer could write a subroutine to perform this calculation. However, this would be extremely inefficient. To avoid having many programmers write very similar subprograms, many commonly used subprograms are supplied in the FORTRAN library supplied with the MICROSOFT

FORTRAN package. The programmer can write the main program so that any of these stored programs are used. However, the programmer does not have to write the subprogram (he does not even have to know its details). These stored subprograms are called *built-in library subprograms*. You can also write subprograms that can be stored on disk and be used by many main programs. We shall discuss this subsequently.

Subprograms are classified into two general categories: *functions* and *subroutines*. Both of these take values from the main program and perform calculations using them. However, the *result* of a FUNCTION can only be a single number(s) while a SUBROUTINE can have many results, some of which may be arrays. We shall start by considering the FUNCTION. Subsequently, we shall discuss the SUBROUTINE.

7.1 THE FUNCTION SUBPROGRAM

In this section we shall discuss the use of the FUNCTION subprogram. Both the writing of the FUNCTION subprogram and the procedure by which the main program calls the FUNCTION must be considered. The writing of the FUNCTION shall be discussed first. We shall start with a simple FUNCTION which adds two numbers.

```
FUNCTION ADD(A,B)                    (7.1a)
ADD=A+B                              (7.1b)
RETURN                               (7.1c)
END                                  (7.1d)
```

The first statement is called the FUNCTION defining statement. It designates that this is a FUNCTION whose name is ADD and that two variables A and B are to be entered from the main program. The rules for naming a FUNCTION are exactly the same as for naming a variable (see Sec. 2.5). For instance, the first letter indicates whether it is an integer FUNCTION or a real FUNCTION. The list of variables, separated by commas, within the parentheses, for example (A,B), are the data to be supplied by the main program. Next, a sequence of FORTRAN statements follows. These can be any of the previously discussed statements, such as arithmetic statements, IF statements, DO loops, etc. These calculations should always result in the calculation of a variable which has the *same name* as the FUNCTION. This is done in statement (7.1b) where we have calculated ADD. In place of a STOP statement, the subprogram has a RETURN statement. All subprograms must have at least one RETURN statement. The RETURN statement

returns control to the main program. The END statement signifies to the compiler that compilation of the subprogram should terminate.
Let us consider a simple program using this FUNCTION.

```
C PROGRAM USING A FUNCTION
      READ(5,1)C,D
1     FORMAT(2F8.3)
C NEXT STATEMENT CALLS FUNCTION
      SUM=ADD(C,D)
      WRITE(5,2)SUM
2     FORMAT('ØANS=',E15.7)                    (7.2)
      STOP
      END
C THE FUNCTION FOLLOWS
      FUNCTION ADD(A,B)
      ADD=A+B
      RETURN
      END
```

Note that the subprogram is listed *after* the main program. It can also be listed before the main program. Now we shall discuss the operation of this program. Two variables C and D are read. The next line is

$$SUM=ADD(C,D) \qquad (7.3)$$

At first glance, ADD(C,D) appears to be an array. However, it is not since there is no DIMENSION statement which dimensions an ADD array. Thus, it must be a FUNCTION. Therefore, statement (7.3) is the *calling statement* of the FUNCTION called ADD. That is, it causes the execution of the function. The variables C and D are to be used in the computation of ADD. In the FUNCTION defining statement, the variables are called A and B. In this case, A is given the numerical value of C and B the numerical value of D. A and B are called *dummy variables*. When the FUNCTION is called, they take on the values specified by the main program. The list of variables in the FUNCTION calling statement must be of the *same length* as the list of variables in the FUNCTION defining statement. Corresponding terms in the list are then equated. We shall consider other examples of this subsequently. The FUNCTION subprogram is now executed. The numerical value of ADD is obtained. The RETURN statement then returns control to the main program and SUM is set equal to the value of ADD. Finally, SUM is printed. A program flowchart for program (7.2) is given in Fig. 7.1.

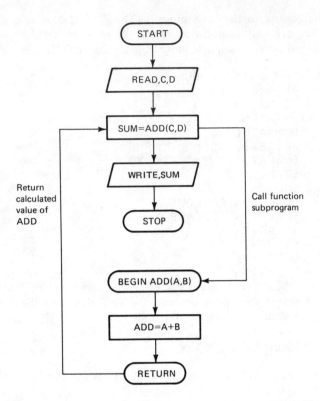

Fig. 7.1 A program flowchart for program (7.2). The statement SUM=ADD(C, D) calls the FUNCTION ADD.

Note that the terminal points for a subprogram are labeled *begin* and *return* (rather than start and stop). The name of the subprogram can be included in the begin block, for clarity.

Let us consider some additional details of the FUNCTION statement. The calling statement contains a list of variables and the defining statement contains a list of the same length. For instance,

$$Y=ABC(X,A,B,C)$$
$$\vdots \qquad\qquad\qquad\qquad (7.4)$$
$$FUNCTION\ ABC(BOX,T,Z,R)$$

Here, we have BOX=X, T=A, Z=B, and R=C. That is, the *order* of the
list of variables and that of the list of dummy variables determines the
assignment of the dummy variables. Note that corresponding variables
must be of the same type. For instance, if the third variable of the list
in the calling statement is an integer variable, then the third variable in
the list of the defining statement must be an integer variable. When the
FUNCTION is compiled and executed, a new variable called BOX is
not set up and stored in a new location in the main storage memory.
What occurs is that BOX now uses the *same storage location* as X. This
results in BOX's having the same numerical value as X. Similarly, T uses
the same storage location as A, etc. In this way, storage space is conserved. Thus, the memory is not likely to become overloaded, which
would cause computation to cease.

This conservation of storage space is helpful. However, at times, it
can lead to difficulties. For instance, consider the following program
sequence.

```
        :
A=12.6
Y=FUN(A)
        :
STOP
END                                                       (7.5)
FUNCTION FUN(Z)
B=Z**2+4.*Z
Z=Z*B
FUN=Z**2
RETURN
END
```

The dummy variable of the FUNCTION is Z. Note that the value of Z
is modified in the FUNCTION, that is, Z=Z*B. Since Z and A share the
same storage location, then the value of A will be changed in the main
program. This new value of A will be used for all subsequent operation
of the main program. (The new Z (that is, Z*B) will be used in all subsequent calculations of the subprogram.) *If we do not want values in
the main program to be changed, then a dummy variable in the FUNC-
TION defining statement should never appear to the left of the equals
sign in any of the statements of the FUNCTION.* To avoid this difficulty
in (7.5) we could replace the last four statements by

Microsoft FORTRAN

```
C=Z*B
FUN=C**2
RETURN
END
```

The variable B in (7.5) and C in the above segment are *internal* variables of the FUNCTION, since they do not appear in the dummy varible list of the FUNCTION defining statement. Thus, B and C are stored in the main storage memory as separate variables and they do not share storage locations with other variables of the main program.

The *names* of symbols used either for the dummy variables of the subprogram or for the internal variables of the subprogram are not related to those in the main program. Indeed, the same variable name can be used for two unrelated variables, one in the main program and the other in the subprogram and they will not interact with each other. For instance,

```
A=12.6
B=4.3
C=11.0
D=ANS(A,C)
.
.
.
END                                          (7.6)
FUNCTION ANS(B,A)
C=B*A
ANS=C**2
RETURN
END
```

This would produce exactly the same results as if the FUNCTION were written as

```
FUNCTION ANS(X,Y)
Z=X*Y
ANS=Z**2                                     (7.7)
RETURN
END
```

That is, in (7.6), when the FUNCTION is executed, the variable B of the FUNCTION uses the storage space of A in the main program, A of the FUNCTION uses the storage space of C of the main program, and C of the FUNCTION is unrelated to C of the main program (that is, they use different storage spaces). This feature of FORTRAN is useful since it allows a subprogram written by one programmer to be used with many main programs without having to change variable names. However, care should be taken since a program such as that of (7.6) can confuse the *programmer*.

Let us consider one further example of a FUNCTION. Let us suppose that we want to enter two variables, a and b, and then compute

$$C = \sqrt{\left|\ \sqrt{|a-b|} - \sqrt{|a+b|}\ \right|}$$

The program which does this is

```
C PROGRAM TO CALCULATE DIFFERENCE OF SQUARE ROOTS
        READ(5,1)A,B
1       FORMAT(2F8.1)
C CALL FUNCTION
        X=ROOT(A,B)
        D=-B
C CALL FUNCTION
        Y=ROOT(A,D)
CALL FUNCTION AGAIN USING
        PREVIOUSLY CALCULATED VALUES
        C=ROOT(X,Y)
        WRITE(5,2)C                                    (7.8)
2       FORMAT(' THE ANSWER IS',E19.5)
        STOP
        END
C THE FUNCTION STARTS HERE
        FUNCTION ROOT(Q,R)
        IF(Q.LT.R)GO TO 100
        ROOT=(Q-R)**.5
        RETURN
100     CONTINUE
        ROOT-(R-Q)**.5
        RETURN
        END
```

Let us consider the FUNCTION. Two values, Q and R, are entered from the main program. Next, the IF statement tests to see if Q is less than R. If the logical expression is true, then $(R - Q)**.5$ is calculated. This value is then returned to the main program. If Q is not less than R, then $(Q - R)**.5$ is calculated and returned to the main program.

Note that the FUNCTION here has two RETURN statements. When either of them is encountered, control is returned to the main program. Each branch FUNCTION of the subprogram is ended with a RETURN statement.

Now consider the main program. A and B are read. Then, X, which is equal to $\sqrt{|a-b|}$ is evaluated using the FUNCTION. Next, Y, which is equal to $\sqrt{|a+b|}$ is evaluated using the FUNCTION and, finally, C, which is equal to $\sqrt{|x-y|}$ is evaluated using the same FUNCTION [see program (4.2) or (4.3)].

We have illustrated a program using a single FUNCTION. Actually, two or more FUNCTIONS may be utilized by the same main program. Also one FUNCTION can call another one. A FUNCTION cannot call itself. If a FUNCTION calls a second one, then the second can call a third one, etc. However, the first FUNCTION cannot be called in this sequence. That is, a loop *cannot* be formed in this way. The FUNC-TIONS are listed in any order before or after the main program. Note that each FUNCTION must have at least one RETURN statement and must terminate with an END statement.

The dummy variable list in the FUNCTION defining statement must consist of a list of valid FORTRAN names. (We shall discuss arrays in the next section.) The list in the calling statement can contain simple algebraic expressions or even constants of the proper type (that is, real or integer). For instance, a valid calling statement is

$$X=FUN(A,3*I-2,33.6) \tag{7.9a}$$

A corresponding FUNCTION defining statement could be

$$FUNCTION \ FUN(X,M,Z) \tag{7.9b}$$

To avoid problems, the beginning programmer should not attempt to change any values entered as expressions or numbers (for example, M and Z should not appear to the left of an equals sign in the FUNC-TION).

7.2 USE OF ARRAYS WITH FUNCTION SUBPROGRAMS

We have considered FUNCTIONS where the variables, entered from the main program, were single variables. Actually, arrays can be entered and manipulated. Remember, however, that the *result* of a FUNCTION is always a single number. Let us consider a simple FUNC-

TION using an array. The FUNCTION will take the sum of all the elements of the array.

```
C EXAMPLE OF A FUNCTION USING AN ARRAY
      DIMENSION A(10)
      READ(5,1)N,(A(I),I=1,N)
1     FORMAT(I4,10F6.1)
      ANS=SUM(A,N)
      WRITE(5,2)ANS
2     FORMAT(' MATRIX SUM IS',E15.6)
      STOP                                          (7.10)
      END
      FUNCTION SUM(B,N)
      DIMENSION B(10)
      SUM=0.
      DO 10 I=1,N
        SUM=SUM+B(I)
10    CONTINUE
      RETURN
      END
```

Note that, in the list of variables, both in the calling statement and in the defining statement, the array is listed *without* its subscripts. The array must be dimensioned *both* in the main program and in the subprogram. To avoid errors, arrays dimensioned in the main program and in the subprogram should be dimensioned *identically*. For instance, in program (7.10), the A array is dimensioned to be a one dimensional array with 10 terms. Then, in the subprogram, the B array, which will use the same storage space as the A array, should be dimensioned to be a one-dimensional array with 10 terms. Errors will not always result if arrays are not dimensioned identically, but they *may*. This is especially true in the case of multiple dimensional arrays. We shall extend these ideas subsequently.

The evaluation of program (7.10) follows the ideas discussed in the last section. When the FUNCTION is called, the dummy array variable B uses the storage space of the A array. The elements of the array are added and control is returned to the main program.

The fact that arrays must be dimensioned in exactly the same way in the subprogram as in the main program can lead to problems. For instance, the same subprogram will often be called more than once during the execution of the main program. Different arrays will be entered from the main program each time that the subprogram is called. These arrays may be of different lengths. Thus, it appears as though a different subprogram would have to be written each time that an array of different size is encountered. This would defeat the purpose of the subprogram. However, FORTRAN provides a means of entering the dimensions of arrays *which appear in the calling statement* as integer variables. These integer variables should also appear in the list of variables of the calling statement. For instance, we could write program (7.10) in the following way:

```
C EXAMPLE ILLUSTRATING DIMENSIONING IN FUNCTIONS
      DIMENSION A(1ØØ)
      NN=1ØØ
      READ(5,1)N
1     FORMAT(I5)
      READ(5,2)(A(I),I=1,N)
2     FORMAT(5F8.2)
      ANS=SUM(A,N,NN)
      WRITE(5,3)ANS
3     FORMAT('ØTHE MATRIX SUM IS',E15.6)          (7.11)
      STOP
      END
      FUNCTION SUM(B,N,NDIM)
      DIMENSION B(NDIM)
      SUM=Ø.
      DO 1Ø I=1,N
        SUM=SUM+B(I)
1Ø    CONTINUE
      RETURN
      END
```

Now, if the FUNCTION were used more than once, the dimension of the B array could be changed by changing the value of the dummy variable NDIM. Note that the second statement which sets NN=1ØØ could be eliminated. We could simply write the calling statement as ANS=SUM(A,N,1ØØ).

When subprograms are dimensioned in this way, the actual "dimensioning" takes place during execution of the program and not during compilation. In fact, true dimensioning must take place during compilation. That is, during compilation, all storage space must be reserved. The DIMENSION statement, which dimensions an array of a subprogram which is a dummy variable in the calling list does *not* reserve storage space, however. This is because these arrays do not use "new" storage space but share it with an array which has been previously dimensioned in the main program. The purpose of the DIMENSION statement in a subprogram is to indicate that the variable in question is an array. This DIMENSION statement is also used in determining how the storage space is shared. For instance, in program (7.11), this indicates that the B array is one dimensional and shares 100 storage spaces with the A array. Thus, the 100 B values have a one-to-one correspondence with the 100 A values.

At times, we use arrays in subprograms that are not part of the main program and are not listed in the FUNCTION defining statement. These must be dimensioned using constants, not variables. This is because storage space must be reserved for these arrays and this must be done during compilation. Thus an actual number must be given in the DIMENSION statement.

Let us illustrate this with an example. We shall write a program which squares all the elements of a two-dimensional array and then adds all the elements of the resulting array.

```
C PROGRAM ILLUSTRATING DIMENSIONING
        DIMENSION A(1Ø,1Ø)
        READ(5,1)N
1       FORMAT(I6)
        READ(5,2)((A(I,J),J=1,N),I=1,N)
2       FORMAT(5F8.3)
        ANS=SUM(A,N,1Ø)
        WRITF(5,3)ANS
3       FORMAT('ØANSWER IS',E15.6)
        STOP
        END
        FUNCTION SUM(B,N,NDIM)
C ILLUSTRATION OF DIMENSIONING                    (7.12)
        DIMENSION B(NDIM,NDIM),C(1Ø,1Ø)
C NEXT SQUARE ELEMENTS PUT IN NEW ARRAY
        DO 1Ø I=1,N
        DO 1Ø J=1,N
          C(I,J)=B(I,J)**2
1Ø      CONTINUE
C SUM ALL ELEMENTS OF NEW ARRAY
        SUM=Ø.
        DO 2Ø I=1,N
        DO 2Ø J=1,N
          SUM=SUM+C(I,J)
2Ø      CONTINUE
        RETURN
        END
```

Note that the use of the C array could be avoided. We could write the arithmetic statement of the second set of DO loops as

SUM=SUM+B(I,J)**2

and not use the C array at all. The first set of DO loops would then be eliminated. However, the C array is deliberated used here for illustrative purposes. The C array is dimensioned numerically while the B array is dimensioned using variable dimensions. Note that this does not create problems since we need only dimension the C array *large* enough. Its dimensions do not have to *exactly* match any of those of the main program.

Let us recall some facts about dimensioning. The DIMENSION statement causes a number of storage locations to be reserved. For instance, in the program just discussed

DIMENSION A(1Ø,1Ø)

causes 100 storage locations to be reserved for A. If N, see program (7.12), is less than 10, then not all of these storage locations will be used. For instance, if the program is run with N=5, then only 25 storage locations will be utilized.

In the subprogram, the B array will share storage space with the A array. The statement

DIMENSION B(NDIM,NDIM)   (7.13)

where we have set NDIM equal to 10, causes the appropriate sharing of storage of the A and B arrays. Again, 100 storage locations must be shared. If N=5, then only 25 storage locations will actually be used.

Care should be taken, especially when multiple dimensioned arrays are used. Let us illustrate this with program (7.12). Suppose that we change the fourth line to

ANS=SUM(A,N,N)

and the value of N is 2. Suppose that all the entered values of the A array are 1. Then, after the implied DO loop is entered, the following values will be stored for A. (They are listed in the storage order of the A array.)

A(1,1)=1
A(2,1)=1
A(3,1)=A(4,1) = ... = A(1Ø,1)=UNKNOWN

```
A(1,2)=1
A(2,2)=1
ALL REMAINING A(I,J)=UNKNOWN
```

Remember than A is dimensioned as a 10 × 10 array in the main program, even though we only want to enter a 2 × 2 array. Now, suppose that when the FUNCTION is executed, in the main program we have

```
NDIM=2
```

Thus, the "program" assumes that the B array is a 2 × 2 array and is stored in the usual order. Since it has 2 × 2 elements, its first four storage locations will correspond to the first four storage locations of the A array.

```
B(1,1)=1
B(2,1)=1
B(1,2)=UNKNOWN
B(2,2)=UNKNOWN
```

Hence, an erroneous result will occur when the program is evaluated since we desire that B(1,2)=1 and that B(2,2)=1. Remember that an array (no matter how large its dimensions) is stored simply as a list. The DIMENSION statement in the FUNCTION is used to align the lists. (Remember that only one set of storage locations is used.) If the dimensions of the array in the FUNCTION are not exactly the same as those in the main program, then the lists will not align properly. Thus, care should be taken to pass the *same* dimension numbers to the FUNCTION as those in the main program. Note that it is not mandatory to do this. However, errors can easily result unless great care is taken.

One final word of caution: *individual* elements of an array cannot be used in the FUNCTION defining statements. For instance, FUN(A(1), A(2),B) is wrong even if the A array is dimensioned in the FUNCTION. On the other hand, individual array elements can appear in the FUNC–TION calling statement.

7.3 FORTRAN LIBRARY FUNCTIONS

Many functions are used repeatedly in very many programs. Such functions are stored in the compiler and can be called by any FORTRAN program which is being executed. They are called *library functions*. To use these functions, they need only be included on the right hand side of an algebraic expression. Let us consider some examples of this. The library function which produces the sine of an angle in radians is

$$SIN(X)$$

For instance, the statement

$$Y=SIN(X) \tag{7.14}$$

sets Y equal to the sine of X. Library functions, as well as ordinary ones need not be alone on the right-hand side of the statement. For instance, the following is a valid FORTRAN expression:

$$Y=A*SIN(X)**2 \tag{7.15}$$

Note that all functions, and not just library ones, can be used in expressions of this form. In general, a FUNCTION can take the place of a variable on the right-hand side of an algebraic expression.

There are very many library FUNCTIONS. A list of the MICRO-SOFT FORTRAN library FUNCTIONS is given in Appendix B. You should study this list to determine the available library FUNCTIONS. There are often several library functions which perform the same type of operation. The functions differ in that one may require real variables and produces a real result and the other may require integer variables and produces an integer result, or they may require integer variables and produce a real result. For instance

$$X=AMAX1(A,B,C,D) \tag{7.16}$$

is a library FUNCTION that sets X equal to the variable in the list which has the largest value. As an example, if the stored values of the variables are A=12.6, B=16.3, C=4.2, and D=1.6, then X=16.3. The library FUNCTION

$$I=MAX\emptyset(K,L,M) \tag{7.17}$$

performs the same operation for integers. In subsequent chapters, we shall discuss double precision and complex variables, which use their own forms of library functions.

Let us illustrate the use of the library function with the following: We want to obtain a solution to the equation

$$\sin \pi x - 0.5x = 0 \tag{7.18}$$

This is called a *transcendental equation*, and must be solved by numerical means. Let us consider a procedure for doing this. A plot of $\sin \pi x$ and $0.5x$ is shown in Fig. 7.2. The solution of the equation occurs when $\sin \pi x = 0.5x$, that is, at x_0, where the two curves intersect. Now suppose that we define a function y such that

$$y = \sin \pi x - 0.5x$$

When $x = x_0$, $y = 0$. Assume that we substitute an arbitrary value of x. If x is less than x_0, then y will be positive since $\sin \pi x$ will be greater than $0.5x$. Similarly, if x is greater than x_0, then y will be negative. Thus, if we guess a value of x_0 and calculate y we can determine if our guess is too large or too small.

Now consider the following computation scheme. From Fig. 7.2 we see that the root lies in the range

$$0 \leqslant x \leqslant 1$$

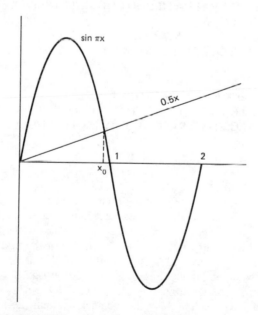

Fig. 7.2 An illustration of the function $\sin \pi x$ and $0.5x$

Divide the range in half. Try $x = 0.5$ as a root. If $y > 0$, then the root lies above 0.5 (i.e., $0.5 \leqslant x_0 \leqslant 1$). On the other hand, if $y < 0$, then $0 \leqslant x_0 \leqslant 0.5$. For the case $x = 0.5$, we will have $y > 0$. Then, $0.5 \leqslant x_0 \leqslant 1.0$. Now divide the new range in half $0.5/2 = 0.25$. Now try $x_0 = 0.5 + 0.25$ (i.e., the middle of the new range). Now if $y > 0$, then $0.75 \leqslant x_0 \leqslant 1$. If $y < 0$, then $0.5 \leqslant x_0 \leqslant 0.75$. Suppose that $y > 0$, then $0.75 \leqslant x_0 \leqslant 1$. Thus, x is located to within 0.25.

Now repeat the procedure. That is, divide the range again, $0.25/2 = 0.125$, and repeat. Now x_0 will be located to within 0.125. By repeating the procedure a sufficient number of times, we can obtain x_0 to whatever accuracy we desire.

Let us consider the accuracy if we cycle 3 times. The accuracy is $1/2^3 = 0.125$. If we cycle 5 times, the accuracy is $1/2^5 = 0.03125$. Thus, in general, the accuracy is 2^{-n} where n is the number of cycles. We should be able to specify the accuracy.

We shall assume that the accuracy is a varaible that can be read in. The algorithm for this program follows and the flowchart is given in Fig. 7.3.

ALGORITHM TO EVALUATE ROOT OF SIN(3.14159*X)−0.5*X=0
READ ACCURACY N
SET INITIAL VALUE OF X:X=0
LOOP TO CALCULATE DIFFERENCE DX, X, AND Y:LOOP FOR
                                                    I=1,N
    DX=1./2**I   (7.19)
    INCREASE X BY DX:X=X+DX
    EVALUATE Y FOR THIS X:Y=SIN(3.14159*X)−0.5*X
    IF Y IS NEGATIVE REDUCE X BY DX:IF(Y.LT.∅)X=X−DX
END LOOP
WRITE, X
STOP

Let us consider the algorithm. First N is read in. Since the DO loop will cycle N times, then, as discussed, N establishes the desired accuracy. The initial value of X is set equal to 0. Now the DO loop is entered. The increment in X is $DX=1/2^I$ where, for the first cycle, I=1. X is incremented by DX and Y is computed. If Y is negative, then the choice for X was too large. Thus, X is reduced by DX. If Y is positive, then the root is greater than the first X. The DO loop is then cycled again using a DX which is half the original one and the procedure is repeated. If the original X was too small then the new X is $(1/2) + (1/2^2)$

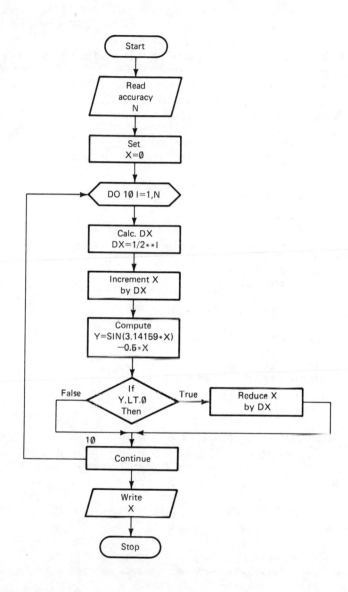

Fig. 7.3 A program flowchart for the algorithm that solves $\sin \pi x - 0.5x = 0$

= .75. If the original X was too large then the new X is $(1/2) - (1/2) + (1/2^2) = .25$. After the first cycle we know that X lies either in the range 0 to 0.5 or in the range 0.5 to 1. That is, we know it to within 0.5, which is the value of the first DX. Similarly, after the second cycle we know the root location to within 0.25. Note that DX is halved with each successive cycle. After N cycles, the value of X will be known to the desired accuracy. Then, this value of X is printed.

A program which implements the algorithm is

```
C  PROGRAM THAT EVALUATES ROOT OF
C  SIN(3.14159*X)-Ø.5X=Ø.
C  ENTER ACCURACY DATA
        READ(5,1)N
1       FORMAT(I6)
C  INITIALIZE X AND DX
        X=Ø.
        DX=1.
C  ENTER LOOP
        DO 1Ø I=1,N                                        (7.20)
          DX=DX/2.
          X=X+DX
          Y=SIN(3.14159*X)-.5*X
C         TEST TO SEE IF X IS TOO LARGE
          IF(Y.LT.Ø)X=X-DX
1Ø      CONTINUE
        WRITE(5,2)X
2       FORMAT('ØX=',E15.7)
        STOP
        END
```

Note that, instead of raising DX to a power, we set its initial value to 1. and then divide it by 2 each time that the loop cycles. This accomplishes the same result but is a more efficient program since we do not have to keep raising a number to a power.

There are other library functions that are given in Appendix B. Now let us consider two library functions that are related to the internal workings of the computer. The first is

PEEK

which allows you to determine the contents of a particular memory location. For instance, when the statement

X=PEEK(1532Ø)

is executed, the values stored in the memory location for X would be the contents of memory location 15320. The number 15320 is a decimal number. However, a hexadecimal number can be entered. Any number preceded by a Z' or X' (a Z and a single quote or an X and single quote) will be interpreted in MICROSOFT FORTRAN as hexadecimal. If you are not familiar with the hexadecimal number system, then the decimal number should be used.

Another function related to the internal workings of the computer is

INP

This is concerned with the input/output ports of the computer. For instance, when

X=INP(128)

is executed, the value stored in the memory location for X is the pesent value at input port 128. If you are not familiar with the internal workings of the computer, then these two functions should not be used.

7.4 ARITHMETIC STATEMENT FUNCTIONS

If a FUNCTION requires only four statements, one of which is an arithmetic statement, that is, *one* in addition to the FUNCTION defining, RETURN, and END statements, then we can write it using only one line within the body of the program. This is called an arithmetic FUNCTION. For instance, consider the following

```
C  ILLUSTRATION OF ARITHMETIC STATEMENT FUNCTION
      ANS(A,B,C)=(A+B+C)*(A-B)
      READ(5,1)X,Y,Z
1     FORMAT(3F9.2)
      D=X+Y
      E=Y-Z
      R=ANS(E,D,X)
      M=ANS(X,Y,Z)
      OUT=R*M+E
      WRITE(5,2)OUT
2     FORMAT('0THE ANSWER IS',E15.7)
      STOP
      END
```
$$(7.21)$$

The first statement defines the arithmetic FUNCTION ANS(A,B,C). Note that A, B, and C are dummy variables, just as they are with ordinary FUNCTIONS. The arithmetic FUNCTION is called in the same way as the FUNCTION subprogram. In the listing of the program the arithmetic FUNCTION must *precede any executable statement*. It follows specification statements. (The only specification statement that we have considered thus far is DIMENSION.)

Since only one statement is allowed in any arithmetic FUNCTION, no DIMENSION statement can be included. Hence, arithmetic FUNC–TION statements cannot use arrays.

Ordinary subprograms are external to the main program and each other (if there is more than one subprogram). The main program, or any subprogram, can call upon any of the subprograms in their execution. This is not true in the case of the arithmetic FUNCTION. It is internal to the program in which it is defined and it can only be used in the main program. Similarly, if a subprogram contains within it an arithmetic FUNCTION, then the arithmetic FUNCTION can only be used by that (particular) subprogram.

The fact the arithmetic FUNCTIONS are internal to their main program (or subprogram) causes a variable, which is not in the calling list, to be treated as a variable of the main program, for instance

```
          CALC(A,B,C)=(A+B+C)*X
          READ(5,1)X,Y,Z
    1     FORMAT(3F8.1)
          R=X*Y+Z
          V=X-Y+R                                    (7.22)
          ANS=CALC(R,V,Z)*CALC(Z,V,Y)
          WRITE(5,2)ANS
    2     FORMAT(' ANS=',E15.7)
          STOP
          END
```

Whenever CALC is executed, the resulting value is the sum of the three variables, which correspond to the dummy variable times the value of X from the main program. Variables listed in the FUNCTION defining statement (for example, A, B, and C) are dummy variables, and are not related to variables of the main program, even if they have the same name. This is the same as in the case of an ordinary subprogram. However, variables not listed in the FUNCTION defining statement (for example, X) are the same as those in the main program. Note that there always must be at least one dummy variable in any FUNCTION.

7.5 THE SUBROUTINE SUBPROGRAM

The FUNCTION subprogram is extremely useful. However, it is limited in that only a single value(s), not arrays, can be returned to the main program. In many cases, it is necessary to calculate and return one or more arrays to the main program. A subprogram, called a SUBROU-TINE, can be used in this case. The SUBROUTINE is very similar to the FUNCTION and almost all of the ideas which we have discussed in Secs. 7.1 and 7.2 are applicable to SUBROUTINES. The method of calling a SUBROUTINE differs from that for a FUNCTION. This provides the added versatility. We shall start by illustrating a simple SUBROUTINE. Let us rewrite program (7.2), now using a SUBROUTINE rather than a FUNCTION.

```
        READ(5,1)C,D
1       FORMAT(2F8.2)
        CALL ADD(C,D,SUM)
        WRITE(5,2)SUM
2       FORMAT('ØANSWER=',E15.6)
        STOP                                        (7.23)
        END
        SUBROUTINE ADD(A,B,E)
        E=A+B
        RETURN
        END
```

Let us consider this. The SUBROUTINE consists of the last four state-ments. The first statement of these is the SUBROUTINE defining statement.

$$SUBROUTINE \ ADD(A,B,E) \qquad (7.24)$$

This is very similar to the FUNCTION defining statement except that the word SUBROUTINE replaces the word FUNCTION. The list of dummy variables is essentially the same as that of the FUNCTION. There is one difference. The *result(s)* of the calculation is now included in the list of dummy variables. Now consider the main program. The SUBROUTINE is called through a special call statement, which is

$$CALL \ ADD(C,D,SUM) \qquad (7.25)$$

That is, it consists of the word CALL followed by the name of the SUBROUTINE with a list of variables. The list of variables are variables of the main program. Note that the variable SUM has not been encountered before. However, when the program was compiled, a storage location was reserved for it. That is, listing a "new" variable in a calling statement will cause the compiler to reserve storage space for it. The "variables" of the calling statement can be simple arithmetic statements or numbers (see cautions at the end of Sec. 7.1). The variables listed in the SUBROUTINE defining statement which correspond to actual variables of the calling statement do not have their own memory location. They use the storage locations of the corresponding variables in the CALL statement list. This is exactly the same as in the case of the FUNCTION. A program flowchart for program (7.23) is given in Fig. 7.4.

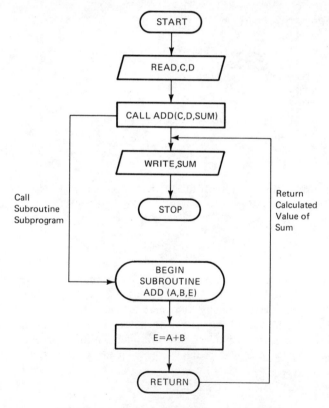

Fig. 7.4 A program flowchart for program (7.23)

When the CALL statement is reached, the SUBROUTINE is executed. During this execution, when the RETURN statement is reached, control is returned to the main program. The next statement executed is the one following the CALL statement. Note that execution of the SUBROUTINE results in the changing of the stored value of (some of) the variables listed in the calling statement. These stored values can then be used subsequently anywhere in the main program. If there are any variables in the list of the calling statement that should not be changed by the execution of the SUBROUTINE, then these should not appear to the left of the equals sign in any of the statements of the SUBROUTINE.

Thus, most of the basic ideas of the SUBROUTINE are the same as those of the FUNCTION. There are some differences. A FUNCTION must have at least one variable in its calling expression whereas a SUBROUTINE can have none. For instance, we could rewrite program (7.23) as

```
      CALL ADD
      STOP
      END
      SUBROUTINE ADD
      READ(5,1)                          (7.26)
1     FORMAT(2F8.1)
      E=A+B
      WRITE(5,2)E
2     FORMAT('ØANSWER=',E15.6)
      RETURN
      END
```

Now the reading and printing are performed in the SUBROUTINE and there is no need to pass variables between it and the main program. We shall consider other aspects of this subsequently.

Let us now illustrate the use of a SUBROUTINE with a one dimensional array. We shall write a program that is to read in two arrays of equal size and multiply the corresponding elements of each. For instance, if we have the arrays

$$A = \begin{bmatrix} 1 \\ 3 \\ 4 \end{bmatrix} \qquad B = \begin{bmatrix} 2 \\ 4 \\ 6 \end{bmatrix} \qquad (7.27a)$$

then the result is to be

$$C = \begin{bmatrix} 2 \\ 12 \\ 24 \end{bmatrix} \qquad (7.27b)$$

A program which produces the desired calculation is

```
C ILLUSTRATION OF MATRIX MANIPULATION
        DIMENSION A(1Ø),B(1Ø),C(1Ø)
        READ(5,1)N
1       FORMAT(I2)
        READ(5,2)(A(I),I=1,N)
        READ(5,2)(B(I),N=1,N)
2       FORMAT(1ØF8.3)                          (7.28)
        CALL MULT(A,B,C,N,1Ø)
        WRITE(6,3)(C(I),I=1,N)
3       FORMAT(' ',1ØE1Ø.3)
        STOP
        END
C       SUBROUTINE STARTS HERE
        SUBROUTINE MULT(D,E,F,N,NDIM)
        DIMENSION D(NDIM,NDIM),E(NDIM,NDIM),
                        F(NDIM,NDIM)
        DO 1Ø I=1,N
          F(I)=D(I)*E(I)
1Ø      CONTINUE
        RETURN
        END
```

In the main program, the arrays are dimensioned. Next, N, the actual size of the arrays is read. Remember that N must be equal to or less than the dimensioned values of the arrays (i.e., 10). Then, the arrays are read and SUBROUTINE MULT is called. Note that in the SUBROUTINE defining statement the arrays are listed *without* their subscripts.

Now let us consider the SUBROUTINE. The arrays which are listed in the SUBROUTINE defining statement are dimensioned using a variable. All the comments concerning dimensioning made in Sec. 7.2 apply here also. The DO loop is used to multiply the corresponding elements of the two arrays. After this is done, control is returned to the main program and the values are printed.

Let us now illustrate the use of a SUBROUTINE with multidimensional arrays. We shall write a program which is to read in two two-dimensional arrays of equal size, square the elements of one, and then add these to the corresponding elements of the other. For instance, if we have arrays with two rows and columns, these calculations are

$$A = \begin{bmatrix} 1 & 2 \\ 3 & 4 \end{bmatrix}, \qquad B = \begin{bmatrix} 5 & 6 \\ 7 & 8 \end{bmatrix} \qquad (7.29a)$$

The results are to be

$$C = \begin{bmatrix} 1 & 4 \\ 9 & 16 \end{bmatrix} + \begin{bmatrix} 5 & 6 \\ 7 & 8 \end{bmatrix} = \begin{bmatrix} 6 & 10 \\ 16 & 24 \end{bmatrix} \qquad (7.29b)$$

The program is

```
C ILLUSTRATION OF MATRIX MANIPULATION
        DIMENSION A(10,10),B(10,10),C(10,10)
        READ(5,1)N
1       FORMAT(I2)
        READ(5,2)((A(I,J),J=1,N),I=1,N)
        READ(5,2)((B(I,J),J=1,N),I=1,N)
2       FORMAT(10F8.3)                              (7.30)
        CALL RUN(A,B,C,N,10)
        WRITE(6,3)((C(I,J),J=1,N),I=1,N)
3       FORMAT(' ',10E10.3)
        STOP
        END
C       SUBROUTINE STARTS HERE
        SUBROUTINE RUN(D,E,F,N,NDIM)
        DIMENSION D(NDIM,NDIM),
                    E(NDIM,NDIM),F(NDIM,NDIM),
                        G(10,10)
        DO 10 I=1,N
        DO 10 J=1,N
        G(I,J)=D(I,J)**2
10      CONTINUE
        DO 20 I=1,N
        DO 20 J=1,N
        F(I,J)=G(I,J)+E(I,J)
```

```
2 Ø        CONTINUE
           RETURN
           END
```

The two-dimensional arrays are dimensioned in the main program. Then, N, the actual size of the array is read. (Note that N must be equal to or less than 10.) The arrays are then read, and the SUBROUTINE RUN is called. Remember that, in the calling statement list, and in the SUB—ROUTINE defining statement, the arrays are listed *without* their subscripts. The array C is calculated and the results printed.

Now consider the SUBROUTINE. The arrays which are listed in the SUBROUTINE defining statement are dimensioned using a variable (see Sec. 7.2). The array G, which is not in the defining statement, must be dimensioned numerically (see Sec. 7.2). The G array is included to illustrate dimensioning. Actually, we do not need this array. The same result could be accomplished by eliminating the first nested DO loop and writing the arithmetic statement as

$$F(I,J)=D(I,J)**2+E(I,J)$$

The FORMAT statements will result in the reading and writing of 10 numbers to a line. In Sec. 6.4 we discussed procedures for reading and writing matrices in more desirable forms.

The SUBROUTINE and FUNCTION are very similar and most of the explanations of Secs. 7.1 and 7.2 are applicable to the SUBROU—TINE. The additional versatility of the SUBROUTINE comes about because of the added flexibility imparted by the calling statement.

Library SUBROUTINES

The MICROSOFT FORTRAN library also contains functions that can be used. We shall consider some of them here. In general, these subroutines should only be used if you are familiar with the internal workings of the computer. The SUBROUTINE POKE allows a number to be stored in a specific memory location. For instance,

```
CALL POKE(15217,128)
```

causes 128 to be stored in memory location 15217.

The SUBROUTINE OUT is used to output data to a specified port of the computer. For instance,

```
      CALL OUT(16,256)
```

outputs 256 to port 16. Variables as well as constants can be used for either of these FUNCTIONS.

The MICROSOFT FORTRAN library also contains subroutines that are used to control the input and output operations, or to perform multiplication and other arithmetic operations. All of these library SUBROUTINEs should only be used by persons who are familiar with machine language and the internal workings of the computer. Their details are discussed in the MICROSOFT FORTRAN manual. When you link your program, any needed library subroutines are called. However, you need not be concerned with their details.

7.6 COMMON STORAGE

We have discussed that the variables in subprogram calling statement lists share storage spaces with the variables in the subprogram defining statement lists (see Secs. 7.1, 7.2, and 7.5). This is useful because it saves storage space. (Actually, in this case, there is one memory location with several names.) In long and complex programs this can be extremely helpful. There is another technique whereby we can cause variable (names) in a main program and subprograms to share storage space if they are not listed in the calling statement list. This is the COMMON statement. At times, it is more convenient to use the COMMON statement than to include the variables in the calling statement. Let us illustrate the use of the COMMON statement by rewriting program (7.23) using it.

```
        COMMON C,D,SUM
        READ(5,1)C,D
1       FORMAT(2F8.2)
        CALL ADD
        WRITE(5,2)SUM
2       FORMAT('ØANSWER IS',E15.6)              (7.31)
        STOP
        END
        SUBROUTINE ADD
        COMMON A,B,E
        E=A+B
        RETURN
        END
```

The variables C, D, and SUM of the main program are said to be placed in *common storage* with A, B, and E of the subprogram. The rules for this common storage are the same as for the lists of variables in subprograms and their calling statements. Thus, C and A share the same storage location. One important rule is that *when variables in a main program and subprogram have been placed in common storage, they should not be included in the lists in the calling and subprogram defining statements.* Thus, in program (7.31), there is no list associated with the SUBROUTINE name. All the variables need not be removed from the list and placed in the COMMON statement. This is a matter of preference of the programmer. (Note that FUNCTION subprograms require *at least one* variable in the list.)

It is important that variables placed in common storage be of the same type and, if arrays are involved, that they are of the same length. For instance, consider the program sequence

```
DIMENSION A(1Ø),B(2,6)
COMMON A,B,C,D
   :                                                    (7.32a)
   :
SUBROUTINE ABC(G,MM,NN,KK)
DIMENSION AA(MM),AB(NN,KK)
COMMON AA,AB,Q,R
```

The DIMENSION and COMMON statements in the main program allocate the first ten locations of common storage to A, the next twelve to B, and the next two to C and D. This constitutes a list of 24 variables. Usually, the form of the list of the COMMON statement in the SUB—ROUTINE is identical with that of the list in the main program. That is, AA would be an array of 10 terms. AB would be a 12 term (2,6) array, and Q and R are each single variables (i.e.,we would set MM=10, NN=2, KK=6).

This type of allocation is least confusing but not necessary. For instance, suppose that we wrote in the SUBROUTINE

```
DIMENSION A1(9),AC(1Ø)                                 (7.32b)
COMMON A1,B1,AC,D1,E,F,G
```

As before, the list of 24 variables in the main program COMMON statement would be aligned with the list in the subprogram COMMON statement. Thus, we would have

A(1)=A1(1)
.
.
.
A(9)=A1(9)
A(10)=B1
B(1,1)=AC(1)
B(2,1)=AC(2)
B(1,2)=AC(3)
B(2,2)=AC(4)
B(1,3)=AC(5)
B(2,3)=AC(6)
B(1,4)=AC(7)
B(2,4)=AC(8)
B(1,5)=AC(9)
B(2,5)=AC(10)
B(1,6)=D1
B(2,6)=E
C=F
D=G

That is, each COMMON statement establishes a list, all arrays are listed in their storage order and the list in the main program and subprogram are aligned to obtain the common storage locations. The list in the subprogram can be shorter than that in the main program. For instance, in statement (7.32b), if we omitted the G, then the storage allocation would be the same except that R in the main program would not be stored in common with a variable in the subprogram. An important fact to remember when COMMON storage is set up is that corresponding variables in the list must be of the same type (e.g., integer, real).

COMMON statements are cumulative. For instance, the following are equivalent.

$$\text{COMMON A, B, C} \qquad\qquad (7.33a)$$
$$\text{COMMON D}$$

and

$$\text{COMMON A, B, C, D} \qquad\qquad (7.33b)$$

COMMON statements can be used to dimension arrays in MICROSOFT FORTRAN. This often proves convenient to the programmer. For instance, the following are equivalent.

```
DIMENSION A(1Ø),B(15)                        (7.34a)
COMMON A
```

and

```
DIMENSION B(15)                              (7.34b)
COMMON A(1Ø)
```

An array must be dimensioned in only *one* place. For instance, in (7.34a) it would be improper to write COMMON A(10), since now the A array would be dimensioned in both the DIMENSION and the COMMON statements.

The individual elements of an array cannot be included in the COMMON statement list. That is, any number following an array (e.g., A(10)) must be a dimension and not a reference to a particular element of the array.

Labeled COMMON Storage — Block COMMON Storage

When a program uses several subprograms and utilizes common storage, the COMMON statement can become cumbersome if the list of variables becomes very long. For instance, checking the list becomes a tedious process for the programmer. This can be avoided by *labeling* or *naming* areas of common storage. Variables can be designated to lie within a certain named common storage area, or *block*. The list of variables in any one storage area must conform to all the rules but the lists in one area are not related to the list in the other areas. Thus, the programmer does not have to work with long lists of variables. Let us consider the procedure for labeling common areas and then discuss their use.

```
COMMON/PLACE/A,B,C/AREA/D,E,F,G                (7.35)
```

This statement designates that variables A, B, and C are to be placed in common storage (with three other variables) in an area called PLACE, while the variables D, E, F, and G are placed in common storage (with four other variables) in an area called AREA. The name of the area can be any that is valid for a FORTRAN symbol. Note that the name of the storage areas is placed within two slashes. Let us illustrate the use of the labeled COMMON with the following program segment.

```
COMMON/PLACE/A,B,C/AREA/D,E,F,G
.
.
.
SUBROUTINE ARE
COMMON/PLACE/X,Y,Z                                             (7.36)
.
.
.
SUBROUTINE ANS
COMMON/AREA/W,U,V,B
```

Here, A, B, and C share storage locations with X, Y, and Z and D, E, F, and G share storage locations with W, U, V, and B. Thus, long lists of variables do not have to be checked. The unlabeled form of COMMON is called *blank* common storage. It can be used in conjunction with labeled common. For instance,

$$COMMON\ BOX,TOY/PLACE/A,B,C/AREA/D,E,F,G \qquad (7.37)$$

would be equivalent to statement (7.35) except that the two additional variables BOX and TOY are placed in the blank common area. We can also designate blank common by designating an area with no name, that is, by writing two slashes with no symbols between them. For instance, the following is equivalent to statement (7.37).

$$COMMON/PLACE/A,B,C//BOX,TOY/AREA/D,E,F,G \qquad (7.38)$$

Note that a single variable cannot be placed in more than one COMMON block.

Common storage can, at times, be used to reduce the overall storage required by the program. For instance, suppose that two different subprograms each use arrays that are internal to the subprograms (for example, the G array in program (7.29)). If these subprograms do not call each other, then only one of these arrays will ever by used at any one time. In this case, these arrays can be placed in common storage. Thus, storage space is conserved. Remember that storage space is reserved for internal variables. Labeled common storage is convenient here since both subprograms can have a labeled COMMON statement to do this. However, this common storage can be ignored elsewhere by the programmer. For instance, he can write other COMMON statements ignoring them as long as they do not use the same block names. The block names should be different from all other names in the program.

The lists of data in the COMMON statements need not be of the same length, for instance

```
COMMON A(1Ø),B,C
   .
   .
   .
SUBROUTINE ABC
COMMON F(6)
```

Now the first six variables of the F array are stored in common with the first ten variables of the A array. In Sec. 7.1 we indicated that a subprogram could be lised either before or after the main program. If there are COMMON statements which list unequal amounts of data, then the program or subprogram containing the *longest* list should appear first.

7.7 THE EXTERNAL STATEMENT

At times, it is desirable for the dummy variables in the list of a subprogram to represent another subprogram and not just a variable. As an example, suppose we want to write a FUNCTION subprogram which takes either the sine or the cosine of a calculated value. For instance,

```
FUNCTION ABC(X,Y,Z,F)
A=X**2+2.*Y*Z
ABC=F(A)                                          (7.39)
RETURN
END
```

If, in the calling statement, we designate that F is SIN, then ABC will equal SIN(A). Similarly, if we designate the F is COS, then ABC will equal COS(A). A calling statement of the form

$$ANS=ABC(Q,R,S,SIN) \qquad (7.40)$$

will accomplish this. However, an additional statement is required. This indicates to the compiler that SIN and COS are functions and not variables. This statement is the EXTERNAL statement. Its form is

$$EXTERNAL \ \ SIN,COS \qquad (7.41)$$

That is, it consists of the word EXTERNAL followed by a list of *subprogram names* which are to be transferred through calling statements. Note that there are no parentheses around the list. For instance, the main program for subprogram (7.39) could be

```
        EXTERNAL SIN,COS
        READ(5,1)ABLE,BOX,C
1       FORMAT(3F8.2)
        TIME=BOX+ABLE+C
        DIST=C*TIME
        ANS=ABC(TIME,DIST,C,SIN)*ABC              (7.42)
                        (TIME,DIST,C,COS)
        WRITE(5,2)ANS
2       FORMAT('ØANSWER =',E15.7)
        STOP
        END
```

Note that the EXTERNAL statement can also be used in conjunction with subprograms written by the programmer and not just with library FUNCTIONS.

7.8 USE OF THE LINKER WITH SUBPROGRAMS

We have assumed that the main program and any subprograms are written at one time and compiled together. In this case, the linking procedure discussed in Sec. 1.3 is used. However, you may write subprograms and want to use them with different main programs. In such cases, it is *not* necessary to rewrite the subprograms and the end (or beginning) of each main program. The following procedure can be used.

Write the subprogram as though it were a separate FORTRAN program and compile it. Now write the main program without the subprogram. The two must be linked. The folllowing procedure can be used. Suppose that the compiled main program is stored in a file called

        PROG1/REL or, equivalently, PROG1.REL

(use the form appropriate to your computer) and that the subroutine is stored in a file called

        PROGS/REL or, equivalently, PROGS.REL

The linking command must list the subprogram as well as the main

program. Then call the linker as discussed in Sec. 1.3. After the asterisk
(*) prompt has appeared (See Sec. 1.3), type the following

$$*PROG1:1, PROS:1-G \quad \textbf{(RETURN)} \qquad (7.43a)$$

If your linker uses / rather than – (see Sec. 1.3) then this would appear
as

$$*PROG1, PROS/G \quad \textbf{(RETURN)} \qquad (7.43b)$$

In (7.43a) we assumed that both programs are on the disk mounted on
drive 1. (Note, see Sec. 1.3, that the procedure for specifying the disk
drive may be different for your computer.) After the linking operation
is complete, the subprogram and the main program will be linked and
will run just as if the subprogram were written with the main program.

   If you want to save a machine language file of the linked program,
then add the name of the machine language file to the list followed by
–N or /N, for instance,

$$*MACH-N, PROG1, PROS-G \qquad (7.44)$$

The order of listing of the files is relatively unimportant unless COM-
MON storage with lists of different lengths are used. In this case the file
with the longest COMMON list must appear first.

   Several subroutines can be linked in this way. For instance, suppose that we have the compiled main program stored in file PROG1 and
that this program uses two subprograms. The compiled subroutines are
stored in SUB1,SUB2. Then these can all be linked and a machine language file set up by typing

$$*MACH-N, PROG1, SUB1, SUB2-G \quad \textbf{(RETURN)} \qquad (7.45)$$

(The dashes are replaced by slashes in some systems. Consult your
MICROSOFT FORTRAN manual for the exact form.) The file name
should be in the form which is specified by your DOS.

   If you write a "program" which consists of several subroutines
and *then* compile it, all of these subroutines can be saved under a single
REL file name. If you want to use any or all of these subprograms,
then you only need include the name of this REL file in your linker
command. Some versions of MICROSOFT FORTRAN have specific
library commands that make setting up of formal library files easier

(see your manual for specific instructions). There is an advantage to using such a formal library. When it is used, only the needed subroutines will be linked to the main program. This saves storage space.

7.9 MODULARIZATION—MORE ON STRUCTURED PROGRAMMING

In Sec. 4.9 we introduced some ideas of structured programming which made it easier to write bug-free programs. We are now in a position to expand upon these ideas.

Modularization

The use of subprograms can be a help in writing debuggable programs since they allow us to break a complex program up into simpler subgroups which can be tested individually. In this case, instead of having to debug a very long, complex program, the programmer works with a series of simpler subprograms which are far easier to debug than a long program since the location of the errors can be more easily detected. Indeed, it is easier to write a complex program in this way. This procedure is also suited to team programming since each member of the team can write a separate subprogram. The process of breaking a program up into groups of smaller subprograms is called *modularization* and the subprograms are often called *modules*. Of course, when the individual modules are written, the structured programming form discussed in Sec. 4.9 should be observed. The technique of writing modularized programs can itself be structured. Let us now consider this.

Top Down Design

A procedure which, when used with modularization, results in very easily written and debugged programs, is called *top down design*. It enables you to write and test small parts of the program as you go along without having to write the complete program and then test it. We start by drawing a diagram that represents the main program and its subprograms. In general, when we plan the original algorithm, we must consider that the program will be broken up in this way so that we plan a main program and subprograms. This program structure can be represented by a diagram called a *hierarchal diagram*. A typical one is drawn in Fig. 7.5. Here we show a main program that calls upon two subprograms *a* and *b*. Subprogram *a* calls upon subprogram *d* while subprogram *b* calls upon both subprograms *c* and *d*.

The actual top down design consists of more than just designing a program in modularized form. The programming is performed in a special way. Let us consider it. We write the main program first. This will be tested *before* the subprograms are written. To do this we replace the actual subprograms with simple ones called *stubs*. The stubs do not perform the actual computations of the subprogram. They simply test that the correct data is entered into it and returned to the main program.

After the main program is checked and we ascertain that it is running properly, each subprogram must be written and checked in turn. If possible, this should be first done without the main program, so a simple program would be written to enter data to the subprogram and print out the results to check that it is functioning properly. After the subprogram is checked, a further check should be made to see that it runs with the main program. The next subprogram is then written and checked.

Now let us consider the program represented by the hierarchal diagram of Fig. 7.5 and consider the steps used in writing it. First, the main program would be written and tested using stubs for all subprograms. Next, subprogram *a* would be written and tested by itself using a stub for subprogram *d*. Next, subprogram *a* would be tested with the main program with stubs for all of the other subprograms. Then, subprogram *b* would be written and tested using stubs for subprograms *c* and *d*. Then, subprograms *c* and *d* would be written and tested. Finally, the complete program would be tested. When we proceed in this ordered way, each small module is tested in turn. Thus, the probability of the occurrence of an error in the complete program becomes very small. If

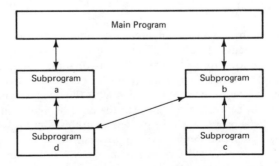

Fig. 7.5 A simple hierarchal diagram

an error does occur in a small module, it is much easier to correct it than it would be to correct a complex long program since it is now obvious where the error has occurred.

EXERCISES

7.1 Describe the operation of the following program

```
       READ(5,1)A,B,C
1      FORMAT(3F8.2)
       Y=MAX(A,B,C)
       WRITE(5,2)Y
2      FORMAT('Ø',E15.7)
       STOP
       END
       FUNCTION MAX(Q,R,S)
       MAX=Q
       IF(MAX,LT.R)MAX=R
       IF(MAX.LT.S)MAX=S
       RETURN
       END
```

Check your results by writing a FORTRAN program and running it on your computer.

7.2 Write a FUNCTION which obtains the average of five quantities. Then write a main program which utilizes this FUNCTION.

7.3 Discuss the storage locations of the variables listed in a FUNCTION defining statement.

7.4 Describe the operation of the following program

```
       DIMENSION A(1ØØ)
       READ(5,1)N
1      FORMAT(I6)
       READ(5,2)(A(I),I=1,N)
2      FORMAT(1ØF6.1)
       ANS=ABC(A,N,1ØØ)
       WRITE(5,3)ANS
3      FORMAT('ØANS=',E15.6)
       STOP
       END
       FUNCTION ABC(X,I,NN)
       DIMENSION X(NN)
       ABC=Ø.
```

```
      DO 1Ø  K=1,I
        ABC=X(I)*I+ABC
      RETURN
      END
```

Check your results by writing a FORTRAN program and running it on your computer.

7.5 Modify program (6.9) so that a FUNCTION is used to obtain the average for each student. [Hint: use a DO loop.]

7.6 Write a FUNCTION which obtains the largest element of a three-dimensional array. The array dimensions are to be entered using variables.

7.7 Discuss the use of FORTRAN library functions.

7.8 Discuss the FORTRAN library function that takes the sine of an angle.

7.9 Write a program that finds the root of the equation

$$\sin \pi x - 0.1\,e^x = 0$$

that lies in the range $0 \leqslant x \leqslant 1$. Start by writing an algorithm and then write the program. Check the program by running it on your computer.

7.10 Write a FUNCTION that finds one root of

$$a_3 x^3 + a_2 x^2 + a_1 x + a_0 = 0$$

Assume that the root location is approximately known. Start by writing an algorithm and then write the FUNCTION. Check the FUNCTION by writing a program and running it on your computer.

7.11 Describe the operation of the following program.

```
        ABC(A,B,C,D)=(A*B)/(C+D)
        READ(5,1)X,Y
  1     FORMAT(2F8.2)
        Z=X+Y
        R=X-Y
        T=ABC(X,Y,Z,R)*ABC(R,Z,Y,X)
        WRITE(5,2)T
  2     FORMAT('ØT=',E15.6)
        STOP
        END
```

7.12 Rewrite program (7.8) using an arithmetic FUNCTION statement. [Hint: use the FORTRAN library function for absolute value (magnitude) in the arithmetic FUNCTION.]

7.13 Describe the operation of the following program. Compare it with the program of Exercise 7.1.

```
        READ(5,1)A,B,C
1       FORMAT(3F8.2)
        CALL MAX(A,B,C,Y)
        WRITE(5,2)Y
2       FORMAT('∅',E15.7)
        STOP
        END
        SUBROUTINE MAX(Q,R,S,T)
        T=Q
        IF(T.LT.R)T=R
        IF(T.LT.S)T=S
        RETURN
        END
```

7.14 Repeat Exercise 7.2 using a SUBROUTINE.

7.15 Repeat Exercise 6.13 using a SUBROUTINE.

7.16 Repeat Exercise 6.14 using a SUBROUTINE.

7.17 Repeat Exercise 6.6 using a SUBROUTINE.

7.18 Repeat Exercise 6.15 using a SUBROUTINE

7.19 Describe the consequences of the following program sequence

```
        COMMON A,B,C,D
        .
        .
        SUBROUTINE ONE(M)
        COMMON Q,R,S,T
```

7.20 Modify the program of Exercise 7.1. Now use COMMON statements. Remember that a FUNCTION must have at least one variable in its defining statement.

7.21 Repeat Exercise 7.20 for the program of Exercise 7.4.

7.22 Write a single statement which is equivalent to the following statements

```
DIMENSION A(1Ø)
COMMON A,B,C
COMMON  D
```

7.23 Modify the program of Exercise 7.13 so that there are no variables in the SUBROUTINE defining statement.

7.24 Repeat Exercise 7.24 for the program of Exercise 7.17.

7.25 Describe the consequences of the following program segment. What must be the values of M, N, and KN?

```
COMMON/NAME/ABLE(5,3),BOX,I/NAME2/
             A,B,C(1Ø),D
 .
 .
 .
SUBROUTINE A(M,N)
COMMON/NAME/ABC(M,N),R,MM
 .
 .
 .
SUBROUTINE  SUM(KN)
COMMON/NAME2/ABC,BOX,AAA(KN),BCD
 .
 .
 .
```

7.26 Discuss the advantages of labeled COMMON storage.

7.27 Write a complete program which accepts three variables, computes the square root of the sum of their squares, and then computes both the sine of this quantity and the common logarithm of this quantity. A single FUNCTION should be used to compute both quantities.

7.28 Repeat Exercise 7.27 using a SUBROUTINE.

7.29 Using any of the procedures discussed in this chapter, write a program which evaluates

$f = (\sin^2 0.1t + \sin^2 0.2t)e^{-0.01t}$

for $t = 1, 2, 5, 10, 20, 50, 100, 200, 500, 1000, 2000,$ and 5000. First write the algorithm; then write the program. Check it by running it on your computer.

7.30 Modify Exercise 7.29 so that

$f_1 = \sin^2 0.1t + \sin^2 0.2t$

and

$f_2 = \cos^2 0.1t + \sin^2 0.2t$

are both evaluated. Write the shortest possible program.

7.31 Write a SUBROUTINE that interchanges two rows of an N by N matrix.

8   *Double Precision*

Ordinary calculations on a digital computer typically require seven significant figures which usually provides sufficient precision. However, there are circumstances when even more precision is required. At times, this high precision requirement is simply due to the fact that extremely high accuracy is demanded. However, the extended precision is usually required because we must overcome the roundoff error in the computer. Let us illustrate this with a simple calculation. Suppose that a computer works with seven significant figures and that we have

```
A=9999999.
B=145.
C=9999998.
```

Now suppose that we add A and B. The sum should be 10000144. However, we only have seven significant figures. Thus, we lost the last significant figures. The result then becomes 10000140. (Note that numbers with more than seven digits can be used since exponential notation is available. However, these numbers can only have seven *significant figures*.) Now let us subtract C. The actual answer should be 146. Now let us consider the effect of roundoff error. In the computer the numbers are stored on an exponential basis. Thus, 10000140 would be expressed as .1000014E8. Similarly, 9999998. would be expressed as .9999998E7. When subtraction is performed, the exponent of the smaller number is usually made equal to that of the larger number. Thus .9999998E7 becomes .09999998E8. However, this now has eight significant figures. As before, only seven are allowed. Thus, the last one is lost and the value used is .0999999E8. Thus, the result of the subtraction (10000140 − 9999990) is 150, which results in a substantial error of 2.74 percent.

Similarly, roundoff error results with multiplication and division. For instance, suppose that we multiply .1234567E1Ø and .9436278E9. The product should be .1164971742E19. However, since we can only work with seven significant figures, the answer stored by the computer will be .1164871E19, resulting in a roundoff error. If we repeat such calculations many times, the loss in accuracy can become very large even though each individual error is itself very small.

To reduce the loss in accuracy due to roundoff errors, compilers are written which allow the precision to be extended. This is known as DOUBLE PRECISION. In most computers, approximately twice as many significant figures are used in DOUBLE PRECISION as in the ordinary mode of operation, which we call *single precision*. Typically, many computers work with seven significant figures in single precision and with 16 in DOUBLE PRECISION. The reader may ask why we do not use DOUBLE PRECISION always since it is so much more accurate than single precision. It is because DOUBLE PRECISION variables require twice as much storage space and require longer execution time, so that the use of DOUBLE PRECISION should be avoided unless it is necessary for accuracy.

We shall now consider the procedures for writing programs which use DOUBLE PRECISION.

8.1 DOUBLE PRECISION—DECLARATION AND PROGRAMS

If we are to use DOUBLE PRECISION, we must declare those variables which are to have extended precision. This is done in a *declaration* statement of the following form

```
DOUBLE PRECISION A,B,C                      (8.1)
```

The declaration consists of the words DOUBLE PRECISION and a list of variables. The DOUBLE PRECISION declaration should precede any executable statements or FORMAT statements. Arrays can also be declared to be DOUBLE PRECISION. For instance,

```
DIMENSION BOX(1ØØ,1Ø)                        (8.2)
DOUBLE PRECISION A,B,BOX,C
```

The dimensioning can be done in the DOUBLE PRECISION declaration statement. For instance, the following is equivalent to (8.2).

$$\text{DOUBLE PRECISION A,B,BOX(1\emptyset\emptyset,1\emptyset),C} \qquad (8.3)$$

The procedure for declaring variables to be DOUBLE PRECISION can be cumbersome if many variables are used. In Sec. 10.2, we shall consider an alternative procedure (which is often superior) for declaring variables to be DOUBLE PRECISION.

When real constants (that is, single precision) were written using the exponential form, we represented 1.236×10^{15} by 1.236E15. When DOUBLE PRECISION is used, the E is replaced by a D. Thus, in DOUBLE PRECISION, the previous number would be written as 1.236D15. If exponential notation is not used, then constants are written the same way in DOUBLE PRECISION as in single precision (for example, 1.24674). Of course, more significant figures can be used in the DOUBLE PRECISION form.

Once the variables have been declared to be DOUBLE PRECISION, the form of the program is essentially the same as for single precision. The only slight modification occurs in the case of formatted input and output statements and in the case of subprograms. These will be discussed in Secs. 8.2 and 8.3. For the time being, replace the E in the field specifier with a D. All the discussions of Chapters 2-6 are applicable to DOUBLE PRECISION. For instance, suppose that we want to modify program (6.32) so that it is executed in DOUBLE PRECISION. The program would become

```
C PROGRAM THAT OBTAINS A FUNCTION
        DOUBLE PRECISION A(9),X,Z
C ENTER DATA
        READ(5,1)N,(A(I),I=1,N),X
1       FORMAT(I3,1∅D6.1)
C EVALUATE FUNCTION
        Z=A(N)
        NN=N-1
        DO 2∅ I=1,NN
        Z=Z*X+A(N-1)
2∅      CONTINUE
        WRITE(5,2)Z
2       FORMAT('∅FUNCTION IS',D25.16)
        STOP
        END
```
$$(8.4)$$

Thus, once the variables have been declared to be DOUBLE PRECISION, the program is essentially the same as before. Note that we have assumed that each item of data can be entered in six spaces. If the data is also to be DOUBLE PRECISION, then more space should be allocated.

If an arithmetic operation is performed in a mixed double precision-single precision mode, then the single precision terms will be converted to DOUBLE PRECISION by adding appropriate zeros. (Note that these DOUBLE PRECISION numbers will be no more accurate than the original single precision numbers from which they were obtained.) Integers will also be converted to DOUBLE PRECISION numbers in mixed mode operations.

Note that all the variables in the program need not be of the DOUBLE PRECISION mode. For instance, consider the statements

```
Z=A+B-C
X=Y*R
```

Here, A, B, C, and Z should be DOUBLE PRECISION since roundoff can cause great loss of accuracy (see the introduction to this chapter). However, Y, R, and X need not be DOUBLE PRECISION since the calculations involving them is not as sensitive to roundoff error. Note that when two nearly equal numbers are subtracted, large percentage errors in the answers can result from small percentage errors in the numbers. For instance, $100. - 99. = 1$. However, if we make a 1 percent error in one number, we have $101. - 99. = 2.$, which yields a 100 percent error in the answer.

Mixed Mode Operation

Let us now consider the result of mixed mode operations. We shall illustrate this with the following simple program segment.

```
      DOUBLE PRECISION D,DBL,B
      READ(5,1)B,A
1     FORMAT(D15.7,F6.3)                        (8.5)
      D=B*A
      C=2*A+D
      DBL=A
      I=DBL
      ⋮
```

When one variable in a mixed mode calculation is DOUBLE PRECISION, the result will be DOUBLE PRECISION. For instance, when D is calculated, the product B*A is taken. Since B is DOUBLE PRECISION, this becomes a DOUBLE PRECISION calculation. That is, the numerical value of A is made a DOUBLE PRECISION number. The variable D has been declared to be DOUBLE PRECISION. Hence, the value for D is stored as a DOUBLE PRECISION value.

Next, C is calculated. First we take 2*A. The integer 2 is converted to real since it multiplies the real variable A. Next, 2*A is converted to DOUBLE PRECISION since it is added to D. Finally, the result is stored as a real (single precision) number since C is real. Note that the excess significant figures are truncated (i.e., thrown away) when this is done.

The statement DBL=A results in the value stored in memory location A being stored as a DOUBLE PRECISION value in a new memory location called DBL. Note that we do not gain accuracy here since zeros are merely added. For instance, if the stored value of A is .1234566, then the stored value of DBL will be .12345670000000. This number can then be used in DOUBLE PRECISION calculations. However, we do not know it to 16 significant figures. That is, we have not improved the accuracy of A by this operation. However, when DBL is used in subsequent calculations, the roundoff error will be less since the operations will be DOUBLE PRECISION.

In the last line, I=DBL, the value of DBL is truncated to an integer. For instance, if DBL=14.7634161121117, then I=14. Suppose that we follow this by DBL=I. Now the integer 14 would be converted into the DOUBLE PRECISION number 14.00000000000000.

8.2 INPUT AND OUTPUT WITH DOUBLE PRECISION

Unformatted input and output statements written in single and extended precision will be identical. Of course, when results are printed, they will contain the appropriate number of significant figures. For instance, an answer in single precision might print as

$\emptyset$.1163467E15

and in DOUBLE PRECISION as

$\emptyset$.1163466846327942D15

Similarly, the data could contain all the signficant figures of DOUBLE PRECISION. However, it is not necessary to do this. For instance, input data of the forms

```
2.
Ø.2D1
Ø.2ØØØØØØØØØØØØD1
```

would all be equivalent.

When formatted input and output are used, *all* the discussions of Chapter 3 apply with one exception. The E format is not allowed. In its place a D format is used. That is, the letter D replaces the letter E in all the FORMAT specifications. Once this is done, all the discussions of Chapter 3 are applicable to DOUBLE PRECISION. As we have discussed, see Sec. 3.3, it is often undesirable to use an F FORMAT specifier for output data. When a D format is used, at least seven columns plus the number of significant digits following the decimal point should be specified. Again, this is identical with the discussion for the E FORMAT. We need not print all the digits when DOUBLE PRECISION is used. If we use extended precision to eliminate the effect of roundoff error on accuracy, then it is undesirable to print the last digits since they probably are in error. Thus, the following program sequence could be a logical one.

```
          DOUBLE PRECISION A(1Ø),B,C
          :
          WRITE(6,21)C                                (8.6)
   21     FORMAT('ØC=',D1Ø.3)
```

8.3 USE OF SUBPROGRAMS

When subprograms are used in DOUBLE PRECISION, we must declare them to be so. This must be done in *both* the main program and in the subprogram. The declaration for FUNCTIONS is different from that for SUBROUTINES. We shall consider them separately.

Functions in DOUBLE PRECISION

Let us consider a program segment which uses a FUNCTION to illustrate its declaration as DOUBLE PRECISION.

```
          DOUBLE PRECISION A,ANS,B(1Ø),C
          :
          C=ANS(A,N)
```

```
    ⋮
    STOP                                                    (8.7)
    END
    DOUBLE PRECISION FUNCTION ANS(Y,N)
    DOUBLE PRECISION Y
    ANS=Y**N+2.*Y**2
    RETURN
    END
```

Let us consider the main program first. All DOUBLE PRECISION variables are declared there. Note that ANS, the result of the FUNCTION is also declared to be DOUBLE PRECISION.

The FUNCTION itself must be declared to be DOUBLE PRECISION. It can be done in the FUNCTION defining statement as illustrated in program (8.7). That is, the words DOUBLE PRECISION are added to the FUNCTION defining statement. Once the declarations have been made, the program and subprograms are written as before.

The same ideas discussed here are used for library FUNCTIONs. For instance, the FUNCTION should be declared to be DOUBLE PRECISION in the main program. Of course, when library FUNCTIONs are used, the programmer does not become involved with the subprogram's internal statements.

DOUBLE PRECISION library FUNCTIONs have names different from those for single precision or for integers. For instance, the library subprogram that takes the natural logarithm for DOUBLE PRECISION variables is

$$DLOG(X) \tag{8.8}$$

The similar library FUNCTION for real single precision variables is

$$LOG(X) \tag{8.9}$$

Thus, the programmer must be careful to choose the proper library FUNCTION.

Subroutines in DOUBLE PRECISION

When SUBROUTINES are used in DOUBLE PRECISION, all extended precision variables must be declared. Note that the SUB-ROUTINE name is *not* a variable in this case, so it does not have to be declared. Thus, a typical program segment would be

```
DOUBLE PRECISION A,B,C,D,X
.
.
CALL RUN(A,B,X,N)
.
.
STOP
END                                          (8.10)
SUBROUTINE RUN(Q,R,S,M)
DOUBLE PRECISION Q,R,S
.
.
RETURN
END
```

We have considered DOUBLE PRECISION declarations in this chapter. In Sec. 10.2 we shall consider a much more convenient, and often more desirable, procedure for declaring variables to be DOUBLE PRECISION.

EXERCISES

8.1   Discuss the need for extended precision calculations.

8.2   Which of the following calculations is more subject to roundoff error? Illustrate your results.

```
X=A+B-C
X=A*B
```

Now consider the program segment

```
X=A*B
Y=C/(X-D)
```

Evaluate this using both ordinary and DOUBLE PRECISION. Use the values

```
A=0.9999999999
B=1.000001
C=1.0000000
D=1.0000000
```

Repeat the results using

```
A=Ø.9999999999
B=3.ØØØØØØ
C=1.ØØØØØØ
D=1.ØØØØØØ
```

To check your results write and run programs on your computer.

8.7 Repeat Exercise 8.4 but now use formatted input and output statements.

8.8 Repeat Exercise 8.4 but now use formatted input and output statements.

8.9 Repeat Exercise 8.6 but now use formatted input and output statements.

8.7 Repeat Exercise 7.2 but now use DOUBLE PRECISION for all calculations.

8.8 Repeat Exercise 8.7 for the program of Exercise 7.5.

8.9 Repeat Exercise 8.7 for the program of Exercise 7.6.

8.10 Repeat Exercise 8.7 for the program of Exercise 7.14.

8.11 Repeat Exercise 8.7 for the program of Exercise 7.15.

8.12 Repeat Exercise 8.7 for the program of Exercise 7.18.

9   *Complex Numbers*

Very often in the fields of engineering, science, and mathematics, calculations are performed which utilize $\sqrt{-1}$. This is commonly designated as i (or sometimes j). Some versions of FORTRAN allow us to perform calculations involving $\sqrt{-1}$. At the present time, MICRO-SOFT FORTRAN does not. However, such operations may be implemented in future versions. Thus, we shall discuss them here. Before discussing such programs, some very basic operations involving such numbers will be considered. The $\sqrt{-1}$ is termed an *imaginary* number. Thus, $i2$. would be an imaginary number equal to 2. times $\sqrt{-1}$. Ordinary numbers (for example, 3, 6, etc.) are called real numbers. Numbers composed of both a real and an imaginary part are called *complex numbers*. For instance, 2. + $i3$. is a complex number.

Let us consider some simple arithmetic operations with complex numbers. When complex numbers are added, their real parts are added and their imaginary parts are added. For instance,

$$3. + i4 + 2. + i6.3 = 5. + i10.3$$

Complex multiplication follows the rules of algebraic multiplication. For instance,

$$(3. + i4.)(4. + i2.) = 12. + i16. + i6. + i^2 8.$$

Noting that $i^2 = -1$, we have

$$(3. + i4.)(4. + i2.) = 4. + i22.$$

Complex division can be illustrated in the following way.

$$\frac{3.+i4.}{2.+i1} = \frac{3.+i4.}{2.+i1.} \cdot \frac{2.-i1.}{2.-i1.} = \frac{10.+i5.}{5.} = 2.0+i1.$$

That is, to obtain the quotient of the division, we multiply both the numerator and denominator by a number which is the same as the denominator except that the imaginary part is replaced by its negative. That is, if the denominator is

$a + ib$

then we multiply by

$a - ib$

This is called the *conjugate*. Note that

$$(a + ib)(a - ib) = a^2 - i^2 b^2 = a^2 + b^2$$

This is a real (ordinary) number. Thus, if we have a ratio of two complex numbers (i.e., division) and we want to obtain the answer as a single complex number, then we multiply the numerator and denominator by the conjugate of the denominator to obtain a complex number as a result of the division.

Complex numbers can be used to represent two dimensional *vectors*. A vector is used to represent something that has both a magnitude and a direction. For example, wind blowing at 10 kilometers/hour in a northerly direction can be represented as a vector of magnitude 10 pointing north. Similarly, forces are often represented by vectors.

Let us see how complex numbers can help us with vectors. Consider that we have a vector b in space, see Fig. 9.1a. Now suppose that we multiply it by -1 so that the vector $-b$ results. That is, b is rotated by $180°$ or, simply, turned around. Thus, we can say that -1 rotates a vector by $180°$ when it multiplies the vector. Now let us define a quantity a that rotates a vector by $90°$ when it multiplies the vector. The vector ab is shown in Fig. 9.1a. If we multiply ab by a again, then it is rotated another $90°$. Thus, $a^2 b = -b$. Since $a^2 = -1$, then $a = \sqrt{-1}$. Thus, we can consider that $i = \sqrt{-1}$ rotates the vector by $90°$. A vector has magnitude and direction. On a two dimensional basis, we can express the coordinates of a vector by its x and y coordinates. Since x and y are perpendicular, we write this as $x + iy$. Using i, we can express a two dimensonal vector as a complex number, see Fig. 9.1b.

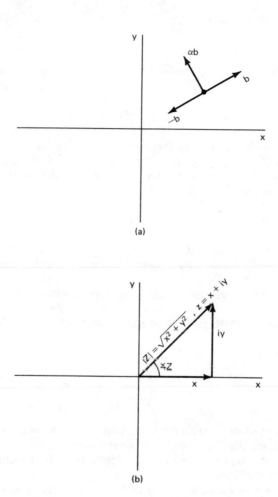

Fig. 9.1 (a) Rotation of vectors; (b) the components of a vector.

Instead of expressing a vector as its real and imaginary parts, we can express it in terms of its magnitude and an angle, see Fig. 9.1b. If the vector is given by $z = x + iy$, then the magnitude of z is given by $|z| = \sqrt{x^2 + y^2}$, while the angle of z is given by $\sphericalangle z = \tan^{-1} y/x$. These results follow from the basic trigonometric relations for a triangle. Similarly, we can write

$$x = |z| \cos \sphericalangle z$$
$$y = |z| \sin \sphericalangle z$$

For instance, if the magnitude of a vector z is 100 and its angle is 30°, then

$$z = 100 \cos 30° + i\, 100 \sin 30° = 86.6 + i\,.5$$

There are several notations that can be used. We have just expressed z in terms of x and iy. This is called *rectangular* form. We can also write it in terms of its magnitude and angle. This is called *polar* form. For instance, we can write

$$z = 100 \ \underline{/30°}$$

We have considered some very basic operations with complex numbers here so that a reader who is unfamiliar with complex operations can follow the discussions of this chapter. Of course, there are far more elaborate operations that can be performed with complex numbers.

There is an alternative procedure for writing complex numbers which is used in FORTRAN. Two equivalent numbers are

$$3. + i4.$$

and

$$(3,4)$$

That is, we can designate a complex number by two numbers enclosed in parentheses. The first number is the real part and the second number represents the imaginary part. This second form is the one which is utilized in FORTRAN.

Let us now consider writing FORTRAN programs using complex quantities. This discussion will, at times, be very similar to that for DOUBLE PRECISION given in the last chapter. For instance, DOUBLE PRECISION uses twice as much storage space as does single precision. Similarly, complex numbers require twice as much storage space as do real numbers because they have a real and an imaginary part. Certain compilers allow double precision complex numbers (see Sec. 10.2). In this case, four times as much storage space is required than that for a single precision real number.

9.1 COMPLEX DECLARATION AND PROGRAMS

FORTRAN provides a very convenient means of programming with complex numbers. Any variable which represents complex numbers must be declared to be COMPLEX. However, once this is done, all the previous discussions of Chapters 2-6 are applicable to COMPLEX operations. There will be slight modifications in the case of input-output statements and in the case of subprograms. These will be discussed in Secs. 9.2 and 9.3.

The COMPLEX declaration statement has the form

$$\text{COMPLEX A,B,RUN,BOX} \tag{9.1}$$

That is, the COMPLEX declaration consists of the word COMPLEX followed by a list of variables. The declaration statement must precede any executable statement.

Arrays can contain complex numbers. They must be declared COMPLEX. For instance,

$$\begin{array}{l} \text{DIMENSION A(1\emptyset),B(12,4),C(15)} \\ \text{COMPLEX A,B,Q,Z} \end{array} \tag{9.2}$$

Note that the C array will consist of real numbers. We can DIMENSION in the COMPLEX declaration statement. For instance, a pair of statements which are equivalent to statements (9.2) is

$$\begin{array}{l} \text{DIMENSION C(15)} \\ \text{COMPLEX A(1\emptyset),B(12,4),Q,Z} \end{array} \tag{9.3}$$

This procedure for declaring variables to be complex can be cumbersome if many variables are used. In Sec. 10.2 we shall discuss an alternative procedure (which is often superior) for declaring variables to be complex.

We shall consider the changes which occur in input-output statements and in subprograms in the next two sections. However, except for these changes, programs using complex variables are similar to those using real variables. For instance, consider the following

```
C EXAMPLE OF COMPLEX NUMBER CALCULATIONS
      COMPLEX A(1Ø),B(1Ø),ANS
         :
         :
```

```
        ANS=A(1)*B(1)
        DO 10  I=2,N
           ANS=ANS+A(I)*B(I)                         (9.4)
10         CONTINUE
        STOP
        END
```

Here, two arrays, A and B, and a variable ANS are declared to be
COMPLEX. We assume that the appropriate statements to cause the
two arrays containing the complex numbers which are to be read are
represented by the three dots. (We shall consider the details of the
terminal input in the next section.) Note that ANS is set equal to the
product of A(1) and B(1), using just the asterisk of "ordinary" multiplication. The computer will take the product of the two complex
numbers when the program is executed. This type of product was
discussed in the introduction to this chapter. The DO loop then causes
ANS to be increased by A(I)*B(I) each time that it is cycled. Thus,
when the DO loop is completed, ANS will be the sum of all the pro-
ducts A(I)*B(I). Finally, the statement represented by the second set
of three dots causes ANS to be printed. Thus, once the variables have
been declared to be COMPLEX, the writing of the program is very
similar to that of the programs which use real variables.

One fact should be noted. The real and imaginary parts of COM-
PLEX numbers must be real numbers, and not integers.

When a variable is set equal to a complex *constant*, the parentheses
"form" indicated previously in this chapter must be used. For instance,
suppose that we want to set A equal to 3. + $i4.$. The appropriate FOR-
TRAN expression is

$$A=(3.,4.)$$ (9.5a)

Similarly, if we want to set A equal to 3. − $i4.$, we would write

$$A=(3.,-4.)$$ (9.5b)

One important fact should be noted. Expressions (9.5) are valid for
constants. However, *neither* of the terms within the parentheses can be
a variable. For instance, A=(X,3.) is invalid even if X is a real variable.
In Sec. 9-3 we shall discuss a procedure for setting a complex variable
equal to one (or two) real variables. We shall also discuss mixed mode
operation there.

9.2 INPUT AND OUTPUT WITH COMPLEX QUANTITIES

When a complex number is to be entered, two real numbers are actually entered, one is the real part and the other is the imaginary part. These numbers should be enclosed in parentheses and separated by a comma, see statement (9.5). For instance, a data line containing two complex numbers would be

(3.,-4.),(6.,8.)

Exponential notation can also be used. For instance,

(3.E+3,2.E-1)

Now let us consider the formatted input and output statements. Here we must take into account that the complex number consists of two real numbers. Thus, provision for these two numbers must be made in the FORMAT statement. For instance, consider the program sequence

```
      COMPLEX A,B
      READ(5,2)A                          (9.6)
2     FORMAT(2F6.3)
```

Two F specifiers are given for the single complex variable A. The data for the input will be

123456789876

This will set A equal to $123.455+i789.876$. Thus, the two parts of the complex number are read using the usual rules for FORMAT specifications given in Sec. 3.1. That is, the real part of A is read from the first six columns of the data card and the imaginary part from the next six columns. Each variable has three decimal places. All the rules given in Chapter 3 apply for the entering of data. However, it must be remembered that each COMPLEX variable consists of two parts.

These ideas also apply to formatted output statements. The basic ideas of Secs. 3.3 and 3.4 apply here. Again, the FORMAT specifier should take into account the fact that two variables must be printed. For instance, consider the program sequence

```
      COMPLEX,A
      A=(1.2,-4.6)                        (9.7)
      WRITE(6,23)A
23    FORMAT(' A=',2E12.3)
```

The printed output would appear as

A=bbb∅.12∅E+∅1bb−∅.46∅E+∅1

where the b's represent blank spaces.

   We have indicated that both halves of the complex number are read or printed with the same FORMAT specifier. This need not be the case. For instance, the last statement of (9.7) could be written as

```
23        FORMAT(' A=',E12.3,E15.5)                    (9.8)
```

In this case, the real part of A will be printed using an E12.5 specification while the imaginary part will be printed using an E15.5 specification. Note that text material can be included between the real and imaginary parts if desired. This could be done by placing the appropriate text material between the FORMAT specifier for the real part and the FORMAT specifier for the imaginary part. For instance,

```
23        FORMAT(' A=',E12.3,'+I',E12,3)
```

9.3 USE OF SUBPROGRAMS

   When subprograms are used with COMPLEX quantities, we must declare them to be so. This must be done in both the main program and in the subprogram. The ideas here are very similar to those given in Sec. 8.3 for DOUBLE PRECISION. We assume that the reader is familiar with the discussion of that section.

COMPLEX Functions

   We shall list a program which uses a FUNCTION to illustrate the basic ideas.

```
COMPLEX A,ABC,B(1∅),C
 :
 :
C=ABC(A,N)
 :
 :
STOP                                                (9.9)
END
COMPLEX FUNCTION ABC(R,N)
COMPLEX R
```

```
ABC=R**N+R**2
RETURN
END
```

All the COMPLEX variables are declared in the main program. Note that the FUNCTION (that is, ABC) is also declared there.

The FUNCTION itself must be declared to be COMPLEX. This can be done in the FUNCTION defining statement by adding the word COMPLEX, as was done in program (9.9).

The same ideas as we have discussed here also apply to COMPLEX library functions. As in the case of DOUBLE PRECISION library functions, COMPLEX library functions take a form different from those for real functions. For instance, the function that takes the square root of a COMPLEX variable is

```
CSQRT(X)
```

One COMPLEX library FUNCTION is especially important since it allows a complex variable to be expressed in terms of one or two real variables. It is CMPLX. For instance,

$$A=CMPLX(B,1.4) \tag{9.10}$$

sets the real part of A equal to the value of B stored in the memory and the imaginary part of A equal to 1.4. Note that B must be a *real* variable. Remember that A=(B,1.4) is not allowed. Only *constants* such as A=(1.2, 1.4) can be used in that type of statement.

COMPLEX Subroutines

When SUBROUTINES are used with COMPLEX quantities, all COMPLEX variables must be so declared. Since the SUBROUTINE name is not a variable, it need not be declared. Thus, a typical program segment would be

```
COMPLEX A,B,C,D
.
.
CALL BOX(A,B,C,M)
.
.
```

```
     STOP
     END
     SUBROUTINE BOX(X,Y,Z,N)                              (9.11)
     COMPLEX X,Y,Z,R
       .
       .
     RETURN
     END
```

Note the variable R in the SUBROUTINE. It is a COMPLEX variable which is internal to the SUBROUTINE.

Mixed Mode Operation

When mixed mode calculations are performed and one of the variables is COMPLEX, then, with the possible exception of DOUBLE PRECISION variables, the other variables will be converted to COM—PLEX. In the following examples let us assume that C, CMP, and CPX have all been declared to be COMPLEX while all other variables are real or integer. Then, if we have

$$C = CMP * A + I \tag{9.12}$$

when the calculations are performed, A is treated as though the following operation were performed

$$CMPLX(A, O) \tag{9.13}$$

When the complex number CMP*A is added to I, then the value of I will first be converted to a real variable and then to a COMPLEX variable. In the case of exponents, the results are somewhat different when the exponent is an integer. Now the exponent remains an integer. For instance,

$$CMP = CPX ** I \tag{9.14}$$

indicates that CPX is to be multiplied by itself I times. Thus, there is no need to convert I. However, when the exponent is a real number, then it is converted to a complex one. That is,

$$CMP = CPX ** A \tag{9.15a}$$

is treated as though the following were written

$$CMP=CPX**CMPLX(A,O) \qquad\qquad (9.15b)$$

(The actual arithmetic involved in raising a complex number to a complex number to a complex power is too involved to be considered here.) Note that some compilers do not allow complex exponents. Such compilers only allow the use of integer exponents when a COMPLEX quantity is raised to a power.

With many compilers, COMPLEX numbers cannot be expressed in DOUBLE PRECISION. In other cases, mixed mode COMPLEX-DOUBLE PRECISION is allowed. Now the operation is essentially the same as that involving mixed mode real and COMPLEX numbers except that, of course, DOUBLE PRECISION rather than real numbers are involved.

It is not allowable to set a COMPLEX variable equal to a real one or vice versa. For instance, A=CMP would be incorrect. Note that this differs from the other mixed mode calculations that we have discussed.

EXERCISES

9.1 Perform the indicated arithmetic operations

    (a) $(3.-i6.) + (7.2+i3.4)$
    (b) $(3.-i6.)(4.-i3.)$
    (c) $(3.-i.6)/(4.+i.3)$
    (d) $(3.-i.6) + (2.+i3.)(3.-i4.)/(1.+i2.)$
    (e) $3\ \underline{/20°}\ +\ 4\ \underline{/30°}$

9.2 Express the following complex numbers in an alternate form

    $(2., 3.)$
    $(1., -4.)$
    $3.-i2.$
    $2.+i6.$
    $2\ \underline{/30°}$

9.3 Describe the operation of the following program

```
         COMPLEX A,B,C
         READ(5,1)A,B
1        FORMAT(2F8.1)
```

```
          A=A*B
          C=A+B*A
          WRITE(5,2)C
2         FORMAT('Ø',E15.7,'+I',E15.7)
          STOP
          END
```

Check your results by running the program on your computer.

9.4 Write a program which accepts three complex numbers and then computes and prints a fourth number which is equal to the product of two of them divided by the third.

9.5 A one-dimensional array can contain up to 100 terms. The elements of the array are complex. Write a program which obtains the product of all the elements in the array.

9.6 Write a program which accepts a two-dimensional complex array. The array can have up to ten rows and columns. The program should produce a one-dimensional array, each element of which is the sum of the terms of one row of the given array. The first term of the new array should be the sum of the terms of the first row, etc.

9.7 There are library FUNCTIONS which obtain the real part and the imaginary part of a complex number. Note that these FUNCTIONS produce real numbers. Use these FUNCTIONS to find the element of a two-dimensional array which has the largest real part. Also find the element which has the largest imaginary part. The array will have no more than 10 rows and 10 columns. Assume that all elements are greater than -10^{-20}.

9.8 Consider a complex number (a, b) where a and b are real numbers. The magnitude of a complex number is defined as $\pm \sqrt{a^2 + b^2}$. Write a program that obtains the magnitude of a complex number. [Hint: see Exercise 9.7.]

9.9 A one-dimensional array consists of up to 100 terms. The elements of the array are complex. Write a program which obtains another one-dimensional array whose elements are the magnitudes of the given array (see Exercise 9.13 for a definition of magnitude of a complex number. Also see Exercise 9.7).

9.10 Discuss the use of library FUNCTION CMPLX(A, B).

9.11 Repeat Exercise 9.4 using a SUBROUTINE.

9.12 Repeat Exercise 9.5 using a SUBROUTINE.

9.13 Repeat Exercise 9.6 using a SUBROUTINE.

9.14 Repeat Exercise 9.8 using a SUBROUTINE.

9.15 Repeat Exercise 9.9 using a SUBROUTINE.

9.16 Write a program that obtains the sum of three COMPLEX vectors. Assume that the vectors are expressed in rectangular form and that the answer is to be expressed in polar form. Check the program by running it on your computer.

10 *Additional Declaration Statements*

We have considered several types of FORTRAN statements which are not executable since they do not control the execution of the program. However, they do provide information to the compiler, that is, they declare something. These are called *declaration statements*. One declaration statement that we have considered is DOUBLE PRECISION, which declares certain variables to be in extended precision. Another declaration statement was the COMMON statement which placed variables in common storage. In this chapter we shall consider additional declaration statements. One declaration procedure will be far more convenient to use than those discussed previously.

10.1 REAL AND INTEGER DECLARATION STATEMENTS

Ordinarily, the FORTRAN convention is that all variables whose names start with the letters I, J, K, L, M, or N are integers and all others are real. However, there are circumstances where it would be convenient for the programmer to start a real variable name with one of the letters from I to N. For instance, suppose we want a real variable called ITEM. This can be done by declaring it to be real. The form of this declaration statement is

        REAL ITEM   (10.1)

We can declare several variables, including arrays, to be REAL. For instance,

        DIMENSION I(1Ø,15)   (10.2)
        REAL I,ITEM,JIG

Dimensioning of arrays can also be done in the REAL declaration statement. For instance, a statement equivalent to statements (10.2) is

$$\text{REAL } I(1\emptyset,15), ITEM, JIG \qquad\qquad (10.3)$$

Note that all variables, except the array I, ITEM, and JIG, whose names start with the letters I through N will be integers. In a very similar way, we can declare certain variables which start with the letters A to H or O to Z to be integers. The declaration statement is

$$\text{INTEGER } ABLE, BOX, Z(1\emptyset,15) \qquad\qquad (10.4)$$

Again, note the dimensioning can take in the INTEGER declaration statement. Note that all other variables whose names start with A to H or O to Z will be real.

Declaration statements should precede any mention of the variables which they declare. The declaration statements must also precede any executable statement. This applies to both main program and to subprograms.

10.2 IMPLICIT DECLARATION

We have discussed declaration statements which can declare a list of variables to be DOUBLE PRECISION or REAL, etc. These are called *explicit declaration statements* since the variables in question are explicitly listed. This explicit listing can often prove to be inconvenient. For instance, suppose a program uses 50 different variables, all of which are to be DOUBLE PRECISION. It would be very tedious to explicitly declare all of these variables. Also, a programmer may often forget to declare one of the variables. This can produce serious errors. There is another declaration procedure that we can use which avoids this difficulty.

It would be desirable to specify variables implicitly so that each one need not be listed. One way of doing this is to declare variables starting with certain letters to be certain types. For instance, in the ordinary convention, variables whose names start with the letters A to H or O to Z are real and those starting with the letters I to N are integers. We can modify this convention by a statement called an IMPLICIT statement. An example of it is

$$\text{IMPLICIT INTEGER}(D) \qquad\qquad (10.5)$$

This statement causes *every* variable which starts with the letter D to be an INTEGER. (Not all versions of MICROSOFT FORTRAN support the IMPLICIT statement.)

The IMPLICIT statement is more versatile than we have indicated. We can specify a range of starting letters. For instance,

$$\text{IMPLICIT DOUBLE PRECISION(A-D,R,X-Z)} \qquad (10.6)$$

This declares all variables starting with the letters A, B, C, D, R, X, Y, and Z to be DOUBLE PRECISION variables. Note that the usual FOR-TRAN conventions apply for all other variables. For instance, those starting with E to H, O, P, Q, and S to W are single precision real. Those variables starting with I to N are integers.

More than one type of variable can be declared in a single IMPLICIT statement. For instance,

$$\text{IMPLICIT DOUBLE PRECISION(A-D,X-Z),REAL(I-K)} \quad (10.7)$$

The rules for locating IMPLICIT statements are very strict. There can be only *one* IMPLICIT statement in a main program and there can be only *one* IMPLICIT statement in each subprogram. The IMPLICIT must be the *first* statement of the main program. It must be the *second* statement of a subprogram. That is, it must *immediately follow* the sub-program defining statement. In MICROSOFT FORTRAN, a program can be named. The IMPLICIT statement then follows the program name. The program is named using a PROGRAM statement which is

    PROGRAM NAME

where the name must start with a letter and must consist of one to six alphanumeric characters. The only exceptions to these rules are comment statements since they are ignored by the compiler. Note that corresponding variables in the main program and in subprograms must be declared in the same way.

An IMPLICIT declaration can be amended by an explicit declaration. For instance,

    PROGRAM ABC
    IMPLICIT DOUBLE PRECISION(A-H,O-Z)   (10.8)
    REAL,ABLE,BOX

(Note that we have named the program ABC.) In this case, all variables starting with A to H or O to Z are DOUBLE PRECISION except ABLE and BOX, which are single precision real.

Microsoft FORTRAN

We shall now discuss a useful feature available on MICROSOFT
FORTRAN. Before discussing this, we shall consider some notation
used with the storage of data. The amount of storage required for a
single precision real variable is called a *word*. Thus, a DOUBLE PRE-
CISION variable requires two words of storage. A word is subdivided
into units called *bytes*. Each word is commonly two bytes. The number
of bytes for storage of variables can be specified in declaration statements. For instance, the following statements are equivalent,

We shall now discuss a feature which is available on only some
FORTRAN compilers. The FORTRAN manual should be checked to
determine if it is available at the reader's location. Before discussing
this, we shall consider some notation used with the storage of data.
The amount of storage required for a single precision real variable is
called a *word*. Thus, a DOUBLE PRECISION variable requires two
words of storage. A word is subdivided into units called *bytes*. Each
word is commonly four bytes. The number of bytes for storage of
variables can be specified in declaration statements. For instance, the
following statements are equivalent

```
        REAL ITEM                              (10.9a)
```

and

```
        REAL*4 ITEM                            (10.9b)
```

The asterisk following the number indicates the number of bytes. Since
the standard storage for a real variable is one word or four bytes, statements (10.9a) and (10.9b) are equivalent.

Let us consider two other equivalent statements.

```
        DOUBLE PRECISION ABLE,BOX              (10.10a)
```

and

```
        REAL*8 ABLE,BOX                        (10.10b)
```

Here, the second statement declares that there are eight bytes of storage
for the real variables ABLE and BOX. Hence, they are DOUBLE
PRECISION variables.

This procedure can be used with IMPLICIT statements. For
instance, consider the following

$$\text{IMPLICIT REAL*4(M),REAL*8(A-D)} \qquad (10.11)$$

This states that all variables whose names start with the letter M are single precision REAL and all variables whose names start with A to D are DOUBLE PRECISION. All other variables follow the standard FORTRAN convention.

The standard number of bytes are as follows: INTEGER, two bytes; REAL, four bytes; DOUBLE PRECISION and COMPLEX, (if available), eight bytes each. With some compilers we can use a combination of DOUBLE PRECISION and COMPLEX. This requires 16 bytes. An IMPLICIT statement using this might appear as

$$\text{IMPLICIT COMPLEX*8(C),COMPLEX*16}$$
$$\text{(Y-Z),REAL*8(A-D)} \qquad (10.12)$$

In this case, any variable whose name starts with the letter C is an ordinary complex variable. If the variable starts with Y or Z, then it is a DOUBLE PRECISION COMPLEX variable. If the variable name starts with A, B, C, or D, it is a DOUBLE PRECISION variable. All other variables follow the standard convention.

The standard storage word length of an INTEGER is two bytes. At times, to conserve storage space, we reduce this storage to one byte. This limits the maximum numerical size of the integer. The storage of integers is such that, with four bytes of storage, the integer can lie between -32768 and 32767. With only two bytes of storage, the integer is restricted to lie between -128 and 127. If integers which are larger than those which can be accommodated by the storage are used, errors will result. If we want to reduce the storage space occupied by some INTEGERS, we could write

$$\text{IMPLICIT INTEGER*1(I-L)} \qquad (10.13)$$

Note that if the byte specification, an asterisk and an integer, is not given, then the standard specification is always assumed. We are limited in the specifications which we can use. For instance, for INTEGER we can use *1 and the standard *2; for REAL variables we can use *4 and *8 for single and DOUBLE PRECISION, respectively; similarly, for COMPLEX (if available) we can use *8 and *16. With MICROSOFT FORTRAN we can specify single byte variables using the specification BYTE.

10.3 THE EQUIVALENCE STATEMENT

At times, a programmer inadvertantly uses two different names for the same variable. For instance, suppose that, in one part of the program, he called a variable NUMB and in another part he called it NUMBER. Since these should be the same, an error will result when the program is run. Thus, much tedious checking and changing must be done to correct the program. This can be avoided. We can declare that NUMB and NUMBER share the same storage location. Hence, they are the same. A COMMON statement *cannot* be used here since its function is to place variables in *main* and *subprograms* in COMMON storage. The statement to be used in this case is the EQUIVALENCE statement. Its form is

$$\text{EQUIVALENCE(NUMB,NUMBER)} \tag{10.14}$$

The EQUIVALENCE statement can be extended. For instance,

$$\text{EQUIVALENCE(A,B,C,D),(I,J,K),(Q,R,S)} \tag{10.15}$$

In this case, the four variables A, B, C, and D all share the same storage location. Also the three variables I, J, and K all share the same storage location which is different from that shared by A, B, C, and D. Finally, Q, R, and S all share a single third storage location. When EQUIVA—LENCE statements are used with arrays, the results can be unexpected. For instance, consider the following.

$$\begin{aligned} &\text{DIMENSION A(1\emptyset),B(1\emptyset)} \\ &\text{EQUIVALENCE(A(1),B(1))} \end{aligned} \tag{10.16}$$

The EQUIVALENCE statement causes A(1) and B(1) to share the same storage location. In addition, the DIMENSION statement does the following: ten *consecutive* storage locations are reserved for A. Similarly, ten *consecutive* storage locations are reserved for B. The storage locations for A(1) and B(1) are made to be the same by the EQUIVALENCE statement. Thus, the storage locations for A(2) and B(2) will be the same, etc. Thus, each element of the A array will be equal to the corresponding element of the B array.

Let us consider some other examples of this.

$$\begin{aligned} &\text{DIMENSION A(1\emptyset),B(7)} \\ &\text{EQUIVALENCE(A(3),B(1))} \end{aligned} \tag{10.17}$$

Here, A(3) and B(1) will share the same storage location. Hence, A(4) and B(2) will share the same storage location (which is different from that shared by A(3) and B(1)). Similarly, A(5) and B(3) will share the same storage location, etc.

As a third example, consider

$$\text{DIMENSION A(2,1\emptyset),B(2\emptyset)}$$
$$\text{EQUIVALENCE(A(1,1),B(1))}$$
(10.18)

Note that the A and B arrays each uses 20 storage locations. Thus, the entire A and B arrays share the same storage locations. Note that the A array is stored in the order discussed in Sec. 6.4. For instance, A(1, 3) shares a storage location with B(5), etc. In MICROSOFT FORTRAN the following can also be used with multidimensional arrays. In the EQUIVALENCE statement, all arrays are considered only as simple lists in terms of their storage order. Only a single number is used to designate this. For instance,

$$\text{DIMENSION A(2,1\emptyset),B(2\emptyset)}$$
$$\text{EQUIVALENCE(A(3),B(1))}$$
(10.19)

causes A(1, 2) and B(1) to share the same storage location. Because of this, A(2, 2) and B(2) share a storage location, etc. Remember that A(1, 2) is the third term in the storage order of the A array. *It is only in* EQUIVALENCE *statements that a single number is used in conjunction with multidimensional arrays.*

When EQUIVALENCE statements are used in conjunction with COMMON storage, there are certain procedures to be observed. Consider the statements

$$\text{COMMON A,B,C}$$
$$\text{DIMENSION D(1\emptyset)}$$
$$\text{EQUIVALENCE(C,D(1))}$$
(10.20)

Three consecutive words are reserved in the COMMON storage areas for A, B, and C, respectively. In addition, ten consecutive words are reserved for the D array. We now make D(1) and C equivalent. Thus, they share the same storage area. D(1) is stored in the COMMON storage area. This has the effect of *extending* the COMMON storage area to contain all of the D array. Thus, now the common area contains twelve words of storage. Note that D(1) and C share the same word.

In this case, extending the COMMON storage area is permissible. However, it is not allowed to extend it *backwards past the first variable*. For instance, the following is an *improper set of statements*.

```
COMMON A,B,C
DIMENSION D(1Ø)                                    (10.21)
EQUIVALENCE(C,D(5))
```

Now C and D(5) share the same storage location. A and B occupy the two words immediately preceding C. Thus, statements (10.21) would make A and D(3) equivalent and B and D(4) equivalent. This is allowed. However, D(1) and D(2) would extend "before" the start of the COM—MON block. That is, the first variable in the COMMON list defines the starting point of COMMON storage. Statements (10.21) attempt to start COMMON storage two words before the defined starting point. This is *not* allowed. Hence, statements (10.21) are improper.

If a group of variables are made equivalent, only one of them can be in COMMON. For instance, the following is *incorrect*.

```
COMMON A,B,C                                        (10.22)
EQUIVALENCE(A,C)
```

The COMMON statement sets up three consecutive words for A, B, and C, where A is stored in the first one and C in the third. The EQUIVA—LENCE statement causes A and C to have the same storage locations. This is contradictory and is improper.

We have illustrated the COMMON statement using blank COMMON. However, the same results would be obtained using labeled COMMON.

EXERCISES

In the following exercises, check your results by writing FORTRAN programs and running them on your computer.

10.1 Rewrite the program of Exercise 6.4 but now call the B array the JJ array. The elements of the JJ array are to be real.

10.2 Repeat Exercise 6.7 but use the symbol T to express the integer powers.

10.3 Repeat Exercise 7.6 but now use the symbol ITEM to represent the array which contains real variables.

10.4 Repeat Exercise 8.3 but now use IMPLICIT statements to declare DOUBLE PRECISION.

10.5 Repeat Exercise 8.4 but now use IMPLICIT statements to declare DOUBLE PRECISION.

10.6 Write an IMPLICIT statement which declares all variables whose names start with A to H REAL, those whose names start with I to N INTEGER, those whose names start with O to T DOUBLE PRECISION, and those whose names start with U to Z COMPLEX.

10.7 Repeat Exercise 8.10 using an IMPLICIT statement for the DOUBLE PRECISION declarations.

10.8 Repeat Exercise 8.11 using an IMPLICIT statement for the DOUBLE PRECISION declaration.

10.9 Repeat Exercise 9.5 using an IMPLICIT statement for the COM—PLEX declaration (if COMPLEX variables can be run on your computer).

10.10 Repeat Exercise 10.4 using the "byte notation."

10.11 Repeat Exercise 10.5 using the "byte notation."

10.12 Repeat Exercise 10.9 using the "byte notation."

10.13 Describe the consequences of the following statement.

```
EQUIVALENCE(A,B,C),(DOG,G)
```

10.14 Describe the consequences of the following statement.

```
EQUIVALENCE(A,B,C),(C,G,H)
```

10.15 Describe the consequences of the following program segment.

```
DIMENSION A(1Ø,1Ø),B(1ØØ),C(2,5Ø)
EQUIVALENCE(A(1,1),B(1),C(1,1)
```

10.16 Repeat Exercise 10.15 for

```
DIMENSION A(1ØØ),B(2Ø),C(2,4)
EQUIVALENCE(A(5),B(3),C(2))
```

10.17 Describe the consequences of the following program segment. Is it valid?

```
COMMON A,B(1Ø),C
DIMENSION D(15)
EQUIVALENCE(B(1),D(3))
```

10.18 Repeat Exercise 10.17 for the program segment.

```
COMMON A,B(1Ø),C
DIMENSION D(15)
EQUIVALENCE (C,B(1))
```

11 *Logical Operations*

In Sec. 4.1 we discussed logical expressions with which we assume the reader is familiar. In this chapter we shall consider logical variables and demonstrate how they can be of help to the programmer.

11.1 LOGICAL VARIABLES AND STATEMENTS

A logical variable can have only one of two values:

.TRUE.

or

.FALSE.

Note the periods at the beginning and end. That is, a logical variable can only be *true* or *false*. This seems very different from other variables which can have numeric values. However, we shall demonstrate their use. To illustrate logical variables, let us consider a simple program

```
LOGICAL L1,L2,L3
A=3.Ø
B=4.Ø
C=5.Ø
L1=A.LT.B
L2=A.GT.C
L3=L1.AND.A-B.GT.C
K=Ø
IF(L3.OR.L1)K=1
```

(11.1)

```
        WRITE(5,1)K
1       FORMAT(I3)
        STOP
        END
```

Let us consider the details of this program. The first statement is a *logical declaration* statement. Thus, first, the variables L1, L2, and L3 are declared to be LOGICAL variables. Note that all LOGICAL variables must be so declared. (The declaration statement must precede any mention of the variables. In some compilers it must precede any executable statement.) Values are then established for the three real variables, A, B, and C. Now we have the *logical statement*

$$L1 = A.LT.B \tag{11.2}$$

A LOGICAL variable can be set equal to a *logical expression* which can have either value .TRUE. or the value .FALSE. . Logical expressions were discussed in Sec. 4.1. All of the discussion there applies here. In particular, the logical operators of Table 4.2 can be used in conjunction with logical variables. The relational operators of Table 4.1 *cannot* operate *directly* upon logical variables. Of course, statements such as (11.2) are valid. For the program that we are considering L1 has the value .TRUE. if A is less than B, and the value .FALSE. if A is equal to or greater than B. Since A is less than B in (11.1), L1 is .TRUE. . Similarly, L2 is .FALSE. . Finally, L3 is .FALSE. since *both* L1 and A−B. GT.C are not .TRUE. . The logical statement of the IF statement will be .TRUE. . (Note that this logical statement is .TRUE. if L3 *or* L1 is .TRUE. .) Hence, K=1 and the value 1 will be printed.

We have used an explicit statement to declare LOGICAL variables. An IMPLICIT statement can also be used. For instance,

$$IMPLICIT\ LOGICAL(L-M),INTEGER(A-H) \tag{11.3}$$

declares that all variables starting with L or M are LOGICAL variables and all values starting with A to H are INTEGER variables. All other variables follow the usual FORTRAN standard.

Let us consider another program to illustrate the use of logical variables. Suppose that we have an array of up to 100 numbers and we want to determine if the numbers 2 and 4 are present and if the number 3 is absent. That is, we want to examine the array and output CONDITION VERIFIED if at least one 2 *and* one 4 are present *and* there are no 3s. If there are no 2s *or* 4s, *or* if a 3 is present, then the output will be CONDITION NOT VERIFIED. The program is

```
C PROGRAM ILLUSTRATING USE OF LOGICAL VARIABLES
      IMPLICIT LOGICAL(L)
      DIMENSION M(1ØØ)
      READ(5,1)N
1     FORMAT(I6)
      READ(5,2)(M(I),I=1,N)
2     FORMAT(1ØI6)
      L1=.FALSE.
      L2=.FALSE.
      L3=.FALSE.
      DO 1Ø I=1,N                              (11.4)
      IF(M(I).EQ.2)L1=.TRUE.
      IF(M(I).EQ.3)L2=.TRUE.
      IF(M(I).EQ.4)L3=.TRUE.
1Ø    CONTINUE
      L4=L1.AND.L3.AND.(.NOT.L2)
      IF(L4)WRITE(5,3)
3     FORMAT('ØCONDITION VERIFIED')
      IF(.NOT.L4)WRITE(5,4)
4     FORMAT('ØCONDITION NOT VERIFIED')
      STOP
      END
```

All variables starting with an L are logical ones because of the IMPLICIT statement. Next, the M array is read in. Then we set three logical variables L1, L2, and L3 equal to .FALSE. . In the DO loop, if there are any 2's in the array, we set L1=.TRUE. . Similarly, L2 and L3 become .TRUE. if there are any 3's and 4's in the array. Now consider the statement

```
      L4=L1.AND.L3.AND.(.NOT.L2)
```

L4 will be .TRUE. if any only if L1 and L3 are both .TRUE. and, in addition, if L2 is .FALSE. (.NOT.L2 is .TRUE.). Note that the parentheses are actually not required in this statement since the .NOT. operation will be performed here before the .AND. operation, see Sec. 4.1. The logical IF causes J to be set equal to 1 if L4 is .TRUE. . Thus, we obtain the desired output. Note that we can combine IF and logical statements. For instance, we could write

```
      IF(L1.AND.L3.AND..NOT.L4)WRITE(5,3)
```

LOGICAL arrays can be used. These are arrays whose elements are logical variables. These arrays can be dimensioned in a DIMENSION statement or in an explicit LOGICAL declaration statement. In MICROSOFT FORTRAN, one byte of memory is assigned to each LOGICAL variable.

11.2 INPUT AND OUTPUT OF LOGICAL VARIABLES

The value of a LOGICAL variable can be read in as data or printed out. If we are to work with LOGICAL values, then a new field specifier must be used since the others which we have discussed, I, F, E, and D, apply only to numbers. This field specifier is the L field specifier. For instance, consider the following segment.

```
      IMPLICIT LOGICAL(L)
      READ(5,2)L1,L2,L3                                    (11.5)
2     FORMAT(3L1)
```

The FORMAT specifier indicates that the LOGICAL information is to be entered in a single column. There are three repeated specifiers. Thus, the values of L1, L2, and L3 are entered in the first three columns of the terminal input. T or F are used as the symbols. Note that commas cannot be used on input to separate the LOGICAL variables on all versions of MICROSOFT FORTRAN.

If the FORMAT statement had been changed to

```
2     FORMAT(3L5)                                          (11.6)
```

then the field for L1 would be the first five columns, the field for L2 columns six to ten and the field for L3 would be columns 11 to 15. T or F should be left adjusted. To avoid difficulties, LOGICAL data should be entered using an L1 field specifier.

Let us now consider output using the following program.

```
      IMPLICIT LOGICAL(A-C)
      D=12.6
      E=15.2
      A=.TRUE.
      B=D.GT.E                                             (11.7)
      C=A.AND.B
      WRITE(6,3)D,A,B,C
```

```
3        FORMAT(' ',E1Ø.3,L3,L5,L2)
         STOP
         END
```

(Here A is.TRUE., B is .FALSE. since D is not greater than E, and C is .FALSE. since both A and B are not .TRUE.) The printed output then appears as

bØ.126E+Ø2bbTbbbbFbF

where the b's represent blank spaces. Note that in output, the LOGICAL values are right adjusted in their designated fields. Thus, the output of LOGICAL data is similar to the output of other data except that an L field specifier is used. Text information can be included with LOGICAL information in the same way that it is with other output material.

11.3 LOGICAL SUBPROGRAMS

Subprograms involving LOGICAL operations can be written. They must be declared to be LOGICAL. Their declaration exactly follows that of Sec. 8.3 for DOUBLE PRECISION subprograms except that the words DOUBLE PRECISION are replaced by the word LOGICAL in the declaration statement.

EXERCISES

11.1 In the following A=6.Ø, B=12.Ø, and C=3.Ø. Determine the value of the LOGICAL variables, Y, R, and Z.

```
Y=A.GT.B.OR.A+B.GT.C
R=Y.AND.A*B.GT.C
Z=A+B.GT.B-3*C
```

11.2 Consider that I and J are two arrays with no more than 100 terms each. Write a program which determines if the I array and the J array have any common terms. Use LOGICAL variables in your program. Start by writing an algorithm and draw a flow-chart. Check your program by running it on your computer.

11.3 Consider a two-dimensional array A(I, J) which has 100 rows and columns. Write a program which determines if all A(I, I) are equal to or greater than all A(I, J). For instance, A(1, 1) is to be

equal to or greater than A(1, 2), A(1, 3)... A(1, 100) and A(2,2)
is to be equal to or greater than A(2, 1), A(2, 3) ... A(2, 100).
Use LOGICAL variables in your program. Start by writing an
algorithm and draw a flowchart. Check the program by running it
on your computer.

11.4 Modify the program (6.9) so that a ∅ is printed if there are no
students whose average is greater than or equal to GRADE and a
1 is printed if there is at least one student whose average is equal
to or greater than GRADE, where the value of GRADE is to be
entered by the user of the program. Use LOGICAL variables in
your program. Check your results by running the program on
your computer.

11.5 Describe the operation of the following program.

```
        IMPLICIT LOGICAL(L)
        READ(5,1)A,B,C,L1,L2
1       FORMAT(3F6.3,3L1)
        LOG=A.GT.B*C
        LAP=(L1.OR.LOG).AND.L2
        L3=.FALSE.
        IF(LOG.AND.LAP)L3=.TRUE.
        WRITE(5,2)LOG,LAP,L2,L3
2       FORMAT('∅',4L2)
        STOP
        END
```

Check your results by running the program on your computer.

11.6 Modify the program of Exercise 11.2 to use a printout of LOGI–
CAL data.

11.7 Repeat Exercise 11.6 for the program of Exercise 11.3.

11.8 Repeat Exercise 11.6 for the program of Exercise 11.4.

11.9 Consider the following logical expression

```
A=B.OR.C.AND.(D.OR.B)
```

where A, B, C, and D are logical variables. Write a program that
gives all values of A for all possible logical values of B, C, and D.
Hint: use DO loops of test value 2 to cycle the logical variables.

11.10 Repeat Exercise 11.16 for the logical expression

```
A=((B.AND.C).AND.(D.OR.(A.OR.C))).OR.(A.AND.B)
```

12 *Manipulation of Alphanumeric Characters*

FORTRAN is a language which is primarily intended to perform mathematical calculations. However, it can also be used to perform manipulations on alphanumeric data and to process text material. For instance, we can write a FORTRAN program which will alphabetize a list of names. This alphanumeric programming makes use of formatted input and output.

12.1 ALPHANUMERIC DATA

FORTRAN provides a simple means of storing alphanumeric character strings. For instance, if we write a statement such as

$$I = 'AB' \tag{12.1}$$

then the character string AB will be stored in the memory location for I. However, it will be stored as a number. There is a coding and decoding arrangement which is such that the character string AB is converted into a number. This number is stored in the memory location for I. Thus, statement (12.1) is equivalent to one which sets I equal to the appropriate integer constant. Thus, to store a character string in a memory location, we can set a variable equal to the desired character string, which is *enclosed in single quotation marks*. Note that the quotation marks indicate that the character string is alphanumeric data and not, for instance, a variable name.

There are limits to the amount of data that can be stored. For instance, an INTEGER can store up to two characters. A single precision REAL variable can store up to four characters. A DOUBLE PRECISION variable can store up to eight characters. Thus, long character strings may have to be stored using more than one variable. We shall illustrate this subsequently.

Let us consider the following program

```
      K='AB'
      WRITE(5,2)K
2     FORMAT(' ',I15)
      STOP
      END
```
(12.2)

The output AB would not be printed. Instead, a number equal to the "code value" of AB would be printed. This is because the "computer" has no way of knowing whether the number stored in the memory location for K actually represents an integer or is a code representation of the data stored. The I15 field specifier indicates that an integer should be printed. Thus, the character string is not printed. If we want to print out the alphanumeric characters, then we must use a special FORMAT field specifier which indicates that the decoding is to be done so that an alphanumeric character field is to be printed. The field specifier is an A field specifier. For instance, if we change program (12.2) to

```
      K='AB'
      WRITE(5,2)K
2     FORMAT(' ',A4)
      STOP
      END
```
(12.3)

then the output of the program would be

bbAB   (12.4)

where the b's represent blank spaces. The alphanumeric character string is right adjusted in its specific field. In this case, the field is the first four columns. The rules for the A field specifier are essentially the same as for the INTEGER field specifier (that is, I). For instance, the number following the A indicates the field size in columns.

Let us consider the input of alphanumeric character strings. Suppose that we have the program segment

```
      READ(5,1)A,B
1     FORMAT(2A4)
```
(12.5a)

The A FORMAT specifier indicates that both A and B are to represent alphanumeric characters. Thus, the appropriate coding will be done. Now suppose that we enter the following data.

```
WILSON
```

This will have the same effect as if we had the following two program statements

```
        A='WILS'
        B='ONbb'
```

where the b's represent blank spaces. These blanks will be stored as part of the alphanumeric data. Note that we do not put the quote marks on the terminal input. If, following statements (12.5a), we have the statements

```
        WRITE(5,2)A,B
2       FORMAT(' ',2A4
        STOP
        END
```
(12.5b)

then the output will be

```
WILSONbb
```

Note that ON is not right adjusted since the two blank spaces are part of the alphanumeric data. Note that commas cannot be used to separate alphanumeric data on input, since they would be interpreted as part of the text.

When the FORMAT statements are written, care should be taken to assure that sufficient field is allowed. For instance, if a 2A3 specifier were used in (12.5b), the output would be WILONb. To be safe, four columns should be allowed for each integer which stores alphanumeric data.

We can use more variables when longer character strings are used. Remember also that eight characters could be stored in each DOUBLE PRECISION variable.

In this section we have represented letter constants as a character string between quotes. The Hollerith notation can also be used (see Sec. 3.6). For instance, the following are equivalent

```
'ABC'
3HABC
```

The Hollerith notation is cumbersome since we must count the number of characters exactly.

Use of H Field Specifier for Data Input

When the H field specifier is used in conjunction with data input, a somewhat different operation results. Let us illustrate this with an example. Consider the program segment

```
       READ(5,27)
27     FORMAT(1ØHABCDEFGHIJ)
```

This calls for the reading of 10 characters of alphanumeric data. These *replace* the 10 alphanumeric characters (that is, ABCDEFGHIJ) in the FORMAT statement. If this FORMAT statement is used subsequently in the program, then the "replaced" alphanumeric string will be used. As an example, consider the following program

```
       READ(5,27)
27     FORMAT(1ØHABCDEFGHIJ)
       WRITE(5,27)                                      (12.6)
       STOP
       END
```

Assume that the terminal input has the following typed on it:

ØANSWER IS

Then the printed output will be

ANSWER IS

Note that, in the example, a carriage control character is included with the input data because it will be the start of a line on output.

The string of characters in the original FORMAT statement is a "dummy string." That is, it could have been any string of alphanumeric characters including blanks. There must be as many characters in the dummy string as called for by the H field specifier (10 in this case).

The H field specifier for data input is often used when headings are to be changed. For instance, suppose that a computer program is used to print a student's grades in all his courses. The H field specifier can be used in order to have each student's name printed with the grades. In the next section we shall consider much more versatile alphanumeric data manipulation procedures.

Note that blank spaces are valid alphanumeric data. For instance if, in the previous example, the data were

ØANSWERႦႦႦ

then the output would be

ANSWER

The three blank spaces of the input would be interpreted as data.

Quotes can be used in place of the H field specifier. For instance, in the previous program, an equivalent FORMAT statement would be

27   FORMAT('ABCDEFGHIJ')

However, in this case it is often more convenient to use the H field specifier since it indicates, at a glance, to anyone who reads the program, the number of alphanumeric characters that can be supplied as data.

12.2 PROGRAMS MANIPULATING ALPHANUMERIC DATA

Let us now illustrate the manipulation of alphanumeric character strings. Let us consider a simple procedure which determines if two names on a list are the same. The names can have up to four characters. The program follows:

```
        REAL NAME(1ØØ)
        READ(5,1)N
1       FORMAT(I3)
        READ(5,2)(NAME(I),I=1,N)
2       FORMAT(A4)
        NN=N-1
        DO 1Ø I=1,NN                              (12.7)
```

```
        KK=I+1
        DO 1Ø K=KK,N
        IF(NAME(I).EQ.NAME(K))GO TO 5
        GO TO 1Ø
5       WRITE(5,3)NAME(I)
3       FORMAT(' ',A4)
1Ø      CONTINUE
        STOP
        END
```

Let us consider this program. We DIMENSION the NAME array to have 100 REAL elements. Next we read in the number of names to be read. Then, the names are read in using an A4 format. Note that each name can be, at most, four characters long. Each name will be on a separate line of data. If the FORMAT had been

```
2       FORMAT(3A4)
```

then there would be three names to each line. Each name will have a field of four characters. Next, the elements of the NAME array are compared. Remember that they are stored as numbers. That is, NAME (1) is compared with NAME(2) . . . NAME(1ØØ), then NAME(2) is compared with NAME(3) . . . NAME(1ØØ), etc. If any two elements are the same, then statement number 5 is executed and the (duplicating) name is printed. If the names are not the same then statement 5 is skipped. Thus, the output of this program consists of all the names which are duplicated.

Now let us consider another program. We shall enter a list of student names and their respective grades. The list that is entered is not in alphabetical order. Let us write a program which prints out the names, with the respective grades, in alphabetical order.

Thus far, we have not presented any information which would indicate how lists can be alphabetized. FORTRAN provides a means for doing this. Alphanumeric character strings are coded into numbers. The code is based on "alphbetical order." For instance, AAAA will have a lower numerical representation than will AABA. Similarly, BAAA will have a higher number code than either AABA or AAAA. Thus, if we arrange the variables which store the alphabetical characters in numerical order, the corresponding character strings will be in alphabetical order.

The program which performs the alphabetizing follows:

```
C AN ALPHABETIZING PROGRAM
      IMPLICIT REAL(N)
      DIMENSION NAME1(1ØØ),NAME2(1ØØ),GRADE(1ØØ)
      READ(5,1)L
1     FORMAT(I3)
      DO 1Ø I=1,L
        READ(5,2)NAME1(I),NAME2(I),GRADE(I)
2       FORMAT(2A4,F3.Ø)
1Ø    CONTINUE
      DO 2Ø I=1,L
        NAME='ZZZZ'
        DO 15 J=1,L                                    (12.8)
          IF(NAME.GE.NAME1(J))GO TO 5
          GO TO 15
5         NAME=NAME1(J)
          K=J
15      CONTINUE
        WRITE(5,3)NAME1(K),NAME2(K),GRADE(K)
3       FORMAT(' ',2A4,F8.Ø)
        NAME1(K)='ZZZZ'
2Ø    CONTINUE
      STOP
      END
```

Let us discuss this program. Three arrays are dimensioned. The names are to be contained in the arrays NAME1 and NAME2. Thus, each name can have up to eight characters. This corresponds to program (12.5). The grade is in the GRADE array. The name and grade will be on each line of data. These are read in the first DO loop.

We shall base our alphabetizing on only the first four letters of the name. Let us consider how this is done.

Now consider the inner DO loop whose object is statement number 15. We set the variable NAME='ZZZZ.' The numerical representation of this will be larger than any number in the NAME1 array since the letters ZZZZ will be the last term in any alphabetical sequence. NAME is compared with NAME1(J), for J from 1 to N. If NAME is equal to or greater than NAME1(J), then the numerical value of NAME is replaced by the numerical value of NAME1(J), otherwise it is unchanged. Also, K is set equal to J. Thus, after the DO loop is cycled, NAME will be numerically equal to the smallest NAME1(J). This corresponds to the alphabetically first name. Note that K will equal the corresponding J. Then, NAME1(K), NAME2(K), and GRADE(K)

are printed. Next, NAME1(K) is set equal to 'ZZZZ.' Thus, the alphabetically first name now becomes the last in the list. The outer DO loop
causes the entire process to be repeated. Now the list has been modified
so that the name which was originally second, now is alphabetically
first. Thus, when the inner DO loop is cycled again, the value of K
corresponding to the number of the second term will be obtained.
Thus, the second name on the list and its grade will be printed and the
process is then repeated. When the outer DO loop is completely cycled,
the complete list will be alphabetized and printed. Note that when the
data for the grades is printed, we use an F8.$\emptyset$ specification to obtain
spaces between the names and the grades. If we had used DOUBLE
PRECISION for the storage of the names, then 16-character names
could have been entered. The string 'ZZZZ' would have to be replaced
by 'ZZZZZZZZ' in the program.

Techniques of this type can be used for other types of character
string manipulations.

EXERCISES

12.1 Discuss the storage of alphanumeric data.

12.2 Describe the operation of the following program.

```
        READ(5,1)A,B
1       FORMAT(2A4)
        WRITE(5,2)A,B
2       FORMAT(' ',2A4)
        STOP
        END
```

12.3 Describe the operation of the following program.

```
        READ(5,1)A,B
1       FORMAT(2F6.3)
        C='YES'
        D='NO'
        IF(A.GT.B)GO TO 5
        WRITE(5,2)C
2       FORMAT(' ',A4)
        STOP
5       WRITE(5,2)D
        STOP
        END
```

12.4 Write a program which accepts a list of words containing up to four characters. Determine if any of the words is BOOK.

12.5 Repeat Exercise 12.4 but now assume that the words can be up to eight characters long and the word to be compared is HOUSE.

12.6 Repeat Exercise 12.4 but now print all the words starting with the letter E.

12.7 Use your computer to determine the numerical values of the integers which store the characters

        AA
        AA
        BA
        ZZ

12.8 Repeat Exercise 12.7 using REAL variables.

12.9 Modify the program of (6.9) so that the students' names can be entered and printed out.

12.10 Modify the program of Exercise 12.9 so that the output is in alphabetical order.

12.11 Modify the program (12.8) so that the alphabetizing is based on all the characters of the students' names.

13 *Some Additional Statements*

In this chapter we shall consider some additional FORTRAN statements which can be of help to the programmer. We shall start by considering some additional FORMAT field specifiers and then some aspects of data handling.

13.1 SOME ADDITIONAL FORMAT FIELD SPECIFIERS

The FORMAT field specifiers that we have considered thus far (that is, D, E, F, H, I, L, and A) are adequate for the input and output of all data. In this section we shall consider some field specifiers which may simplify these operations and help the programmer.

The P FORMAT Specifier

When data is printed using an E or D specifier, the first number printed is always a zero. For instance, a number printed using an E10.3 specifier could be

$$-\emptyset.126\text{E}+12 \tag{13.1a}$$

Most people would rather see this written as

$$-1.26\text{E}+11 \tag{13.1b}$$

There is a procedure which we can use to modify the printing of the output so that it appears in the form of (13.1b) rather than in the

form of (13.1a). To perform this modification, a 1P is placed before the
E or D specifier. For instance,

```
          WRITE(6,2)A                                    (13.2)
2         FORMAT(' ',1PE1Ø.3)
```

would result in the value of A's being printed as in (13.1b). Note that
the numerical value that is printed is *not* changed by this specification.

Once a scale factor (that is, a P specifier) has been given in a
FORMAT statement, it is in effect for the remainder of that (single)
FORMAT statement. For instance, the following two FORMAT state-
ments are equivalent.

```
1         FORMAT(1PE1Ø.3,1PE15.5,1PD2Ø.9)          (13.3a)
```

and

```
1         FORMAT(1PE1Ø.3,E15.5,D2Ø.9)              (13.3b)
```

If, in any one FORMAT statement, we want to remove the 1P specifier,
we use a ØP specifier. For instance,

```
4         FORMAT(1PE1Ø.3,D2Ø.9,ØPF7.3)             (13.4)
```

Here, the 1P specifier applies to the E1Ø.3 and the D2Ø.9 specifiers, but
ØP, which is the equivalent of having no P specifier, is applied to the
F7.3 field specifier. The 1P specifier should never be used with the F
field specifier. It will have the effect of multiplying all results by 10.
Thus, great confusion can result if a 1PF specifier is used. Its use should
be avoided except by the most experienced programmers.

Actually, we can specify nP where n is an unsigned integer constant.
However, with the exception of 1P and ØP, this specification has little
use and should usually be avoided except by the most experienced
programmers. See the MICROSOFT FORTRAN manual for full specifications of the P specifier.

The X FORMAT Field Specifier

Very often, when we print data, we want to insert blank spaces
for readability. For instance, consider the program sequence

```
            A=-36.6
            B=-47.2                                                   (13.5)
            WRITE(6,3)A,B
3           FORMAT(' A=',E1Ø.3,'    B=',E1Ø.3)
```

The resulting printing would be

A=-Ø.366E+Ø1   B=-Ø.472E+Ø1

The blank space before the A is a carriage control character. The three blank spaces before the B are actually printed as spaces. This is done to make the line more readable. Having to count spaces in the FORMAT specification can be tedious. A more convenient way is to use the X field specifier. Let us illustrate this. A FORMAT statement equivalent to that of (13.5) is

```
3           FORMAT(' A=',E1Ø.3,3X,'B=',E1Ø.3)    (13.6)
```

The use of 3X inserts three blanks at the corresponding point in the printout. As a further example, consider

```
6           FORMAT(' A=',E1Ø.3,5X,'K=',I3,3X,'Z=',      (13.7)
                                             E12.5)
```

Here there will be five spaces before K= in the printout and three spaces before Z= is printed. Thus, the X specifier is of the form nX, where n is an unsigned integer. This causes n spaces to be skipped at the corresponding place when the output is printed.

The X field specifier can also be used for data input. For instance, consider the following

```
            READ(5,1)A,B                                      (13.8)
1           FORMAT(F6.3,3X,F8.2)
```

Here, A will be entered in the first six columns. Information entered in the next three columns would be ignored and B would be entered in the next eight columns.

The G FORMAT Field Specifier

When floating point numerical data is printed, we usually use an E or D field specifier. It is often dangerous to use an F specifier since important significant figures may be lost if the number becomes too large or too small. However, data printed in the F FORMAT is often more easily read by the user of the program. For instance,

$$396.123 \tag{13.9}$$

is more readable than

$$\emptyset.396123E+\emptyset3 \tag{13.10}$$

It would be desirable to have a FORMAT field specifier which automatically switches from an F specifier to an E (or D) specifier when the number becomes too large or too small to be properly printed using the F specification. Such a field specifier does exist. It is called the G field specifier. Let us illustrate its use.

```
      WRITE(6,2)A                                         (13.11)
2     FORMAT(' ',G11.4)
```

This specifies that A is to be printed in the first 11 columns using four significant figures. For instance, some values of A could be

```
36.37
-261.4
3.183
∅.127
-∅.1∅∅
```

If the magnitude (absolute value) of A is less than 0.1 or greater than 9999, then the specifier automatically becomes an E11.4 specifier. For instance, if A equals 19999, then printing only the last four significant figures would result in 9999's being printed which results in the loss of the most signficant figure. The E11.4 specifier, or, equivalently, the G11.4 specifier, results in the printout of

```
∅.1999E+∅5
```

Thus, only the least significant figure is lost. In general, the field specifier has the form $Gw.d$, where w and d are unsigned integers, w represents the width of the field and d represents the number of significant figures. If the number to be printed has an absolute value which lies in the range

$$0.1 < r < 10^d \tag{13.12}$$

then the d *most* significant figures are printed with no exponential information. If the magnitude of the number is *equal to or less* than 0.1 or *equal to or greater* than 10^d, then exponential notation is used. The specifier then acts as though it were E*w.d* or D*w.d* depending on whether the variable is a single precision or DOUBLE PRECISION variable. Since the G specifier causes automatic switching to the exponential form, w should be large enough. That is, it should be at least such that

$$w > d + 7 \qquad\qquad (13.13)$$

(see Sec. 3.3)

When REAL numbers are printed using a G field specifier, and the exponential form is not used, the results are slightly different than those obtained using an F field specifier. For instance, if we have a G11.4 specifier, then a column of the data might appear as

```
123.6
12.41
1.796
```

while with an F11.4 field specifier, we would have

```
123.6∅∅∅
12.41∅∅
1.796∅
```

Thus, the decimal points are aligned using the F field specifier. If long tables of numbers are to printed, this is an advantage to the reader.

13.2 THE DATA STATEMENT

Often, when we write a program, we wish to specify the initial values of certain variables. For instance, we might want to state

```
PI=3.14159
```

or to state that all the elements of an array are initially 1.0. We could write FORTRAN arithmetic statements which do this. However, these require execution time. There is a more convenient statement called a

DATA statement that can be used to specify the *initial* value of certain variables. It does not consume execution time. This can be an important saving of computer time. Note that we stress the word *initial*. The procedure that we use will cause the value of the variables to be specified during *compilation*. These variables can subsequently be changed during the execution of the program. However, the DATA statement cannot be called during *execution* to "reinitialize" the data. One other restriction should be mentioned. The DATA statement cannot be used to initialize variables in COMMON storage. We shall consider a procedure for this in the next section. The DATA statement has the basic form

$$\text{DATA } X,Y,I/2.16,31.8,26/ \tag{13.14}$$

That is, it consists of a string of variables followed by a string of numbers enclosed in slashes. Statement (13.14) has the effect of initializing the values to be

$$\begin{aligned} X &= 2.16 \\ Y &= 31.8 \\ I &= 26 \end{aligned} \tag{13.15}$$

That is, each variable is set equal to the number, enclosed in slashes, which follows it.

There is another form which can be used for the DATA statement. It is

$$\text{DATA } X,Y,Z/12.6,15.8,-31.6/,A,I/19.2,3/ \tag{13.16}$$

Here the intial values are X=12.6, Y=15.8, Z=−31.6, A=19.2, and I=3. That is, we can have a list of variables separated by commas, followed by a pair of slashes, which enclose an equal number of constants separated by commas. Corresponding terms are then equated. There is a comma following the second slash and the entire procedure can be repeated again.

At times we repeat a constant many times in a DATA statement. MICROSOFT FORTRAN has a convenient feature. If n^*, where n is an unsigned integer constant, is placed before a constant, it has the effect of repeating the constant n times. For instance,

$$\text{DATA } X,Y,Z/3^*6./ \tag{13.17}$$

is equivalent to

$$\text{DATA } X,Y,Z/6.,6.,6./ \tag{13.18}$$

Any declaration statement concerning a variable used in a DATA statement must precede the DATA statement.

If an array is listed without any coefficients, then the whole array is initialized in its storage order. For instance, consider the following

```
DIMENSION A(2,2)                    (13.19)
DATA A,B/Ø.,1.,2.,3.,4./
```

In this case, the initial values are A(1, 1)=0., A(2, 1)=1., A(1, 2)=2., A(2, 1)=3., and B=4. .

Character and LOGICAL data can also be initialized. The LOGICAL variables must be so declared prior to the DATA statement.

```
DIMENSION A(1Ø)
LOGICAL L                           (13.20)
DATA A,B,C/12*1./,L,I/.TRUE.,'ANS'/
```

Now the A array and the values of B and C are initialized to 1., L is set equal to .TRUE. and I to 'ANS'.

One important fact should be noted. The DATA statement as we have discussed it cannot be used in conjunction with variables placed in COMMON storage. In Sec. 13.3 we shall discuss a procedure that allows us to do this.

13.3 THE BLOCK DATA SUBPROGRAMS

The DATA statement cannot be used to initialize any variable in COMMON storage. However, a special form of subprogram called a BLOCK DATA subprogram can be used to establish the initial values of variables in COMMON storage. The BLOCK DATA subprogram is nonexecutable. It operates during compilation only and *cannot* contain executable statements, nor can it be called by the main program. Let us consider a simple BLOCK DATA subprogram.

```
BLOCK DATA SUB
DIMENSION C(5)                      (13.21)
```

```
COMMON/BLOCK1/A,B,C/BLOCK2/D,E,F
DATA A,C,E/1.6,5*4.9,7.3/
END
```

Note that the subprogram starts with the words BLOCK DATA and a subprogram name (in this case SUB), and ends with END. The DATA statement is as discussed in Sec. 13.2. The effect of (13.21) is to specify the initial value of A as 1.6, each element of the C array as 4.9, and E as 7.3. Note that all the data in COMMON storage does not have to be initialized. However, the COMMON statement(s) must contain *all* the variables in any block that is listed. All values of the COMMON BLOCK that are initialized must be initialized in the same BLOCK DATA subprogram.

If an IMPLICIT statement is used in a BLOCK DATA subprogram, it must be the second statement in the program. For instance,

```
BLOCK DATA START
IMPLICIT LOGICAL(C)
COMMON A,B,C,D(15)
DATA A,C,D/1.3,.TRUE.,15*0.0/
END
```

Here we have identified that the initial value of A is 1.3, that of C is .TRUE., and that all the elements of the D array are initially 0.0. Note that the BLOCK DATA subprogram can be used with blank COMMON as well as with labeled COMMON storage.

13.4 THE ENCODE AND DECODE STATEMENTS

MICROSOFT FORTRAN provides two statements that allow the programmer to change the internal format of stored data. All data is stored as binary numbers. However, these numbers will vary with the form of the data. For instance, if you enter an integer using an I field specifier, a certain binary number will be stored. If you enter the same integer using an A field specifier, a different binary number will be stored. Suppose that you want to enter some numbers as characters, since they were part of the data used by a word processing program. For instance, they might be grades. However, in addition to the word processing, you may also want to use these numbers in arithmetic calculations. If the numbers were entered using an A field specifier, they could not be used in numerical calculations (e.g. multiplication, addition). We shall now consider two statements that allow the con-

version of data from one form to another so that we could use these
entered integers in numerical calculations.

The first statement that we shall consider is ENCODE. For instance, the statements

$$\begin{aligned} &\text{ENCODE(ARR,2)A,B,C} \\ 2 \quad &\text{FORMAT(3F)} \end{aligned} \tag{13.22}$$

convert the data stored in the computer's internal format into ASCII
code. Note that ASCII code is the code that is used to transmit data to
and from the computer and its peripherals. For instance, data is supplied to the line printed in ASCII code. The variable ARR must be an
array. ENCODE is analogous to a WRITE statement. Now that the data
stored in the ARR array is in ASCII form, it can be read using a different FORMAT specification, just as if it were being entered from the
terminal, and the data can be converted to the desired internal storage
form. A statement analogous to the READ statement is used for this
conversion. It is DECODE, for instance

$$\begin{aligned} &\text{DECODE(ARR,3)A1,B1,C1} \\ 3 \quad &\text{FORMAT(3A4)} \end{aligned} \tag{13.23}$$

Statements (13.22) and (13.23) will take data entered as real and con
vert it into character form. It is assumed here that the values for A, B,
and C are those which normally represent characters. A table of ASCII
codes is given in the MICROSOFT FORTRAN manual.

Now let us consider a program that inputs three characters that are
assumed to be chosen from 0, 1, 2, 3, 4, 5, 6, 7, 8, and 9. These will
then be converted to integer form, which can then be used in calculations. In the following program, I, J, and K represent characters, while
I1, J1, and K1 represent integers. For instance, subsequent arithmetic
calculations could be performed using I1, J1, and K1.

```
    DIMENSION IA(3)
    READ(5,1)I,J,K
1   FORMAT(3A1)
    ENCODE(IA,2)I,J,K
2   FORMAT(3A1)
    DECODE(IA,3)K1,J1,K1        (13.24)
3   FORMAT(3I1)
    WRITE(5,4)I1,J1,K1
```

```
4         FORMAT(' ',3I1)
          STOP
          END
```

EXERCISES

13.1 Modify the following FORMAT statement so that the exponential data is printed with a 1P FORMAT.

```
          WRITE(6,21)A,B,C
21        FORMAT('Ø',2E1Ø.3,E15.4)
```

Use your computer to verify the results.

13.2 Modify the following FORMAT statement so that data printed with an E or D field specifier is printed with a 1P specifier but all other field specifiers are unchanged.

```
          WRITE(6,22)A,B,C,D
22        FORMAT('Ø',F6.1,2E1Ø.3,F7.2)
```

Use your compuer to verify the results.

13.3 Repeat Exercise 13.2 for

```
          WRITE(6,23)A,B,I
23        FORMAT('ØA=',E1Ø.3,'B=',F6.1,'I=',I4)
```

13.4 Modify the following FORMAT statement so that when the output is printed, there are five blank spaces before B= and ten blank spaces before C=.

```
          WRITE(6,5)A,B,C
5         FORMAT('Ø','A=',E1Ø.3,'B=',E1Ø.3,'C=',E1Ø.3)
```

13.5 Use the G FORMAT to modify the following FORMAT statement. Make the expression as short as possible.

```
21        FORMAT(' ',2E1Ø.3,F1Ø.3)
```

Use the computer to verify your results.

13.6 The output of a program can consist of an integer which lies between 1 and 9999. It is desired that the output be of the form ANSWER=64. There are to be no blank spaces between the equals sign and the answer. Write a program segment which will accomplish this.

13.7   Describe the effect of the following statement

    DATA A,B,C/1.2E3,-1∅.7,4.63/,D,E/4.1,∅.∅/

Use your computer to verify your results.

13.8   Repeat Exercise 13.7 for

    DIMENSION A(3)
    DATA A/1.,2.,3./

13.9   Repeat Exercise 13.7 for

    DIMENSION A(1∅∅),B(2,2∅)
    DATA A,C/1∅1*∅.∅/,B,C/4∅*1.∅,3.∅/

13.10   Repeat Exercise 13.7 for

    DIMENSION A(5∅)
    DATA A/2∅*1∅.1,3∅*2∅.∅/

13.11   Write a DATA statement which sets an array of 100 terms and three other variables equal to 0.0 initially.

13.12   When will the BLOCK DATA subprogram be used?

13.13   Describe the consequences of the following program

    BLOCK DATA TEST
    IMPLICIT,LOGICAL(L)
    COMMON A(3),B,C,L
    DATA A,B/3*2.∅,4.6/,C,L/2.3,.TRUE./
    END

13.14   Write a BLOCK DATA subprogram which sets the initial value of all the elements of an array A of DIMENSION A(5,10) to zero. The array A is to be in COMMON storage.

13.15   Describe the operation of the ENCODE and DECODE statements. Write and run a program to verify your discussion.

14 *Debugging Programs*

When a program is written, it often contains some errors. Actually, almost no long programs are written which are without errors. An error in a program is called a *"bug"*. Thus, correcting the error is called *debugging* the program.

We have discussed techniques of structured programming which make it easier to write programs with few errors and which make it easy to locate them. However, even when these techniques are used, errors occur and must be corrected. We shall consider the location of program errors (bugs) in this chapter.

The errors can be in one of two categories. The first type can be detected during compilation. For instance, the grammatical rules of FORTRAN may have been violated. As an example, suppose a statement was written as A+B=C. This is not allowed. Such *syntax errors* are detected by the compiler and an error message is printed on the screen to help the programmer correct his errors.

The second type of error results when the program can be compiled properly but does not produce the results that the programmer intended. This may be a *logical error*. Let us consider a trivial example. Suppose that we want to write a program which adds two numbers. If, instead of writing C=A+B, we wrote C=A−B, a perfect FORTRAN program would result. However, the answer will be incorrect.

Another type of error in the second category is an *execution error*. Suppose that a program contains a statement

$$I = M**K$$

where, during execution, the values of M and K have been computed to be 100 and 250, respectively. In this case, an integer overflow will result and the correct results will not be obtained.

All types of bugs can, and often do, occur in programs. In this chapter we shall consider the procedures for correcting bugs.

The first debugging procedure is done simply be rereading the program. After a programmer gains experience, many bugs can be spotted in this way. However, especially in long program modules, there usually are errors which will not be found by rereading alone. They will be detected during complilation or after the program has been executed and the results are available. We shall start our discussion by considering the correction of bugs that can be discovered during compilation.

14.1 DEBUGGING OF ERRORS DETECTED DURING COMPILATION

If a statement or group of statements violates the rules of FOR–TRAN, the program cannot be properly compiled. In this case, computation ceases and an error message is given. The MICROSOFT FORTRAN compiler has many error messages which are given in the MICROSOFT FORTRAN manual. These can be very helpful in debugging the program since they supply the programmer with information about what is wrong with his program. At times, errors do actually "get through" the compiler. Programs should always be checked with sample data before they are considered finished.

The error message usually lists the FORTRAN statement(s) that results in the compiler's detecting an error. At times, those statements indicated are actually correct. For instance, consider the sequence

```
C PROGRAM SEGMENT WITH AN ERROR
        DIMENSION A(1Ø)                                    (14.1)
        DO 1Ø I=1,15
1Ø      B(I)=A(I)
```

The program has forgotten to DIMENSION the B array. Thus, statement 1Ø cannot be properly compiled. Thus, although statement 1Ø is correct, it will be pointed to by the error message. However, when such error messages occur, experience teaches the programmer to check for DIMENSION statements. The compiler may generate an error message each time the B array appears. If B is not dimensioned, the compiler will think that it is a FUNCTION to be supplied when linking is performed. Statement 1Ø then cannot be correct since the FUNCTION is on the wrong side of the equals sign. As the programmer becomes more experienced, his ability to interpret error messages increases. Thus, the process of debugging becomes a faster one.

Let us consider some other errors that can be detected during compilation and which will result in the printing of error messages. The simplest ones are errors in spelling. For instance, if we write

2   FORNAT(F6.3)
             ↑   (14.2)

the N should be an M.

Another common error is forgetting to number a statement. For instance, FORMAT statements, objects of DO loop, or GO TO statements must all be numbered.

There can be errors in syntax. For instance,

A=(BUG)(ERROR)

Here the asterisk has been omitted. That is, we should have A=BUG* ERROR. Other characters that are often forgotten are commas and parentheses.

Often, especially if the program has many arrays, the programmer will forget to DIMENSION one (or more) of them.

When long programs are written, the programmer may forget the name of a variable. For instance, if an average is computed, AVE may be used as the variable name in one part of the program and AVEG in another. Suppose that we have

AVE=(A+B+C)/3.
    :
    :
MARK-1.3ᵡAVEG

The compiler will assign a memory location to AVEG. Its numerical value will be meaningless and improper results will be obtained.

We have considered errors that commonly occur. However, there are others.

14.2 DEBUGGING ERRORS THAT OCCUR DURING EXECUTION

After a program has been successfully compiled, execution is attempted. At times, the execution fails. Actually, some errors produce a warning message but computation is allowed to proceed. Other errors

cause computation to cease. A list of errors is given in the MICROSOFT
FORTRAN manual. For instance, there can be an overflow, or a divide
check can result. In this case, the program must be checked to see why
a number(s) becomes too large, or why division by zero was attempted.
For instance, consider the following program segment.

```
C PROGRAM SEGMENT WITH AN ERROR
        DIMENSION B(1∅)
        ⋮
        ⋮
        A=12.6
        SUM=∅.                                          (14.3)
        DO 1∅ I=1,1∅
           SUM=SUM*B(I)
1∅         CONTINUE
        C=A/SUM
```

In this case, SUM=$\emptyset$. Note that when the DO loop is executed, SUM=
SUM*B(I) always results in zero. Thus, a divide check will occur at the
last statement. Usually, overflows or underflows or divide checks result
from more complex errors. Sometimes overflow and underflow result
because the data produces extremely large or small values, although the
program is "correct." At times, a simple modification of the details of
the program can avoid the problems. However, other times, relatively
sophisticated techniques must be used.

Let us consider a case where errors can result even though the program is mathematically correct. Suppose that we want to compute the
function

$$v = 1 + q(\frac{f}{f_0} - \frac{f_0}{f}) \tag{14.4}$$

where $q = 100$, $f_0 = 10^{10}$, and f is to take on the values

1.0000001 × 10^{10}, 1.0000002 × 10^{10} and 1.0000003 × 10^{10}

f/f_0 and f_0/f will both be very close to one. For instance, if we have
$f = 1.0000001 × 10^{10}$, then

$f_0/f = 0.9999999$

while

$$f/f_0 = 1.0000001$$

Thus, a small percentage error in f/f_0 and/or f_0/f can produce a large percentage error in the difference between them, see the introduction to Chapter 8. Thus, roundoff can cause the answer to be substantially in error. Hence, a FORTRAN statement such as

$$V=1+Q*(F/F\emptyset-F\emptyset/F)$$ (14.5)

would be mathematically correct but could lead to erroneous results. Let us see how this could be corrected.

Let us write f in the following way

$$f = f_0 + \delta$$ (14.6)

Note that we know δ accurately. For instance, if

$$f = 1.0000001 \times 10^{10} \text{ then}$$

$$\delta = 0.0000001 \times 10^{10} = 1000$$

Now we can write

$$f/f_0 = 1 + \delta/f_0$$

Then

$$f/f_0 - f_0/f = 1 + \delta/f_0 - \cfrac{1}{1 + \cfrac{\delta}{f_0}}$$

Manipulating, we have

$$f/f_0 - f_0/f = \frac{1 + \dfrac{\delta^2}{f_0^2} + \dfrac{2\delta}{f_0} - 1}{1 + \delta/f_0}$$ (14.7)

The inaccuracy in the previous calculation resulted because of the need to subtract two almost equal quantities. The same type of subtraction results here. Note that δ/f_0 will be very small so that

$$1 + \frac{\delta^2}{f_0^2} + \frac{2\delta}{f_0} \approx 1$$

However, now we can perform the subtraction exactly since it is done in the equation. That is, it is done algebraically (using letters). Thus,

$$1 + \frac{\delta^2}{f_0^2} + \frac{2\delta}{f_0} - 1 = \frac{\delta^2}{f_0^2} + \frac{2\delta}{f_0} = \frac{\delta}{f_0}(2 + \frac{\delta}{f_0}) \tag{14.8}$$

This is exact. Note that in computing

$$\frac{\delta}{f_0}(2 + \frac{\delta}{f_0})$$

no subtraction of nearly equal quantities results and the attendant roundoff error is eliminated. Thus, a much better FORTRAN statement than (14.5) would be

```
V=1.+Q*(DELT/FØ)*(2.+DELT/FØ)/(1.+DELT/FØ)              (14.9)
```

It is assumed that the necessary value(s) of DELT is entered prior to this statement. Note that this procedure requires that we know DELT accurately. However, in problems of this type, this is usually the case. That is, we usually express f in terms of its difference from f_0 so that δ (or, equivalently, DELT) is known exactly.

Other types of errors can occur during execution. The simplest is having a result printed with an improper FORMAT statement. Such errors were discussed in detail in Sec. 3.3. We assume that the reader is familiar with this material.

Real and integer modes often cause problems. For instance, suppose that we want to calculate $2^{1/i}$ for values of i ranging from 2 to 10. The following program segment appears to do it.

```
C PROGRAM SEGMENT WITH AN ERROR
        DO 1Ø I=2,1Ø
        X=1/I                                          (14.10)
        Y=2.**X
1Ø      CONTINUE
```

However, for any value of I, the calculated value of X will be 0. Note that 1/I is the division of two integers. Thus, any fractional part will be discarded, see Sec. 2.6. Since X is a real variable, the integer 0 will then be converted to the real value 0., which will be the value stored in the X location. We can correct program (14.10) by writing

$$X = 1./I$$

Now the division is a mixed mode operation and the proper value of X will be obtained. We could also replace the single statement by

$$AI = I$$
$$X = 1./AI$$

Another type of error that commonly occurs during execution results when the coefficient of an array is larger than the value dimensioned for the array. For instance, consider the program sequence

```
DIMENSION A(100)
    .
    .
    .
K=(M+I)*N
A(K)=B+1.
```

where we assume that M, I, N, and B are quantities entered or calculated in the program. Suppose that, for certain input data, K is greater than 100. The A array is only dimensioned to have 100 storage locations. Then, if K is greater than 100, the memory location of A(K) is an improper one, see Sec. 6.1. It may be a location reserved for another variable. In this case, erroneous numerical results will be obtained for that variable or any other variables that depend on it. Unpredictable results can occur with this type of error. Great care should be taken in those program which calculate the subscripts of an array to see that this type of error does not occur.

Programs should always be checked to see if they produce the correct results. That is, "hand calculations" (or those using desk calculators) should be performed to see if the results check with those obtained by the computer. Of course, the fact that the program works with one set of input data does not guarantee that it will work with all sets of input data. Thus, several sets of typical data should be checked. Also, the program itself should be studied to see if the potential for execution errors exists.

Logical Errors

There are circumstances when a program is executed and run where there are no execution errors of the type discussed and results are obtained. However, they are wrong. There are two causes for such errors. The data may be erroneously entered (e.g. the wrong number

was typed). This can be checked by having all entered data printed out.
Then, the printout can be checked to determine that the data has been
entered properly.

The other cause for the incorrect results is that there is a logical
error in the program. That is, it is a perfectly good FORTRAN program
but it calculates something other than desired. Again, all programs
should be checked using "hand calculations" to determine that they
are operating properly.

Let us now discuss a logical error. We shall do this by discussing a
simple program with a logical bug. Suppose that we want to obtain the
sum of all the elements in a one-dimensional array. Let us attempt to
do it with the following program.

```
C PROGRAM WITH LOGICAL ERROR
        DIMENSION A(1ØØ)
        READ(5,1)N
1       FORMAT(I3)
        READ(5,2)(A(I),I=1,N)
2       FORMAT(1ØF5.1)
        SUM=Ø.                                    (14.11)
        DO 1Ø I=1,N
          SUM=A(I)
1Ø      CONTINUE
        WRITE(5,3)SUM
3       FORMAT(' ',E15.7)
        STOP
        END
```

This program will always print the value of SUM which is equal to the
value of A(N). The bug is that the statement preceding the CONTINUE
statement should be

$$SUM=SUM+A(I) \qquad (14.12)$$

In a simple program, the error might be seen by an inspection of the
program. In a long program it might not be as obvious. To find the
error, it would help to check each segment of the program. For instance,
we could modify the program in the following way.

```
C PROGRAM WITH A DEBUGGING STATEMENT
        DIMENSION A(1ØØ)                          (14.13)
```

```
         READ(5,1)N
1        FORMAT(I3)
         READ(5,2)(A(I),I=1,N)
2        FORMAT(10F5.1)
         SUM=0.
            DO 10 I=I,N
         SUM=A(I)
C           DEBUGGING STATEMENT
         WRITE(5,5)SUM,A(I)
5           FORMAT(2E15.7)
10       CONTINUE
         WRITE(5,3)SUM
3        FORMAT(' ',E15.7)
         STOP
         END
```

Now SUM and A(I) are printed each time that the DO loop is cycled. It then would become evident that the value of SUM is equal to the current value of A(I) and the bug would be detected. Often, comment statements are inserted before and after the debugging statements. This is done so that these error-correcting statements can be easily detected by the programmer and removed after the program is debugged.

The general procedure for locating a bug which cannot be easily detected is to enter simple data. For instance, in the above example, we could make N small (for example, 4) and keep A(I) as easily manipulated terms (for example, 1.0, 2.0, etc.). Then, we calculate small segments by hand (or with a desk calculator) to see what all the values (not only the final results) should be. Run the program with the debugging statements added and check to see that the values obtained are correct. Continue in this way through each segment of the program module until the bug is located.

At times, this type of check can be done without using the computer. The programmer must follow each step of the program and carry out the calculations by hand, just as the computer would. The danger here is that the programmer knows what calculations *should* be made. Thus, even if the statement says SUM=A(I), he may calculate SUM= SUM+A(I).

One further word of comment: bugs will occur in almost every program. The beginning programmer will make them in simple programs. The advanced programmer will make them in more detailed programs. Bugs should not be discouraging to the programmer and debugging should be considered a part of program writing.

14.3 EDITING OF PROGRAMS

At times, after a program has been written, it is desirable to edit it. For instance, for purposes of debugging, we might want to insert or change statements. Alternatively, we might wish to correct a typographical error. MICROSOFT FORTRAN has a very powerful editor which allows us to make such changes easily. We shall now discuss it.

In Sec. 1.3 we discussed the use of the editor for simple operations. There we considered the entering of a program and the entering and exiting of the editor. We also discussed how to insert lines into a program and the replacement of existing lines. We shall now discuss more sophisticated editing commands. We assume that you are familiar with Sec. 1.3.

Single Line Editing—Alter Mode

If a statement has an error, it need not be retyped. Changes can be easily made by using the alter mode of the editor. This mode has very simple commands that can be used to change a single character, insert strings of characters and to delete characters. The editor is entered as discussed in Sec. 1.3. An asterisk * prompt appears indicating that you are in the editor command mode. The alter mode is entered by typing **A** followed by the line (*not* FORTRAN statement) number. For instance, suppose that we have line number 8ØØ, FORTRAN statement number 2

$$\emptyset\emptyset8\emptyset\emptyset2 \quad FORGAT('\emptyset',2E15.7) \qquad (14.14)$$

There is a typographical error. The G should be replaced by an M. Now suppose that we are in the editor mode and that the asterisk prompt has appeared. Type **A8ØØ**

A8ØØ (RETURN)

(Note that RETURN and ENTER are equivalent.) The following will appear on the screen

$$\emptyset\emptyset8\emptyset\emptyset \qquad (14.15)$$

and we are ready to edit the line.

When we make changes in a line, there is a *cursor* that is used. The cursor points to the character that is to be changed. Only those parts of the statement that have been pointed to by the cursor appear on the screen. Statement (14.15) indicates that the pointer is at the start of the line. Thus, no part of the statement has yet been printed. The cursor must be moved to the desired position. There are several procedures for doing this, and each involves typing a character(s). These are:

(SPACE)

Typing a single space moves the cursor one position to the right. If the space is preceded by a number, then the cursor moves that many spaces. For instance,

3 (SPACE)

(the parentheses are not typed) moves the cursor three spaces to the right and

−2 (SPACE)

moves the cursor two spaces to the left. The characters will be printed as the cursor moves "over them."

For instance, in the example of (14.15), if we type one space, then the line will appear as

Ø Ø 8 Ø Ø 2

If we now type 8(SPACE), the line will appear as

Ø Ø 8 Ø Ø 2   FOR   (14.16)

Note that the cursor had been moved one space previously. We are now in a position to correct the error. Before discussing how this is done, let us complete the discussion of the motion of the cursor. We shall list the various cursor control letters.

W   If W is typed, the pointer will move to the start of the next word. A number can also be typed preceding W. For instance, 2W will advance the cursor two words and −3W will move the cursor back three words. A word is a collection of alphanumeric characters without a space. The space ends a word.

→   The right arrow shifts the cursor to the end of the line.

L   Typing **L** causes the entire line to be printed and positions the cursor at the start of the line. This allows you to inspect the entire line before or during editing.

P   Typing **P** causes the entire line to be printed, as in the case of L. However, now the cursor position is unchanged. It is not moved to the start of the line.

(ENTER)   Typing **ENTER** or, equivalently, **RETURN**, causes the
or   printing of the remainder of the line and ends the editing
(RETURN) of the line. The changes you have made are saved in the computer's memory. You are returned to the editor command mode and the * prompt appears.

Replacement of Text

Now that we have discussed the procedures for moving the cursor, we can consider the procedures for changing the text.

C   Typing **C** allows you to change a single character. For instance, suppose that we have (14.14) and have moved the cursor as indicated in (14.16). If we then type **CM**, the following will appear.

ØØ8ØØ2   FORM   (14.17)

The G has been replaced by an M. If we now type **ENTER** (or **RETURN**)

ØØ8ØØ2   FORMAT('Ø',2E15.7)   (14.18)

will be printed and the editing of the line will be completed. A number can be typed before the **C**, for example **3C**. Now the next three characters will be changed to the three characters that you type in. If, in (14.18), you move the cursor so that you have

ØØ8ØØ2   FORMAT('Ø',   (14.19)

then, typing **6C3D17.4** will result in

ØØ8ØØ2   FORMAT('Ø',3D17.4)   (14.20)

If you type –4C, then the four characters preceding the cursor will be changed. You can end the change by typing ESC or, equivalently, BREAK. For instance, if you type 1∅C and only want to change three characters, to QWE, type 1∅CQWE(BREAK).

R   The R command is similar to the C command. If you type 3R followed by text and then ESC or BREAK, then the next three characters following the cursor will be replaced by the text. Note that, in this case, the new text can be longer or shorter than the replaced text. If a negative integer precedes R, (e.g. –6R), then the six characters to the left of the cursor will be replaced by the text.

Addition of Text

The following instructions are used to add text to an existing line.

I   Typing I causes the succeeding text to be inserted starting at the cursor position. The text must be terminated with an ESC or, equivalently, BREAK. You can also terminate the insertion by typing a carriage return or ENTER. This also terminates the editing of the line. You are returned to the editor command mode and the * prompt appears. Your changes are saved.

B   Typing B or kB, where k is a positive integer, inserts k blank spaces. If k is omitted, it is assumed to be 1. For instance, 3B causes three blanks to be inserted at the cursor position

G   Typing kG followed by a character causes that character to be inserted k times at the current cursor position. For instance, 5GW causes WWWWW to be inserted.

X   The X is typed when text is to be added at the end of the line. The cursor is moved to the end of the line and any text material that is entered from the keyboard is added to the line. This must be terminated by a BREAK or, equivalently, ESC, a carriage return, or ENTER. Typing X is equivalent to moving the cursor to the end of the line and typing I. If –X is typed, then the insertion is made at the beginning of the line.

Deletion of Text

The following instructions are used to delete text from an existing line.

D   Typing **D** causes the character at the cursor position to be deleted. The deleted character will appear on the screen surrounded by pairs of exclamation points. For instance, if we have the line

ØØ1ØØC   A COMMEENT   (14.21)

and if the cursor is positioned so that the screen appears as ØØ1ØØC A COMM, and **D** is typed, then ØØ1ØØ A COMM!!E!! will appear. The E has been deleted. Typing **kD** will cause the next **k** characters to be deleted. Typing **–kD** causes the **k** characters to the left of the cursor to be deleted. The back arrow is equivalent to **–1D**.

H   If **H** is typed, the remainder of the line to the right of the cursor is deleted, and new text can be added just as though an **I** were typed. This insertion must be terminated in the same way as if an **I** were used (see the **I** instruction).

K   If **K** followed by a character is typed, all characters up to (but not including) the typed character will be deleted. For instance, **KG** will cause all characters from the cursor to the next occurrence of G to be deleted. If **kKG** is typed, then all characters up to the **k**th occurrence of G will be deleted. If there is no G, then the command will be ignored.

T   Typing **T** causes the remainder of the line to the right of the cursor to be deleted. If **–T** is typed, the line to the left of the cursor will be deleted. Control is returned to the editor and the * prompt appears.

Z   Typing **Z** causes words to be deleted. If **kZ** is typed, the next **k** words will be deleted. If **–kZ** is typed, the **k** words to the left of the cursor will be deleted. If the cursor is in the middle of a word, the part of the word to the right (left) of the cursor will be deleted and counted as one word.

Ending and Restarting Alter Mode

We shall now consider the commands that are used to end the editing of a line in the alter mode. Typing a carriage return, **ENTER**, or **A** ends the editing of a line. All the editing is saved. The line has been changed. The complete line is printed.

E   If **E** is typed, the line editing is ended as in the previous paragraph except that now the remainder of the line is not printed.

N   There are times when you feel that the editing is in error and
or   you want to cancel all the changes. If you type **N** or **Q**, the
Q   editing of the line will be terminated and all the changes will be lost. The line will be the same as it was before. You are returned to the editor command mode and the * prompt reappears. Typing a shift left arrow has the same effect as **N** or **Q**, but you remain in the editing mode. The changes are canceled and the cursor is placed at the beginning of the line.

Finding Text

We have considered that the cursor is moved over a single character or over a number of characters at a time. There is a convenient procedure for moving the cursor. It can search for specific text. (This is done in the alter mode.)

S   Typing **S** followed by a character will cause the cursor to be positioned before the next occurrence of the character. If **S** is preceded by an integer, **kS**, then the cursor is positioned before the **kth** occurrence of the character. For instance, 3SG will position the cursor before the third occurrence of G to the right of the present cursor. A –2SG will position the cursor after the second occurrence of G to the left of the present position of the cursor. If the specific character cannot be found, then the cursor is not moved.

We have discussed the basic ideas of the alter mode, line-changing operations. Your MICROSOFT FORTRAN manual should be consulted for additional information.

Global Search and Substitute

The editor allows the entire program, or specific lines of it, to be searched for text. The location of the specific text will be identified. In addition, if you so desire, the existing string of text can be replaced by a different string. These commands make extensive use of the **BREAK** or, equivalently, **ESC** key. When this key is pressed, a $ appears on the screen. We shall use the symbol $ to specify that **BREAK** or **ESC** is pressed. Note that you cannot press the dollar sign key for this purpose. A range of lines is indicated by a colon. For instance,

$$1\emptyset\emptyset:3\emptyset\emptyset \hspace{3cm} (14.22)$$

specifies the range of lines from $1\emptyset\emptyset$ to $3\emptyset\emptyset$. If you want to find the location of a string, type

F1ØØ:3ØØØ,5$STRING$

The first five lines containing STRING in lines $1\emptyset\emptyset$ to $3\emptyset\emptyset\emptyset$ will be printed on the screen with their line numbers. Then lines can be edited if desired. The number 5 is called the *limit*. If you want to find all occurrences of a string, just enter a limit that you know is larger than the number of lines containing text, or simply omit the limit as in

F1ØØ:3ØØØ,$STRING$

We can also substitute one string for another. These need not be of the same length. If the F is replaced with an S and a second string follows the first string, then a replacement will be made. For instance, consider

S1ØØ:3ØØØ,5$STRING$LIST$

the first five lines containing STRING in lines $1\emptyset\emptyset$ to $3\emptyset\emptyset\emptyset$ will be printed with every occurrence of STRING replaced by LIST. Note that more than 5 STRINGS may be replaced.

If you want to perform a search and substitution in the entire program, type the range as

↑:✲

In this case, the up arrow stands for the first line in the program and * stands for the last line.

We have discussed the most important aspects of global search and substitution here. For other details, consult the MICROSOFT FOR-TRAN manual.

General Commands

We shall now expand on some of the instructions given in Sec. 1.3.

I   This command followed by **RETURN** or **ENTER** allows you to insert lines. When typed at the start of the editing session, it numbers successive lines in increments of $10/$ starting at 100. If you type

$$In_1, n_2 \text{ (RETURN)} \tag{14.23}$$

then lines will be inserted starting at number n_1 with an increment of n_2. Both n_1 and n_2 must be unsigned integers. For instance, suppose you want to insert three statements between lines 500 and 600. Type

$$*I530,20$$

Now lines will be inserted starting with 530 in increments of 20, i.e., 530, 550, 570, and 590. Since line 600 already exists, the insertion procedure will automatically stop. That is, an existing line will be neither written over nor skipped over. If you want to terminate the insertion before such an automatic termination, type **BREAK** (or **ESC**) after you have entered the last line and typed **RETURN** (or **ENTER**). Be sure you type **RETURN** before you type **BREAK** (or **ESC**). In (14.23), n_2 is called the increment. The normal increment is 100. However, once (14.23) is used, the increment is changed to n_2, and it will remain n_2 unless another command of the form of (14.23) is given or until the editing session is ended. If you do not want to change the increment from 100 in this semipermanent fashion, then replace the comma in (14.23) by a semicolon.

$$*In_1; n_2 \text{ (RETURN)} \tag{14.24}$$

D   The **D** is used to delete lines when you are working in the edit command mode. For instance, if you type

$$*D5\emptyset\emptyset \text{ (RETURN)} \qquad\qquad (14.25)$$

then line $5\emptyset\emptyset$ will be deleted. If you type

$$*Dn_1:n_2 \text{ (RETURN)} \qquad\qquad (14.26)$$

then all lines between n_1 and n_2, inclusive, will be deleted. The symbol ↑ represents the first line and the symbol * represents the last line. Then

$$*D1\emptyset\emptyset\emptyset:* \text{ (RETURN)}$$

causes all lines from $1\emptyset\emptyset\emptyset$ to the end of the program to be deleted.

R   The **R** command allows you to replace lines. It is a combination of the deletion and the insertion. For instance,

$$*Rn_1:n_2,n_3 \qquad\qquad (14.27)$$

is equivalent to $Dn_1:n_2$ followed by In_1,n_3. The comma can be replaced by a semicolon as in (15.24). If you just want to replace line n_1, type **Rn_1**.

P   Typing **P** causes a line to be listed on the screen.

$$*Pn_1:n_2 \text{ (RETURN)} \qquad\qquad (14.28)$$

causes all lines n_1 to n_2 to be displayed on the screen. The ↑ and * can be used as range specifiers. Typing **P2$\emptyset$ (RETURN)** causes line $2\emptyset$ to be displayed.

L   If **P** is replaced by **L**, the information will be displayed on the line printer if one is available. If you do not have a line printer, do not type **L**. It will cause the computer to "lock up" and you will have to reboot the system and the results of the editing session will be lost.

The current line is the one that was just edited or printed. The period (.) can be used to represent the current line. For instance, **P.** will cause the current line to be printed. **A.** causes the alter mode to be entered for the current line. If you type down arrow, the next line will be printed (and become the current line). Typing **BREAK** (or **ESC** or up arrow on some computers) causes the line preceding the current one to be printed. This then becomes the current line.

Renumbering Lines

At times, it is desirable to renumber some or all of the lines to make room for new statements. The basic form of the renumbering command is

$$\text{*N}n_1;n_2=n_3:n_4 \text{ (RETURN)} \tag{14.29}$$

n_3 and n_4 specify the range of old numbers that will be renumbered. They will be renumbered starting with number n_1 with an increment of n_2. For instance,

$$\text{*N5}\emptyset\emptyset\emptyset;2\emptyset=5\emptyset\emptyset:1\emptyset\emptyset\emptyset \text{ (RETURN)}$$

will cause lines $5\emptyset\emptyset$ to $1\emptyset\emptyset\emptyset$ to be renumbered starting with line number $5\emptyset\emptyset$ and using increments of $2\emptyset$ (i.e. $5\emptyset\emptyset\emptyset$, $5\emptyset2\emptyset$, $5\emptyset4\emptyset$, . . .). Note that if the semipermanent colon is replaced by a comma in (14.29), then the "permanent" increment will be changed from $1\emptyset\emptyset$ to n_2.

If the range is omitted, the entire file will be renumbered. For instance,

$$\text{*N3}\emptyset\emptyset;5\emptyset \text{ (RETURN)}$$

will cause the entire file to be renumbered. The starting line number will be $3\emptyset\emptyset$ and the increment will be $5\emptyset$ (i.e., $3\emptyset\emptyset$, $35\emptyset$, $4\emptyset\emptyset$, $45\emptyset$, . . .). If the increment is omitted, the "permanent" increment will be used.

$$\text{*N8}\emptyset\emptyset=5\emptyset\emptyset:1\emptyset\emptyset\emptyset$$

will cause lines in the old range $5\emptyset\emptyset$ to $1\emptyset\emptyset\emptyset$ to be renumbered starting with line number $8\emptyset\emptyset$ and using the permanent increment. (Note that the permanent increment can be changed as discussed.)

If the starting number n_1 of (14.29) is omitted (i.e. N;2Ø=5ØØ: 1ØØØ) then the starting number is set equal to n_3. If the range is omitted, then the starting number is the same as in the original program. For instance, N;2Ø=5ØØ:1ØØØ is equivalent to N5ØØ;2Ø=5ØØ:1ØØØ. Also, N;2Ø will cause the program to be renumbered with increments of 2Ø.

Suppose you want to make room in the middle of a program, for instance, between lines 1ØØØ and 2ØØØ. Also suppose that there are presently 1Ø lines there, separated by increments of 1ØØ. If we type

$$*N1ØØØ;1Ø=1ØØØ:2ØØØ$$

then renumbering of these lines in increments of 1Ø (1ØØØ, 1Ø1Ø, 1Ø2Ø, 1Ø3Ø, . . . , 1Ø9Ø) will result.

Thus, the renumbering command can be helpful when reorganizing files. Note that the editor will *not* permit you to renumber to change the sequence of lines or to cause one line to write over another.

Exiting the Editor

After you are finished editing, you exit the editor by typing E and a new file name, see Sec. 3.1. A new name must be used since the editor will not write over existing files, or set up two files with the same name on one disk. In this way, you will always have a back-up file. Do not keep too many back-up files since this can become confusing. On some computers this back-up is automatic.

The E command exits the editor. You can save a file without exiting by typing W. For instance,

$$\text{W PROG/FOR:1 (RETURN)} \qquad\qquad (14.30)$$

will store the edited file under the name PROG/FOR on disk drive 1. (The file should be named in a way that is suitable for your DOS, see Sec. 1.3.)

If you want to exit the editor without saving the changes, simply type

$$\text{Q (RETURN)} \qquad\qquad (14.31)$$

This will return you to the DOS without saving any changes. If you had previously saved a file using the W command, that file will still be saved.

Index File

When your file becomes long enough, the editor generates a second file called an *index file*. You need not be concerned about the index; it is merely used by the editor to speed up the operation. The name of the index file is the same as that of the original file, except that the first letter of the file extension becomes a Z. For instance, if the file name is

PROGRAM/FOR

then the index file will be called

PROGRAM/ZFO

It will be stored on the same disk as the program.

A word of caution is required. If you rename your program, it may be possible to confuse the editor. For instance, suppose that you have edited a program called ABC/FOR; its index file is called ABC/ZFO. When you debug a program, you may edit it several times. Each time that you exit the editor, you must rename the file. Suppose that you edit ABC/FOR and name the edited program ABC1/FOR. Its index file will be ABC1/ZFO. Now suppose that you have to edit ABC1/ZFO. In order to avoid having too many back-up files, and too many names to remember, you might delete ABC/FOR and rename ABC1/FOR to be ABC/FOR. Now the editor will assume that ABC/ZFO is the index file. Thus, the wrong index file will be used. This can cause disastrous operation. You should delete ABC/ZFO and then rename ABC1/ZFO to be ABC/ZFO. Now the correct index file will be used. However, this can easily lead to mistakes. The index file should be deleted if there is any possibility of a mixup. Remember that if a file is changed in *any* way, do not edit it if there is an old index file with the same name (except for the Z in the extension) on the disk.

We have considered the features of the editor that apply to FOR-TRAN. There are other editing details that are given in the MICRO-SOFT FORTRAN manual.

EXERCISES

14.1 Obtain a complete list of error statements for your computer.

14.2 Write some programs with deliberate spelling errors (for example, DINEMSION). Run the program and study the error messages.

14.3 Write programs with deliberate grammatical errors. Run them and study the error messages. Include such errors as forgetting to DIMENSION an array and forgetting to number the object of a DO loop.

14.4 Discuss the procedures for finding logical errors in programs.

14.5 The following program is used to obtain a number in the following way. Enter two arrays, square all the elements of the first (original) array, and then obtain the sum of all the elements of that (new) array and the second one. Also obtain the sum of all the elements of the two original arrays (not necessarily in that order). Find the bugs in the program.

```
       DIMENSION A(1Ø,1Ø),B(1Ø,1Ø)
       READ(5,1)((A(I,J),I=1,1Ø),J=1,1Ø)
       READ(5,1)((B(I,J),I=1,1Ø),J=1,1Ø)
       SUM=Ø.
       DO 1Ø I=1,1Ø
       DO 1Ø J=1,1Ø
         SUM=SUM*A(I,J)+B(I,J)
1Ø     CONTINUE
       DO 2Ø I=1,N
       DO 2Ø J=1,N
         A(I,J)=A(I,J)*2
2Ø     CONTINUE
       DO 3Ø I=1,N
       DO 3Ø J=1,N
         SUM=A(I,J)+B(I,J)+SUM
       WRITE(5,2)SUM
2      FORMAT('Ø',E15.7)
       STOP
       END
```

14.6 A program is to be written which is to calculate

$$x = (a - \frac{b}{c})(d + 1 - f)$$

The value b/c will be close to a and we can express $b = ac + \delta_1$. Similarly, $d \approx 1, d = 1 + \delta_3$, and $f = 2 + \delta_2$. The quantities δ_1, δ_2, and δ_3 are known accurately. Write a program that minimizes roundoff error.

14.7 Discuss the operation of the following program. For what values
of the input quantities will be correct results be obtained?

```
        DIMENSION A(1ØØ),B(1ØØ)
        READ(5,1)N,K
1       FORMAT(2I6)
        DO 1Ø I=1,N
1Ø      A(I)=N*I
        M=K*6
        DO 2Ø J=1,1Ø
          MM=J+M
2Ø      B(MM)=A(MM)**2
        SUM=Ø.
        DO 3Ø JJ=1,1Ø
3Ø      SUM=SUM+B(JJ+M)
        WRITE(5,2)SUM
2       FORMAT('ØSUM=',E15.7)
        STOP
        END
```

14.8 Edit one of your programs. Use all of the procedures discussed
in Sec. 14.3.

15 Storage, Retrieval, and Entering of Data

In this chapter we shall consider the storage and retrieval of data. A variety of topics will be discussed here. We shall start by considering how to minimize the main storage space required during execution of a program. Some aspects of entering of data that we have not yet discussed will then be considered. Finally, we shall discuss the storage on and retrieval of records from magnetic tapes and floppy disks.

15.1 PROGRAMMING TO REDUCE THE NEED FOR MAIN STORAGE

When a program is executed, all the variables are stored in the main storage memory (see Sec. 1.1) All computers, no matter how large, have a limit to their main storage. Typical small computers store between 16,000 and 65,000 bytes. During execution, the machine language program is also stored in the main storage. Thus, many programs require a great deal of storage space. This must not exceed the capabilities of the main storage. Hence, programs often should be written to minimize the amount of storage required.

One procedure for doing this is to use nonexecuted commands wherever possible. For instance, if initial values are specified using DATA statements or BLOCK DATA subprograms, then no core storage space is needed for commands. For instance, the statements

```
DIMENSION A(1ØØØ)                                    (15.1)
DATA A/1ØØØ*1.Ø/
```

set all the elements of the A array equal to 1.0 during compilation and no machine execution is required. On the other hand,

```
        DO 10 I=1,1000
10      A(I)=1.0
```
(15.2)

require both main storage space for the executable command and use execution time. Note, however, that statements such as (15.2) must be used when a program is to be executed many times without recompilation. For instance, suppose that the last executed statement is a GO TO statement that directs control to the first statement. A DATA statement will *not* be useful in such cases.

One very important procedure for saving main storage space is to not use arrays unnecessarily. For instance, suppose we have two arrays and we want to add the corresponding elements of each. We could use the following program sequence

```
        DIMENSION A(50,50),B(50,50),C(50,50)
        DATA C/2500*0.0/
        .
        .
        DO 10 I=1,50
        DO 10 J=1,50
10      C(I,J)=A(I,J)+B(I,J)
```
(15.3)

Here we have set the initial value of the elements of the C array equal to zero with a DATA statement which saves some storage space. However, what we should question is whether we need the C array at all. For instance, suppose that, in subsequent calculations, we never use the A array and/or the B array. Then, we can rewrite program segment (15.3) as

```
        DIMENSION A(50,50),B(50,50)
        .
        .
        DO 10 I=1,50
        DO 10 J=1,50
10      A(I,J)=A(I,J)+B(I,J)
```
(15.4)

Now, in all subsequent calculations, we use A(I, J) in place of C(I, J). Of course, this assumes that we do not use the original A array subsequently. Note that program (15.4) has 2500 (that is, 50 × 50) less variables than does program (15.3). Each real variable requires four bytes. Thus, the saving in storage is considerable.

The conservation of storage space can require some sophisticated programming. We have illustrated some simple procedures in this section. However, they are often very helpful in saving storage space.

15.2 THE END AND ERR OPTIONS

When data is being read, occasional problems occur. At times, an error in reading occurs. For instance, suppose that data is being read from a floppy disk. It may have a faulty spot. The computer may sense this and terminate computation. Other problems can occur. For instance, the program may call for the reading of 1000 data items from the disk but only 800 items are supplied on the disk. If we use an ordinary READ statement, then execution cannot proceed and all computations will be lost. We can include expressions within the READ statement so that if the END of the data is encountered or if a reading error occurs, execution does not cease, but control is transferred from the READ statement to a specific statement in the program. Thus, some execution can continue.

$$READ(6,2,ERR=4\emptyset)A,B,C \qquad\qquad (15.5)$$

This is equivalent to the statement

$$READ(6,2)A,B,C \qquad\qquad (15.6)$$

except that if a reading error occurs, control in the program is transferred to statement number 4∅. (Any valid statement number can be used in place of 4∅.) For instance, we could have

```
        READ(6,2,ERR=4∅)A,B,C
        :
        :
        STOP
4∅      WRITE(2,5∅)                              (15.7)
5∅      FORMAT(' READING ERROR')
        STOP
        END
```

(We assume that 6 refers to the appropriate disk drive.) Now, if a reading error occurs, we have the information printed out. At times, we read in enough information to perform some computation even though a reading error occurs. For instance, suppose some calculations were performed prior to the reading of A, B, and C. Statement 4∅ could have the results of these calculations printed.

If the last data item is reached on a floppy disk, an end of file (EOF) mark is encountered. If all the data called for has not been read, then execution is terminated unless the END option is used with the READ statement. This has the following form

$$READ(6,3,END=3\emptyset)A,B,C,D,E,G \qquad (15.8)$$

If the end of the data is reached before the sixth item is read, control is transferred to statement number 3∅.

The END and ERR options can be used simultaneously. For instance,

$$READ(6,4,END=4\emptyset,ERR=5\emptyset)A,B,C \qquad (15.9a)$$

The order of END and ERR is unimportant. For instance, statement (15.15a) is equivalent to

$$READ(6,4,ERR=5\emptyset,END=4\emptyset)A,B,C \qquad (15.9b)$$

The END and ERR options only apply to the particular READ statement with which they are used. If there is more than one READ statement, each one can have its own END and ERR options. Some or all of the statements to which control is tranferred can, at the programmer's option, be the same.

The END option is often used when the total amount of data is unknown. For instance, we may not know how much information is contained in a file, but we do know that the file contains less than 1000 items. In this case we can write

```
      K=∅
      DO 1∅ I=1,1∅∅∅
      READ(6,2,END=5∅)A(I)
      K=K+1
       .
       .
       .
1∅    CONTINUE
5∅    CONTINUE
```

Now the DO loop will be terminated after 1000 items are read or after an EOF is encountered. Hence, if the file only contains 750 items, the loop will be terminated after 750 items are read. Note that K will equal the total number of data items read and can be used in subsequent calculations.

15.3 RANDOM, DIRECT, AND SEQUENTIAL ACCESS STORAGE

In this section we shall discuss the various types of storage techniques that are used in a digital computer. In the following two sections we shall discuss the FORTRAN statements that are used to enter and return data into and from floppy disks. These are the most convenient storage devices commonly used with microcomputers.

Storage devices can be characterized by the speed at which data can be entered and returned from them. For instance, the fastest storage and return is in the main storage memory. This is termed a *random access* storage device since the time required to enter or retrieve data is independent of the data's location in the memory. It may seem as though the main storage memory should be used for all storage. However, main storage memory is relatively expensive. Thus, its size is limited. The storage in microcomputers ranges between 16,000 and 65,000 bytes. Main storage memory is used for the storage of data needed for execution of the program and the machine language necessary to direct the operation of the program. In general, all operations being executed have their data and instructions stored in the main memory storage.

There are times when we want to store large programs or great quantities of data which will be used at a later time. It would be wasteful of storage space to keep this in main storage memory. Several other forms of storage exist. Information can be stored on magnetic disks. The information is entered or removed by heads which can be positioned over the disk. This is somewhat like the ordinary tape recorder, except that now the heads can be positioned. In order to obtain data, the head must move to the point on the disk where the data is stored. This is a mechanical operation. It is slow in comparison with the electronic operation of main storage memory. On large, hard disk drives, to reduce the time required for a head to reach a desired position, several heads are used. Thus, one head is always relatively close to the desired position and the amount of motion is reduced. Floppy disk drives are simpler than hard disk drives, and only one head is used. These devices are said to provide *direct access* storage.

There is also storage on magnetic tape. Information is entered on or read from a magnetic tape using a device which may be an ordinary tape recorder. If information is stored on one end of the tape and the head is positioned over the other end of the tape, then the entire tape must be wound in order to obtain the desired data. This type of storage is said to have *sequential access* since the information is stored on the tape in sequence and we must "run through" the tape until the desired material is obtained. The access time on tapes is large and many seconds may be required to obtain the data. Floppy disk storage is much more convenient. We shall discuss its use here. We shall see that both direct and sequential access files can be written on floppy disks.

15.4 SEQUENTIAL ACCESS DISK FILES

We shall now discuss the reading and writing of sequential access disk files. Each item on a file is called a *record*. For instance, if 100 numbers are stored, each of them may be a separate record. In a sequential file, each record is read or written in sequence. For instance if, in the previous list of 100 numbers, we only require the sixty-fifth item, we would have to read the preceding 64 items of data. This means that extra time must be spent in reading. In the next section we shall discuss direct files where a particular record can be read directly. However, sequential access is often no problem since we frequently read or write the entire file. We shall see that sequential access may also have other advantages.

If a file is read or written, it must first be opened. The opening operation performs the necessary operations required for reading from or writing to the disk. In MICROSOFT FORTRAN there are several means for opening a file. The most convenient is with a library subroutine called OPEN.

The calling statement differs from system to system. For instance, in TRS-80 MICROSOFT FORTRAN, we use

CALL OPEN(LUN,file name,record length)(15.10)

Here LUN is an integer supplying the logical unit number, file name represents the file name, password, and disk drive (as specified by the DOS), and the record length is an integer that specifies the number of bytes for each record. For instance, normal integer data requires two bytes, reql data requires four bytes, etc. (see Sec. 10.2). An example of (15.10) is

CALL OPEN(6,'NUMB/DAT:1 ',4)   (15.11)

Here the LUN is 6, file name is NUMB/DAT, and the file will be stored on the disk in drive 1. Note the space between DAT:1 and the quote. It should be included. Each record will be four bytes long.

The LUN should be used in any READ or WRITE statement. For instance, we have previously used 5 and 2 in these statements as the LUNs for the terminal and line printer, respectively. We can actually redefine LUNs using the CALL OPEN statement. However, it is probably less confusing not to do so. We shall use 6, 7, 8, and 9 for the LUNs of the disk drives.

With other DOSs, the form of the OPEN statement may differ. For instance, it may be of the form

```
CALL OPEN(LUN,file name,drive)          (15.12)
```

In this case, the record length is fixed. Your MICROSOFT FORTRAN manual should be consulted to obtain the correct form. The file name is written as specified by your DOS.

The CALL OPEN statement is not the only way of opening a file. However, it is the most convenient one since a file name can be specified. If the CALL OPEN is not used, MICROSOFT FORTRAN will open the file under a default name which depends upon the LUN. For instance, if we have a WRITE statement that uses a LUN of 6, e.g. WRITE(6,3)A, then the file will be opened under the name FORTØ6/DAT (or FORTØ6.DAT).

After the operations on a file are complete, the file should be closed. The statement

```
ENDFILE a                               (15.13)
```

closes a file. *a* should be an integer constant or integer variable equal to the LUN in question.

Let us illustrate this with a program that writes 100 numbers to the disk.

```
        DIMENSION A(12Ø)
        DO 1Ø I=1,12Ø
          A(I)=I
1Ø      CONTINUE
        CALL OPEN(6,'NUMB/DAT:1 ',6)
        DO 2Ø I=1,12Ø
          WRITE(6,1,ERR=3Ø,END=3Ø)A(I)      (15.14)
1         FORMAT(' ',E15.7)
2Ø      CONTINUE
3Ø      ENDFILE 6
        STOP
        END
```

Note that we allow six bytes for each record. Two store the number and two others store the carriage control character. Note that a carriage control character is *not* needed in all versions of MICROSOFT FORTRAN when we write to the disk. In this case, we can change the FORMAT statement to

```
1        FORMAT(E15.7)                          (15.15a)
```

and the CALL OPEN statement becomes

```
         CALL OPEN(6,'NUMB/DAT:1 ',4)           (15.15b)
```

Now let us write a program that reads the data written by program (15.14). It is

```
         DIMENSION B(120)
         CALL OPEN(6,'NUMB/DAT:1 ',6)
         DO 10 I=1,200
             READ(6,1,ERR=20,END=20)C,B(I)
1            FORMAT(A1,E16.2)
10       CONTINUE                               (15.16)
20       ENDFILE 6
         WRITE(5,3)(B(I),I=1,120)
3        FORMAT(' ',10F6.2)
         STOP
         END
```

Each record of the file contains a blank space and a number. With each READ operation, C reads the blank from the record. Note that we do not do anything with C. However, it must be read since all data must be read in sequence from a sequential file. The specification of the record length for READ must be the same as that used when the record was written.

Note that the DO loop calls for the reading of 200 records. Since program (15.14) only placed 120 records on the disk, the END option terminates reading in this case. There are times when we want to know how many records are in a file. The following modification of program (15.16) accomplishes this.

```
         K=0
         DO 10 I=1,200
             READ(6,1,ERR=20,END=20)C,B(I)
             K=K+1
1            FORMAT(A1,E16.2)                    (15.17)
10       CONTINUE
20       ENDFILE 6
```

When the loop terminates, K will be equal to the number of records read. In this case, the final value of K will be 120.

If your version of MICROSOFT FORTRAN does not require carriage control characters, then the CALL OPEN statement can be written as

$$\text{CALL OPEN(6,'NUMB/DAT:1 ',4)} \qquad (15.18a)$$

and the READ and FORMAT statements become

```
     READ(6,1,ERR=2Ø,END=2Ø)B(I)            (15.18b)
1    FORMAT(E16.2)
```

Unformatted Input/Output

MICROSOFT FORTRAN allows disk input and output in an unformatted form. In this case, the data is transmitted and stored in exactly the form of the binary code used by the computer. This form is convenient since the programmer does not have to write FORMAT statements, but FORMATted files can be read and printed from the DOS just as programs can. This may not be the case for unformatted files. The main advantage of the unformatted form is that it takes much less room on the disk. With the formatted form, even if no carriage control characters are used, each record must start on the equivalent of a separate line. This wastes disk space. This is not true in the unformatted case.

To write unformatted READ and WRITE statements, simply omit the FORMAT number from within the parentheses of the READ and WRITE statements. As an example, we shall rewrite programs (15.14) and (15.16) in unformatted form. These are

```
     DIMENSION A(12Ø)
     DO 1Ø I=1,12Ø
       A(I)=I
1Ø   CONTINUE
     CALL OPEN(6,'NUMB1/DAT:1 ',4)            (15.19)
     DO 2Ø I=1,12Ø
       WRITE(6,ERR=3Ø,END=3Ø)A(I)
2Ø   CONTINUE
3Ø   ENDFILE 6
     STOP
     END
```

and

```
      DIMENSION B(12Ø)
      CALL OPEN(6,'NUMB1/DAT:1 ',4)
      DO 1Ø I=1,2ØØ
        READ(6,ERR=2Ø,END=2Ø)B(I)
1Ø    CONTINUE                                    (15.20)
2Ø    ENDFILE 6
      WRITE(5,3)(B(I),I=1,12Ø)
3     FORMAT(' ',1ØF6.2)
      STOP
      END
```

When a sequential file is opened, data can be read from the first record and then read from each record in sequence. Assume that there is a pointer that points to the next record. Opening the file sets the pointer to the beginning of the file. We can also reset the pointer to the beginning of the file using the statement

    REWIND n   (15.21)

where n corresponds to the LUN in question. On some versions of FORTRAN there is a statement that will backspace the pointer just one record. It is

    BACKSPACE n   (15.22)

where n is again a LUN. This is not presently implemented in MICRO-SOFT FORTRAN, although it may be in the future.

Care must be taken with sequential access files. If you open a file and WRITE to it, any previously existing file with the same specifications (name and drive number) will be lost.

We have assumed that the LUN and record length were supplied as data to the OPEN subprogram in the form of integer constants. Actually, the LUN and record length can be in the form of integer variables. In addition, the file name can also be in the form of a variable. In the case of the file name, the data must be stored in an array and the array name, without coefficient, replaces the file name in the OPEN specification list. We shall rewrite program (15.20) to illustrate the use of variables in the CALL OPEN statement.

```
      DIMENSION B(12Ø),W(4)
      READ(5,24)(W(I),I=1,4)
24    FORMAT(4A4)
      L=6
```

```
          LL=4
          CALL OPEN(L,W,LL)
          DO 1Ø I=1,2ØØ                              (15.23)
             READ(6,ERR=2Ø,END=2Ø)B(I)
1Ø        CONTINUE
2Ø        ENDFILE 6
          WRITE(5,3)(B(I),I=1,12Ø)
3         FORMAT(' ',1ØF6.2)
          STOP
          END
```

The W array is used to store the file name which is entered from the terminal. There are four elements in the W array. Hence, 16 characters can be specified for the file name, password, and disk drive. The size of the W array can be increased if a longer specification is desired.

15.5 DIRECT ACCESS DISK FILES

Some versions of MICROSOFT FORTRAN allow the direct access of records in a file. (This is sometimes called random access. We use the term "direct access" since this is not true random access.) In this case, we can READ from or WRITE to a specific record without having to read all the intervening records or rewriting the entire file. The details are similar to those for reading and writing sequential access files except that an additional specification, REC, is added to the READ or WRITE statement, for instance

$$WRITE(6,1,REC=I,ERR=5\emptyset,END=5\emptyset)A(I) \qquad (15.24)$$

Now we write the record numbered I. Let us illustrate the use of direct access by writing a program that is equivalent to (15.14) in that it stores the elements of an array on disk.

```
          DIMENSION A(12Ø)
          DO 1Ø I=1,12Ø
             A(I)=I
1Ø        CONTINUE
          CALL OPEN(6,'NUMB2/DAT:1 ',128)
          DO 2Ø I=1,12Ø,2
             WRITE(6,1,REC=I,ERR=5Ø,END=5Ø)A(I)
1            FORMAT(' ',E15.7)
2Ø        CONTINUE                                   (15.25)
          DO 4Ø I=2,12Ø,2
             WRITE(6,1,REC=I,ERR=5Ø,END=5Ø)A(I)
```

```
4Ø      CONTINUE
5Ø      ENDFILE 6
        STOP
        END
```

Note that first we enter record numbers 1, 3, 5, 7, 9 . . . 119 and then records 2, 4, 6, . . . 120. This is not sequential. However, if we examine the file on the disk we would see that the records will be stored in the order 1, 2, 3, ... Thus, the records are stored in sequence even though we have not written them in sequence. Direct access seems attractive. However, it has a disadvantage. Note that we have used a record length of 128 bits. This is wasteful of storage space on the disk since we only need six bytes. The number of bytes required for a direct access record will vary with the version of MICROSOFT FORTRAN. Your manual should be consulted for the proper length. In any event, direct access storage may require more disk space than sequential access. If you simply use a direct access WRITE statement to open a file, without a CALL OPEN, see Sec. 15.4, then the correct record length for direct access will automatically be assigned to the file, but then you cannot name your files. The record length will still be greater than that required in the sequential access case.

In (15.26) we list a program that uses direct access to read the file generated in (15.25). Note that we have picked out several "random" records to read and that we do not have to read the intermediate records.

```
        DIMENSION B(12Ø)
        CALL OPEN(6,'NUMB2/DAT:1 ',128)
        DO 1Ø I=1,2ØØ,1Ø
           READ(6,1,REC=I,ERR=2Ø,END=2Ø)C,B(I)
1          FORMAT(A1,E16.2)
1Ø      CONTINUE                                    (15.26)
2Ø      ENDFILE 6
        WRITE(5,3)(B(I),I=1,12Ø,1Ø)
3       FORMAT(' ',1ØF6.2)
        STOP
        END
```

We have illustrated direct access with formatted READ and WRITE statements using carriage control characters. On some versions of MICROSOFT FORTRAN, the carriage control character can be omitted. In addition, with some versions of MICROSOFT FORTRAN, nonformatted READ and WRITE statements can be used. In each of these cases

$$REC=n \qquad\qquad (15.27)$$

where n is an integer constant or variable, must be inserted into the READ and WRITE statements as described for programs (15.25) and (15.26). For instance, the READ statement of program (15.23) would be

```
READ(6,REC=I,ERR=2Ø,END=2Ø)B(I)
```

EXERCISES

15.1 Modify the following program so that the required storage space is minimized.

```
       DIMENSION A(1ØØØ),B(1ØØØ),C(1ØØØ)
       READ(5,1)N
1      FORMAT(I4)
       READ(5,2)(A(I),I=1,N)
2      FORMAT(E16.7)
       DO 1Ø I=1,N
         B(I)=A(I)**2
         C(I)=B(I)*(A(I)+B(I))
1Ø     CONTINUE
       WRITE(5,3)(C(I),I=1,N)
3      FORMAT('Ø',E15.6)
```

15.2 Discuss the use of the END and ERR options.

15.3 Discuss the various types of storage and their advantages and disadvantages.

15.4 Discuss the consequences of the following program segment.

```
       DIMENSION K(1ØØ)
       CALL OPEN(6,'FILE/DAT:1 ',8)
       DO 1Ø I=1,1ØØ
1Ø     K(I)=I
       DO 2Ø I=1,1ØØ
2Ø     WRITE(6,2,ERR=3Ø,END=3Ø)K(I)
       FORMAT(' ',I3)
3Ø     ENDFILE 6
```

```
STOP
END
```

Use the computer to verify your results.

15.5   Can the disk storage space in the previous problem be reduced?

15.6   Write a program to read the file created in Exercise 15.4. Check the program by running it on your computer.

15.7   Rewrite the program of Exercise 15.4 without using carriage control characters.

15.8   Write a program to read the file of Exercise 15.7. Check your program by running it on your computer (if possible).

15.9   Rewrite the program of Exercise 15.4 but now use an unformatted READ statement.

15.10 Repeat Exercise 15.8 for the program of 15.9.

15.11 Repeat Exercise 6.6 but now output the data to a disk.

15.12 Repeat Exercise 6.23 but now store the data in disk files.

15.13 Repeat Exercise 15.11 but now use direct access files.

15.14 Repeat Exercise 15.12 but now use direct access files.

15.15 Compare sequential and direct access files.

APPENDIX A:
A Glossary of
Microsoft FORTRAN
Terms

In this appendix we shall list the various terms and expressions used in FORTRAN. An example of their use will be given as will the section in which they are defined.

Term	Example	Section
Alphanumeric data	I='ABC'	12.1
.AND.	IF(A.LT.B.AND.D.GT.C)	4.3
Arithmetic statements		
addition and	A=B+C	
subtraction	A=B−C	2.1
multiplication and	A=B*C	
division	A=B/C	2.2
exponentiation	A=B**2	2.2
hierarchy		2.3
Arithmetic statement		
function	ABC(A, B)=A*B+C**2	7.4
ASSIGN	ASSIGN 2 TO N	4.6
BACKSPACE	BACKSPACE2	15.4
BLOCK DATA		13.3
CALL	CALL ABC(X, Y, N)	7.5
Carriage control		
character	'Ø'	3.3
COMMENT	C A COMMENT	1.3
COMMON (blank)	COMMON A,B,C	7.6
COMMON(labeled)	COMMON/ABC/A,R,N/BOOK/D,E	7.6

Term	Example	Section
COMPLEX	COMPLEX ABLE, BOX	9.1
CONTINUE	20 CONTINUE	4.2
DATA	DATA A, BOX, C/1∅.5, 5., ∅.∅/,	
	H/1∅/	13.2
DECODE	DECODE(B,3)X,Y,Z	13.4
DIMENSION	DIMENSION A(1∅∅), BOX(2, 15)	6.1
DO	DO 1∅ I=1, N	5.1, 5.2, 5.3
DO, implied	READ(5,1)(A(I),I=1,N)	6.4
DOUBLE	DOUBLE PRECISION A,	
PRECISION	BOX(1∅∅)	8.1
ENCODE	ENCODE(A,2)Q,R,S	13.4
END	END	3.5
END=	READ(5,2,END=40)A,B,C	15.2
ENDFILE	ENDFILE6	15.4
.EQ.	IF(J.EQ.KEE)THEN	4.3
EQUIVALENCE	EQUIVALENCE(A,B),(C,D(1),E(2,4))	10.3
ERR=	READ(5,1,END=2∅,ERR=4∅)	15.2
EXTERNAL	EXTERNAL SIN,COS,FUN	7.7
.FALSE.	Y=.FALSE.	11.1
FORMAT	FORMAT(' A=',E1∅.3)	3.1, 3.2,
		3.3, 3.4
Field specifier		
A−alphanumeric		12.1
D−double precision		8.2
E−exponential		3.1, 3.3
F−real		3.1, 3.3
G−general		13.1
H−Hollerith		3.4, 12.1
I−integer		3.1, 3.3
L−logical		11.2
P−scale factor		13.1
X−space		13.1
FORTRAN		
characters	A,B,C	1.2
FUNCTION	FUNCTION BOX(A,B,C)	7.1
.GE.	IF(X+Y.GE.A−B)THEN	4.3
.GT.	IF(A.GT.B)THEN	4.3
GO TO (assigned)	GO TO I,(1∅,2∅,3∅)	4.6
GO TO (computed)	GO TO(1∅,2∅,3∅),K	4.5

Term	Example	Section
GO TO	GO TO 1∅	
(unconditional)		4.4
IF (arithmetic)	IF(X+Y − Z)1∅,2∅,3∅	4.1
IF (logical)	IF(X.GT.Y)A=1∅	4.3
INP	X=INP(128)	7.3
IMPLICIT	IMPLICIT INTEGER(A-C)	10.2
INTEGER	INTEGER ABLE(1∅),BOX	10.1
.LE.	IF(A.LE.B)THEN	4.3
LOGICAL	IMPLICIT LOGICAL(L)	11.1
LOGICAL,		
hierarchy		4.3
.LT.	IF(A.LT.B)THEN	4.3
LUN		15.3
.NE.	IF(I.NE.J)THEN	4.3
.NOT.	L=.NOT.(L1.EQ.L2)	4.3
.OR.	IF(A.LT.B.OR.I.EQ.K)THEN	4.3
OPEN	CALL OPEN(6,'NUMB/DAT:1 ',8)	15.5
OUT	CALL OUT(16,256)	7.5
PAUSE	PAUSE'136'	4.11
PEEK	X=PEEK(16,42∅)	7.3
POKE	CALL POKE(15,127,63)	7.5
PROGRAM	PROGRAM ADD	10.2
READ (formatted)	READ(6,2)N,(A(I),I=1,N)	3.1
READ (unformatted)	READ(6,ERR=3∅,END=5∅)A(I)	15.5
READ (direct access)	READ(6,2,ERR=3∅,END=2∅)A(I)	15.5
REAL	REAL ITEM(1∅)	10.1
RETURN	RETURN	7.1
REWIND	REWIND6	15.5
STOP	STOP	3.5
SUBROUTINE	SUBROUTINE ABC(X,Y)	7.5
.TRUE.	L=.TRUE.	11.1
Variable names		2.5
WRITE(formatted)	WRITE(6,2)A,(B(I),I=1,N)	3.3
WRITE (unformatted)	WRITE(6,ERR=5∅,END=3∅)A(I)	15.5
WRITE (direct access)	WRITE(6,2,ERR=5∅,END=3∅)A(I)	15.5
XOR	IF(A.XOR.B)GO TO 1∅	4.3

APPENDIX B:
Microsoft FORTRAN
Library Functions

In this appendix we shall list the MICROSOFT FORTRAN library FUNCTIONS. Since these subprograms are all FUNCTIONS, they give a single answer. We shall indicate the type of variable that results (for example, READ, INTEGER) and also the type of variable used in the argument(s). The following abbreviations will be used in this type designation: I=INTEGER; R=REAL; D=DOUBLE PRECISION; L= LOGICAL.

Definition	FUNCTION	Type of FUNCTION	Type of argument(s)
e^x (exponential)	EXP(X)	R	R
	DEXP(X)	D	D
$\sqrt{x}$ (square root)	SQRT(X)	R	R
	DSQRT(X)	D	D
$\log_{10} x$ (common logarithm)	ALOG10(X)	R	R
	DLOG10(X)	D	D
$\ln x$ (natural logarithm)	ALOG(X)	R	R
	DLOG(X)	D	D
$\sin x$ (sine of x in radians)	SIN(X)	R	R
	DSIN(X)	D	D
$\cos x$ (cosine of x in radians)	COS(X)	R	R
	DCOS(X)	D	D
$0 \leqslant z \leqslant \pi$ $\tan^{-1}(x)$ [$z=\arctan x$] $-\dfrac{\pi}{2} \leqslant z \leqslant \dfrac{\pi}{2}$	ATAN(X)	R	R
	DATAN(X)	D	D

Definition	FUNCTION	Type of FUNCTION	Type of argument(s)
$\tan^{-1}(x/y)$ $[z=\arctan(x/y)]$	ATAN2(X,Y)	R	R
$-\pi \leqslant z \leqslant \pi$	DATAN2(X,Y)	D	D
$\tanh x$ (hyperbolic tangent of x)	TANH(X)	R	R
$|x|$ absolute value of x	IABS(I)	I	I
	ABS(X)	R	R
	DABS(X)	D	D
Convert from integer to single	FLOAT(I)	R	I
or double precision real	DFLOAT(I)	D	I
Convert from real to integer	IFIX(X)	I	R
Convert real to double precision	DBLE(X)	D	R
by adding zeros			
Convert double precision to real	SNGL(X)	R	D
saving most significant figures			
Truncation of x. Largest integer	INT(X)	I	R
equal to or less than $|x|$ times	AINT(X)	R	R
the sign of x	IDINT(X)	I	D
Nearest whole number	ANINT(X)	R	R
(roundoff)	DNINT(X)	D	D
Nearest integer	NINT	I	R
	IDIND	I	D
Transfer of sign $|x|$sgn(y) where	SIGN(X,Y)	R	R
sgn$(y) = 1$ $(y > 0)$	ISIGN(I,J)	I	I
$= 0$ $(y = 0)$	DSIGN(X,Y)	D	D
$= -1$ $(y < 0)$			
(magnitude of x times the			
sign of y)			
Largest value of two or more	AMAX$\emptyset$(I1,I2, . . .)	R	I
arguments max$(x_1, x_2, \ldots)$	AMAX1(X1,X2, . . .)	R	R
	MAX$\emptyset$(I1,I2, . . .)	I	I
	MAX1(X1,X2, . . .)	I	R
	DMAX1(X1,X2, . . .)	D	D
Smallest value of two or more	AMIN$\emptyset$(I1,I2, . . .)	R	I
arguments min$(x_1, x_2, \ldots)$	AMIN1(X1,X2, . . .)	R	R
	MIN$\emptyset$(I1,I2, . . .)	I	I
	MIN1(X1,X2, . . .)	I	R
	DMIN1(X1,X2, . . .)	D	D
Positive difference	DIM(X1,X2)	R	R
$x_1 - \min(x_1, x_2)$	IDIM(I1,I2)	I	I
	DDIM(X1,X2)	D	D

Definition	FUNCTION	Type of FUNCTION	Type of argument(s)
Modular arithmetic remainder of x_1/x_2, example $\text{Mod } \dfrac{10}{3} = 1; \text{Mod } \dfrac{12}{5} = 2$	MOD(I1,I2)	I	I
	AMOD(X1,X2)	R	R
	DMOD(X1,X2)	D	D

Index